Dialogue
with a Nonbeliever

DIALOGUE
WITH A NONBELIEVER

About Science and the Limits of Knowledge,
the Big Bang and Evolution,
Ancient Christianity & Modern Heterodoxy

by **Bogdan-John Vasiliu**

second edition

December, 2016

Table of Contents

Table of Contents 5

Foreword.. 10

1. The Fools and the Wise Ones 13

2. Is There a God? I Want to Know! 17

3. Limits of Knowledge 20

   3.1. Limits in Knowing the Present 23

      3.1.1. Objects and Phenomena in Front of Us...................... 23

      3.1.2. Objects and Phenomena that We Ourselves
          Don't Have Access to 24

      3.1.3. Shape of the Earth.. 24

      3.1.4. Rotation of the Earth.. 28

      3.1.5. Vaccines 32

      3.1.6. Christmas Bonuses 41

      3.1.7. Everyday Life 42

      3.1.8. Complex Systems.. 46

   3.2. Limits in Knowing the Future 48

   3.3. Limits in Knowing the Past 53

      3.3.1. Cars in the Parking Lot.. 53

      3.3.2. The Trip to the Moon... 55

      3.3.3. Forensic Investigations 57

      3.3.4. Ancient History.. 61

   3.3.5. An Extremely Absurd Theory.............................63

4. Billions of Years?... 69
   4.1. Some Basic Things 69
      4.1.1. Can the Universe Be Eternal? 69
      4.1.2. Science's Account...71
   4.2. Age of the Universe...72
      4.2.1. The Laws of Physics 73
      4.2.2. Distance to the Stars.....................................73
      4.2.3. Dark Energy..77
      4.2.4. Background Radiation 79
      4.2.5. Dark Matter..80
      4.2.6. Comets 81
      4.2.7. Starlight and Time.......................................82
      4.2.8. Natural and Supernatural Explanations...........84
      4.2.9. The Sub-Atomic Universe 87
   4.3. Age of the Earth 93
      4.3.1. Radiometric Dating......................................93
      4.3.2. Equilibrium of Radioactive Isotopes 99
      4.3.3. Helium in Zircon Crystals............................ 100
      4.3.4. Sodium in Seas and Oceans.......................... 103
      4.3.5. Recorded History 104
      4.3.6. Dendrochronology.................................... 105
      4.3.7. Ice Layers.. 109

5. Can Living Beings Evolve? 113
   5.1. Complexity of Life..114
      5.1.1. Complexity of Cell Machines 114
      5.1.2. Protein Folding... 119
      5.1.3. The Soul Quickens the Body......................... 123
      5.1.4. The Soul and the Heart Transplant................ 125
      5.1.5. The Right Explanation 127
   5.2. Origin of Life 129

5.2.1. Spontaneous Generation? 129

5.2.2. Maximum Number of Tries 132

5.2.3. Chirality 136

5.2.4. The Monkeys and the Typewriter 137

5.3. Can Living Beings Evolve
into Different Life Forms? 141

5.3.1. Genetic Recombination 141

5.3.2. Genetic Mutations 144

5.3.3. Irreducible Complexity 146

5.3.4. Are There Any Beneficial Mutations? 148

5.3.5. The Problem of the Intermediate Stages 151

5.3.6. Bacteria and the Citrates 156

5.3.7. Changes Observed in Today's Life Forms 156

5.4. Controlled Evolution? 158

6. Lack of Fossils **162**

6.1. The Fossil Record 162

6.2. What Do the Evolutionists Say
about the Fossils? 166

6.3. Twenty Fossils 171

7. Other Arguments **177**

7.1. Vestigial Organs 177

7.2. Ontogeny Recapitulates Phylogeny? 180

7.3. Is Evolution a Scientific Theory? 180

7.4. Ethical Arguments 184

7.5. Joshua's Long Day 185

7.6. Noah's Flood 194

7.7. Dinosaurs 198

8. The True Religion **201**

8.1. Some Basic Beliefs 206

8.1.1. Creation.. 206

8.1.2. Revelation... 214

8.1.3. About Islam.. 215

8.2. What Are Heaven and Hell? 219

8.3. Hell in the Vision of the Orthodox Church 224

8.3.1. Saint John of Damascus....................................... 224

8.3.2. Saint Theophan the Recluse 225

8.3.3. Saint Paisios of Mount Athos............................ 226

8.3.4. Saint Silouan the Athonite 229

8.3.5. Saint John Maximovitch..................................... 229

8.3.6. Saint Nephon.. 231

8.3.7. Saint Paul the Apostle... 233

8.3.8. Saint Isaac the Syrian 233

8.3.9. Saint Nicholas Cabasilas..................................... 234

8.3.10. Saint Maximus the Confessor 235

8.3.11. Saint Gregory the Great.................................. 236

8.3.12. Egyptian Paterikon... 238

8.3.13. The Encyclopedia.. 239

8.3.14. Dostoyevsky.. 239

8.3.15. About Metaphors 241

8.3.16. Conclusion about Hell...................................... 243

8.3.17. Sartre's Hell... 244

8.3.18. A Sinner in Heaven.. 246

8.3.19. Eternity 250

8.4. Why Are There So Many Religions? 252

8.5. Aliens...266

8.6. The Eastern Orthodox Church 277

8.6.1. About Humility... 280

8.6.2. About Icons 285

8.6.3. Worship and Veneration 289

8.6.4. Confession... 293

8.6.5. Communion 294

8.6.6. Holy Objects 296

8.6.7. About Sinful Believers 298

8.6.8. About Roman Catholics 300

8.6.9. Religious Exclusivism 305

8.6.10. Books 308

8.7. Other Questions 310

8.7.1. The Movie Zeitgeist 310

8.7.2. Old Testament Law 312

8.7.3. Old Testament Worship 316

8.7.4. Old Testament Wars 321

8.7.5. Unknown Mistakes 323

8.7.6. About Birth Control 327

8.7.7. About Repentance 333

9. Epilogue 341

Foreword

Is there a God? People come to know the fact that there is a God in multiple ways.

Some, during wartime, clearly hear a voice telling them to move away from the place where they had found shelter and, a few moments after they leave, a bomb destroys that shelter. Such a story we hear from a person known for his efforts to find Noah's Ark.

Others first come to believe that there is a devil, and only after that do they understand that there must also be a God. There were cases of people who got involved in the paranormal, trying to communicate with the "dead" and with other "well meaning" spirits. Later, some of these people realized they were actually talking with the devil.

Others say that the best proof that there is a God is that He hears us when we cry out to Him. A Romanian Orthodox Christian believer gave this answer to a fellow countryman who was asking what proof we have that there is a God.

Others notice that every time they say or do something bad—something that their conscience tells them is bad—something bad immediately happens to them, too. After many such "coincidences," they come to admit the fact that there is "Someone" up there Who is watching every step of their lives.

But the most common and most obvious way to know that there is a God is to look around us, at everything surrounding us, and realize that there has to be a Creator who created us, the animals, the plants, this planet and the entire universe.

To counter this obvious reasoning, modern science has come up with the theories of the Big Bang and evolution. The Big Bang theory claims that the universe began to exist about 14 billion years ago, following a big explosion that led to the formation of stars and planets, all with no divine intervention. Then, the evolution theory claims that inanimate matter, somehow, again with no divine intervention, organized itself into the first living organism. This organism, the evolutionists say, started to reproduce and to evolve, and, during billions of years, and also without any divine intervention, eventually turned into the living organisms we see today: people, animals and plants.

We read in the Bible that Thomas did not believe that Christ had risen from the dead until he saw Him with his own eyes. And then Christ told him:

> «*Thomas, because you have seen Me, you have believed. Blessed are those who have not seen and yet have believed.*»[1]

I understand that these words could also mean *blessed are those who believed in God without seeing many arguments*, or *blessed are those who obey all the rules of the Church without trying to find out their purpose*, or *blessed are those who are fully confident that God had very good reasons for all the rules He has left for us in His Church, even though we don't know those reasons.*

Dear reader, if you want to be one of those blessed ones, then you can put this book aside and forget it was ever written. I was not one of those blessed ones; my faith was weak and it needed arguments, it needed answers. And God helped me find those arguments and answers. I am neither a theologian nor a priest, so I have no authority to teach other people. Therefore, in this book I try not to be a teacher for anyone, but only to offer other people, too, the arguments and the answers that God helped me find, with the hope that they will also be useful to them as they were useful to me.

This book is the result of more than ten years of researching the arguments for and against the theories of the Big Bang and

---

[1] John 20:29.

evolution, a study that also implied the search for the right religion and the true Church of Christ. And because that research required countless contradictory discussions with evolutionists, this book is structured as a dialogue, too. The characters Daniel, Michael and John are fictitious. None of them are meant to be an exact replica of the author or of one of the evolutionists mentioned before. Most stories related in the book are based on true events, but the true identities of those involved remain hidden.

This edition is not a real translation. I wrote the original in both Romanian and English, so this edition is actually an original, too. To express this in other words, it was translated by the author himself.

The reader is warned that some of the footnotes refer to articles and books written by evolutionist or atheist scientists. Those references are only listed for those who want to know in detail science's account of the origin of life and the universe. Most of the footnotes with creationist references refer to articles and books written by Protestant scientists, and some of those works contain, in addition to the scientific arguments, theological opinions, too. The reader is warned that many of those theological opinions are considered to be wrong, heretical, by the Eastern Orthodox Church. Therefore, those works can only be useful for their scientific contribution to the refuting of the theories of evolution and the Big Bang, and in no way for the theological opinions that can be found in some of them.

The author
February 18th, 2016

1. The Fools and the Wise Ones

On Sunday morning, Daniel woke up late, like he used to do every Sunday. He got out of bed, washed himself, skipped breakfast and, just before noon, he left home to meet his friend, John.

Daniel and John were both the same age: 27. They had been to college together, had graduated in the same year and had both found well-paying jobs, though in different companies. Neither of them was married, but John was planning to get married in a few months. Daniel had broken up with his girlfriend a few weeks ago, so for now, marriage was, for him, an event way too distant in time. Sometimes the two men saw each other on Sundays, to have lunch together.

On his way to the restaurant, Daniel took a shortcut because he was a little bit late. He passed by a church and slowed down for a second. The service had just finished and the people were going home. Most of them seemed to be in their 50s, but among them Daniel also saw a few young ones, here and there.

'Losers,' he said to himself. 'I can't understand why they are wasting their time like this… It's Sunday, you can sleep longer or do a lot of other useful things. Why would you waste your time in church?'

John had arrived and was waiting for Daniel near the entrance of the restaurant. They sat down at a table and started to browse through the menu. They had seen each other last week, so they didn't have too many new issues to discuss. After enumerating the latest movies and songs recently released, there followed a short debate about the newest computer technologies.

Then a short silence set in, during which the waiter brought their food.

After thinking for a few seconds, Daniel mentioned the people he had seen at the church:

"On my way here, I passed by a church, and I saw some people who had stayed there a few hours. When I passed by, I think the service had just finished and they were going home."

"OK, so?"

"And I don't understand why those people are wasting their time there... Some of them, very few, were young, about our age."

"I think I understand what you want to say. To you, it seems foolish to spend two or three hours in church on Sunday mornings. To you, those people seem to be idiots."

"Exactly."

"It's obvious," John said, "that if indeed there is no God, those people are the greatest losers on the face of the earth, because they're wasting their lives for nothing. You know, besides two or three hours Sunday morning, there are a lot of other things that their religion is asking of them, and which affect their lives profoundly."

"Yes, that's true."

"But it is equally obvious that, however, if there is a God, then maybe the greatest losers are us and the other people like us, who never go to church."

"Maybe... But how do you know that there is a God?" asked Daniel.

"I don't know."

"Then why go to church? Besides, there is more than one religion. And every one of them claims to be the true one..."

"Because you just mentioned that there are multiple religions, here's an extreme example. Do you remember the attacks of September 11, 2001?"

"Of course, everybody remembers."

"Well," John said, "I don't know whether there is a God or not, but even two nonbelievers like me and like you have to admit, although it may be very hard for them, that if the religious beliefs of those terrorists are true, in the afterlife they will be in heaven accompanied by 70 virgins each, and we are going to be in hell."

"You're joking."

"Not at all, I'm very serious. But there are three *ifs*. *If* there is a God. *If* Islam is the true religion. And *if* their interpretation of the Quran is the correct one. You have to admit that *if* these three conditions are met, the 19 terrorists were some of the wisest men in the world, while the atheists and all those of other religions are just some losers."

"I really, really hope that it isn't so," Daniel said.

"I hope that, too."

"So we both hope. But for me, hope is not enough. I would like to know for sure. So how do we *know* whether it is or it isn't so?"

John didn't say anything. Daniel went on:

"You say you're a nonbeliever, but sometimes you seem to be on religion's side."

"I'm not a believer," answered John. "But I'm not a complete nonbeliever, either. I simply don't want to think about religion now; I have more important things to do. I'll think about God and religion when I'm old. So let's say I'm a temporary nonbeliever."

Daniel pondered for a few seconds, then said, smiling:

"You're not going to like this, but I have to tell it to you: Even a temporary nonbeliever like you has to admit, although it may be very hard for him, that if he dies before getting old, he won't have time to think about God and religion anymore and, if there is an afterlife, he will be counted with the nonbelievers."

"Yes, I have to think about this possibility, too, but not right now," John said, also smiling.

"And now let's get back to my problem. You want to wait till old age to figure out whether there is a God or not. But I don't want to wait that long. Maybe there is no God, but I want to know for sure, so I can live my life without worrying that after death I'll be asked why I didn't go to church, to the mosque or to the synagogue. Or to the Buddhist temple."

John laughed.

"And how exactly did you think to proceed in order to find out for sure?"

"I thought," Daniel said, "about going to see a priest and ask him what exactly makes him think there is a God. Maybe this way I'll see that there are no serious arguments."

"I want to know what the priest will answer, too."

2. Is There a God? I Want to Know!

Daniel postponed seeing the priest for a few weeks. He didn't know any priests, and he also had no religious friends. Besides, it seemed to him that his question was a little bit weird and he won't be taken seriously. Eventually, one Sunday around noon, he stopped in front of the church he had noticed before. This time it was a little bit later in the day and almost everyone was gone. He got closer to the door, trying to see whether anyone was still inside. He noticed a young man, maybe a few years older than him, who was also getting ready to leave.

"Hi," Daniel said.

"Hi," the young man replied.

"I'm looking for the priest."

"He just left, actually everybody has left. I'm locking the church and I'm leaving, too. Can I help you with anything? I have the priest's phone number if you want to talk to him."

"No, no, I wanted to ask him something face to face."

"Then, if you have a personal question for him, you'll have to wait till next Sunday. But if it's a question related to the church or to the religious services schedule, you can ask me. I'm Michael and I take care of the church when the priest is not here. Do you want to schedule a religious service, a marriage or a baptism?"

"My name is Daniel. I have a problem and I was wondering if he could help me. I wanted to ask him... I wanted to ask him a rather unusual question... I wanted to ask him how does he know that there is a God?"

A short silence followed.

"It's a really important problem for me," Daniel added quickly, thinking that he was not being taken seriously.

Michael looked at him for a few seconds. Daniel was silent.

"How does the priest *know* that there is a God?" Michael asked eventually.

"Yes, or how do you know? Or how does any believer know that there is a God?"

'What makes you guys dedicate so much of your lives to this God, how can you be so sure that He exists?' Daniel added to himself.

"Or how do I *know*... I'm afraid you're asking the wrong question. What kind of *know* do you have in mind? You want to know whether God exists the same way you know, for example, what your height is, what the speed of light is or what the distance to the moon is?"

"Exactly, how can you prove scientifically that God exists, what tangible, observable proof is there?" Daniel asked, already thinking that Michael had no solid arguments.

"Some time ago I asked myself a similar question," Michael said.

"And what answer did you find?"

"Look, I am neither a priest, nor a scientist. However, if you want to find out my opinion, if you want to know how it is possible to argue scientifically for the existence of God and if you have time to listen to me, let's sit down on this bench in front of the church and set some things straight. Like every modern man, you seem to put great trust in science."

"Of course, science has advanced so much during the past few decades. Science has offered us electronic devices, space travel, modern medicine, laser surgery and so many other things."

"Yes," Michael said, "science has advanced greatly during the past hundred years. And this advancement gives the modern man the illusion that he can do anything, that he can measure anything, that he can investigate anything and that he can find all the answers through science... Well, I have to disappoint you a little. If you have the time and the patience to listen to me, I'll try to prove to you that, despite all this scientific progress, our power of investigating the reality we live in is, however, very limited. I mean we're not, even by far, capable of determining, or measuring all the things we'd like to know. Actually, the most important things are completely beyond our capabilities of knowing and investigating scientifically. And I'll explain it to you step by step."

"I'm listening," Daniel said.

3. Limits of Knowledge

"Some basic things first," Michael said. "To each one of us, it seems that he or she knows very many things, from very many areas. About our day to day life; about the apartment or house we live in; about our friends and acquaintances; about the city we live in; about our country; about the history of our country; about the history of the world; about the human body; about animals and plants; about the planet we live on; about our solar system; about our galaxy; about the universe; about religion. We add new knowledge almost every day. However, only a very small part of this knowledge we have was acquired by direct observation and experiment, that is, empirically[1]. The vast majority of our knowledge was acquired from other sources, mainly from other persons, from books and from TV."

"So far, I agree," Daniel said.

Michael went on:

---

[1] Empirical: capable of being verified or disproved by observation or experiment. (Merriam-Webster)

From a scientific point of view, empirical knowledge is knowledge acquired only through the senses and by experiments performed in a laboratory.

The principle of empirical verifiability is the principle that claims that only statements that are empirically verifiable or logically necessary are cognitively meaningful. Obviously, this is an error. The principle of empirical verifiability is not logically necessary, nor can it be empirically verified, therefore it is declared null by its own rules.

"A part of the knowledge we have is related only to ourselves, for example, we know the address we live at, we know our height, and so on. Another part is about the history of mankind, for example, we all know from history that Hannibal[2] crossed the Alps with a rather large army. A part of this information is important to us, for example, our monthly income. Another part is not that important, for example, unless you like history, I don't think you care too much about Hannibal's crossing of the Alps."

"I agree, usually Hannibal is the last thing on my mind," Daniel smiled.

"And now a very important observation: Anything we observe or experience ourselves, we accept it immediately as true, because we have seen it ourselves, with our own eyes. We don't need arguments to make us believe what we see in front of us. For example, you know for sure how many rooms there are in the apartment or house you live in, because you have seen them yourself, with your own eyes, countless times. You need no arguments for this: you've seen them yourself. Now you know for sure that there is a green bench in front of this church, because you're sitting on it right now. You need no arguments to come to believe that this bench exists."

"Obviously, I see it with my own eyes."

Michael thought for a few seconds, then went on:

"But any other information we receive, from any other source, is not immediately accepted as certainly true, because it is not something we have seen with our own eyes. There is *something* inside us that filters this information, and that *something* either accepts it or rejects it. Many times the information is supported by arguments. These arguments, too, are filtered by that inner *something* and are either accepted or rejected. In short, everything, absolutely everything that is not in front of our eyes goes through this filtration process."

---

[2] Hannibal Barca (247 - 183 BC), Punic Carthaginian general, considered one of the greatest military commanders in history. He led a couple of campaigns against ancient Rome. The year of his death is uncertain (181 - 183 BC).

"Are you calling it '*something* inside us' because you don't really know what that *something* is?" Daniel asked.

"I strongly believe that that *something* is the human soul or, more precisely, the predisposition of the human soul to believe or not to believe something, or even the desire to believe or not to believe something. I also believe that man's soul, depending on its free will, is either helped by the grace of God, or influenced by the lies of the devil. But because now you might not believe in the existence of the soul, because now you might believe that that *something* is the psyche or our brain, I'll keep calling it that *something*. It is also called subjectivity, bias or even prejudice, and it has a reputation for being a bad thing. Have you ever been told that you were being subjective?"

"Countless times," Daniel admitted.

"However, I'm going to show to you that that *something* can be both good and bad, and that it is present everywhere, in all aspects of our lives."

"How about some examples?"

"Soon. One more observation and we'll move on to examples. I was telling you that the inner *something* filters every piece of information, every argument that is offered to us. But it doesn't do this randomly, it has some reasons, some internal causes; and depending on those inner reasons, it accepts or rejects the information and the arguments that it encounters. I will give you many examples in which you'll clearly see that *something* working differently for different people. You'll see situations in which the same information and the same arguments are offered to several people, and each one of them accepts or rejects them in a different way. It is very important that we stop at this, that is, at noticing the filtration process and its result, and in no case should we try to guess the reasons for which someone accepts or rejects a certain piece of information or argument. In no case should we label those who filter the information differently than us as being stupid, idiots, retarded, mean or otherwise. Later, I'll explain to you why. And now let's move on to examples, so you'll understand what I was trying to say."

"I can't wait," Daniel said, "you have made me curious. But does this have anything to do with the arguments for the existence of God?"

"Of course. But before analyzing those arguments, we have to briefly analyze our capacity of knowing the world we're living in. I mean, we have to realize which are the limits of knowledge."

3.1. Limits in Knowing the Present

3.1.1. Objects and Phenomena in Front of Us

Michael went into the church and returned a few moments later with a book.

"Let's start with the present," he said, "because here we have the greatest capabilities to investigate scientifically the world we're living in. In this present we can determine and measure very many things. Look, for example, at the building in front of us: If we want to know how wide it is, we can very easily measure it with a measuring tape. I don't think you'll ever hear people arguing about the size of that building, because it can be measured right away. In the same way, we can measure the distance to the moon, the speed of sound, the speed of light, the chemical properties of various substances, and so on. And we can do this because we have them at our disposal all the time, in front of our eyes. The building, the light, the sound, the chemical substances, and all the rest are immediately accessible to anyone who wants to study them. You won't hear anyone arguing over these subjects, because they can be measured anytime by anyone who has the necessary devices."

"Of course," Daniel said, "this is called scientific research."

3.1.2. Objects and Phenomena that We Ourselves Don't Have Access to

Michael went on:

"But let us look at something else now. In our city there is a big bank in whose vault the citizens can keep valuable objects. Can you measure how thick the vault's door is?"

"No, I can't," Daniel said. "But if I worked at that bank, I could."

"Aha! Here we have to make an important observation: Although the thickness of the vault's door can be measured very easily, it cannot be measured by me or by you, but only by very few of the bank's employees. If the bank publishes an ad in a local newspaper and claims that the vault's door is 30 centimeters[3] thick, then we have our first example of information acquired empirically by others, and which is offered to us in order to believe it. We can see the ad in the newspaper and, if it seems interesting to us and we memorize it, the thickness of the vault's door will be added to the multitude of information we already have. But, unlike the width of the building mentioned before, this time we have no possibility to verify with our own eyes whether the information is true or not."

"I understand," Daniel said, "some things we simply don't have access to ourselves, but other persons do have access, and we hope that those persons will tell us the truth."

3.1.3. Shape of the Earth

"Exactly. Now we move on to something a little bit more difficult," Michael went on. "Can you see with your eyes the shape of the earth?"

"Not really… Only if you're an astronaut."

"That's true. For someone on the ground, observing the shape of the planet is not something as simple and obvious like

---

[3] 30 centimeters (cm) = 11.81 inches (11' 13/16").

measuring the width of a building or the thickness of a door. However, even if you're not an astronaut, you can still see certain things. First, if you're on the seashore with a set of binoculars and you're looking at a ship that's moving away from the shore, you'll see that the ship seems to sink below the horizon line. The bottom part, although larger, disappears before the top part. And second, during a lunar eclipse, you can see that the shadow of the earth on the surface of the moon is always round."

"Yes," Daniel said, "this is how people realized for the first time that the earth was round."

"And now we will see, also for the first time, that inner *something* I told you about in action, leading different people to different conclusions. The shape of the planet cannot be seen from the ground in the same way that you can see, for example, the shape of an apple you're holding in your hand. In other words, the earth is not entirely in front of our own eyes. What can be seen from the seashore is not the shape of the planet, only a ship that seems to be sinking. The conclusion that the earth is round is only a deduction, an interpretation of the observation that the ship seems to be sinking. Although this reasoning seems very obvious to us, *something* inside some people, however, simply rejects it. Those people still believe that the earth is flat. There are extremely few of them, granted, but they exist. They claim that the ship that seems to be sinking is just an optical phenomenon."

"How is something like this possible? What about the shadow of the earth during lunar eclipses?"

"They say the shadow could look round because the moon is also round, and because the earth is shaped like a disk."

"This is absurd," Daniel said… "I've never met such a person."

"I've only met one. You see, it's possible that I was wrong just before, when I spoke about 'those' who believe the earth is round, maybe I should have spoken in the singular, maybe that person is the only one in the world who still believes something like that."

"And how do they, or how does he, explain the thousands of photographs and movie clips from space, in which it can be seen clearly that the planet looks like a sphere?"

"They're all fake, obviously. Can you imagine how many thousands or maybe tens of thousands of people, of different nationalities and religions, would have to be involved in such a conspiracy, to hide from the rest of the world the fact that the earth is flat?"

"Yes, exactly."

"I tried to explain to him that he was wrong, but I couldn't convince him. His inner predisposition was way too strong for my arguments."

"You know," Daniel said, "I think the problem could be solved rather easily. If there are more such persons, they could collect money and build a small rocket, with a camera and a transmitter attached to it, and they could launch it into space. The rocket would send them photos of the earth from an altitude of a few thousand kilometers[4] and the problem would be clarified for them, too."

"I'm afraid you're underestimating the power of one's predisposition to reject even a very solid argument, when his or her inner *something* is very well motivated. You see, if there is a global conspiracy that fakes the photos sent by astronauts from space, then certainly those conspirators could also intercept the photos sent back by their rocket, and could replace them with some fake ones, in which the earth looks like a sphere."

"This is downright ridiculous! Why would anyone believe something like that? Does the shape of the earth have any religious significance? Is this a matter of faith?"

"As far as I understand, the shape of the earth has no religious significance, as Saint Basil the Great also says.[5] Some would go even further and say that turning an insignificant matter into a matter of faith is a heresy, a rather serious sin. However, I believe that God looks at the heart of the man, at his inner motives

---

[4] 1,000 km = 622.28 miles.

[5] St. Basil the Great, *Hexaemeron*, Homily IX.

that make him believe or not believe something, as it is written in the Bible:"

«But the Lord said to Samuel, "Have no regard for his outward appearance, nor for the maturity of his stature, because I have refused him. For man does not see as God sees; for man looks at the outward appearance, but the Lord sees into the heart."»[6]

Michael went on:

"Therefore, my opinion is that if one has a strong and simple faith, and he doesn't understand the scientific arguments, and he believes that the earth is flat, then this can do much good to his soul, and it can get him closer to God, even though his belief is wrong and has no religious significance. And at the same time I believe that if one is being motivated by hatred, by self-love, by the desire to always be right or by other bad motives, then such a belief would do harm to his soul even if the earth were indeed flat. But only God knows the inner motives of each one of us; that's why we have to refrain from judging anyone. Instead, we are more than encouraged to judge ourselves and our own inner motives."

"You said hatred could be a reason. Hatred against whom?"

"Hatred against the modern world, against modern science, against the scientists, and so on. Hatred is a very dangerous feeling, no matter against whom it is directed. When you hate someone you tend to not believe anything he has to say, or, even worse, to believe exactly the opposite, which can be very dangerous, even if that someone were the devil himself. Imagine that someone tells you nine truths, in order to gain your trust, and then a lie, to deceive you. But you think you know what he's up to, and you suppose, incorrectly, that he's telling you lies and only lies, and so you take the nine truths as lies as well."

"I understand," Daniel said. "This is dangerous, indeed."

---

[6] 1 Kingdoms 16:7 (NKJV: 1 Samuel 16:7).

"The desire to always be right may also be dangerous, even if we are truly right, as we are warned by Saint John of the Ladder[7], a Christian monk who lived in the 6th and 7th centuries:"

> He whose will and desire in conversation is to establish his own opinion, even though what he says is true, should recognize that he is sick with the devil's disease.[8]

"Interesting idea, so as you understand it, from a religious point of view, what matters the most are the inner motives, which are known to God alone. OK, it was interesting to see where hatred can lead. We can move on now."

3.1.4. Rotation of the Earth

"Now let's look at something even more difficult to determine, namely the rotation of the earth. Unlike the shape of the earth, which can, however, be observed with our own eyes if we get into space, there is no way to observe the rotation of the earth; it can only be deduced. It cannot be observed because there is no absolute reference system at rest, against which we can relate. From the surface of the earth it seems that we are at rest and the entire universe is rotating around us. From the surface of the moon it seems the same, that the moon is at rest and the universe is rotating around it."

"Yes," Daniel said, "I know the problem from physics; we don't have an absolute reference system."

"Exactly. Because of this, the rotation of the planet can only be deduced, not observed, like you observe the rotation of a car's wheel. And the experiments are rather simple, namely Foucault's

---

[7] He is named "of the Ladder" because of his book titled *The Ladder of Divine Ascent* (also known as *The Ladder of Paradise*, or briefly *The Ladder*). He is also known as St. John Scholasticus, St. John Sinaites or St. John Climacus.

[8] St. John Climacus (of the Ladder), *The Ladder of Divine Ascent*, translated by Archimandrite Lazarus Moore, Harper & Brothers, 1959, Step 4:48.

pendulum and the gyroscope. Everybody can set up something like that at home and can observe that the pendulum's plane of swing is not fixed, it rotates with an angular velocity that depends on the geographical latitude."[9]

"I remember this experiment from physics," Daniel said, "it was the first serious proof that the earth was rotating."

"A more difficult experiment can be done with the gyroscope. If you hold a gyroscope in your hand, you notice that no matter how you move and rotate the handle, the direction of the disk's rotation axis remains unchanged as long as the disk keeps spinning. And if you try to change the direction of that axis, you notice immediately that it resists. However, if the rotation axis is turned toward the sun or some stars, it rotates very slowly, following the star that it points to."

"Obviously. Actually, that axis is fixed, it is the earth that is rotating."

"OK, and now we'll see again that inner *something* in action. Although to us, the two experiments I just described look very convincing, some people, called geocentrists, continue to believe that the earth is fixed and that the rest of the universe is rotating around it. There are very few of them, granted, but still a few more than those who believe that the earth is flat."

"I'm very curious to know," Daniel said, "how do they explain the very precise rotations of the pendulum and the gyroscope? How can a mindless object like the gyroscope know which way and at what speed the sun is moving?"

"They say there is a universal force that rotates the universe around the earth, and it is that force that also rotates the pendulum and the gyroscope."

"To me this seems absurd," Daniel said. "Why isn't it rotating other objects, too? For example, if I hang a sheet of paper on the ceiling lamp, why isn't that universal force rotating it? If you spent a few thousand euros on a powerful telescope, you could

---

[9] The angular velocity of the pendulum's plane is given by the formula $360° \times \sin(\text{latitude}) / \text{day}$. At $45°$ latitude, the velocity is $254.56° / \text{day}$.

see with your eyes the geostationary satellites as light dots that stay motionless in the sky. All stars move from East to West, but they remain all night in their fixed position. Why aren't they falling down, if the earth is fixed? Or why aren't they moved by that force that is rotating the universe?"

"This proves how powerful that inner *something* is," Michael said; "it can annihilate almost any argument."

"Yes, maybe…"

"Although I don't know for sure, I still want to tell you that it is possible that the earth was once fixed and the universe was rotating around it. If it has ever been so, it was only in the primordial world, before the sin of Adam and Eve, which resulted in the corruption of the entire creation and the change of the laws of the material world. We'll talk about this later, if you want to listen. Nowadays, it would only be possible for the universe to rotate around the earth if the laws of physics outside our planet were completely different. But in this case, the engineers who are launching satellites and other space vehicles and are tracking their trajectories for many years would have certainly noticed this by now."

"Maybe there's a conspiracy in there, too," Daniel said smiling ironically.

"And if there were a conspiracy, I wonder how many thousands or tens of thousands of people, from so many countries and so many religions, would have to be involved in that conspiracy? Another alternative for geocentrism would be for the laws of physics to be the same all over the universe, but for God to continuously perform miracles in order to keep the celestial bodies on unnatural orbits around the earth. This is not impossible; God is all-powerful and He can do anything, but I don't really believe that He's doing this. Although I'm a believer and I believe in miracles, I don't believe this scenario because I see that usually matter behaves according to some natural laws pre-established by God, the law of gravity being one of them. God intervenes and performs a miracle only in some situations, and with a certain purpose. For example, when an apple's stem dries up, the apple falls to the ground because of the law of gravity. There is no need for God to send an angel to take the apple and put it down."

"Does the motion or the non-motion of the earth have any religious significance?" Daniel asked.

"I don't think it has any religious significance. As for those who believe that it has such significance, I have the same opinion as about those who believe the earth is flat. If their inner motives are good, such a belief, kept despite the fact that the entire world makes fun of them, can do much good to their souls, even though it is wrong. But if their inner motives are bad, such a belief would do harm to their souls even if the earth were indeed standing still. Of course, we must not and we cannot judge other people's motives, but it is everyone's duty to analyze his own motives and to get rid of the bad ones."

"I understand," Daniel said. "So you think that, from a religious point of view, in such cases it doesn't matter how correct the opinion is, but the inner motives that determine that inner *something* to incline one way or another."

"Yes, this is my opinion. This is how I understand it, that God looks at the heart of the man, not at what we see on the outside."

After a few moments of silence, Michael went on:

"Some time ago I met someone, a very religious person, who was totally against the system."

"The 'system' being who?" Daniel asked.

"By the 'system' he meant modern government, modern science and some secret societies that are suspected by some people to be ruling the world from behind the scenes. Well, yes, from a religious standpoint, this system is indeed diabolical: It makes abortion legal and presents it as something normal; it teaches the theories of Big Bang and evolution in schools and on TV as they were the only possible explanations, and so on. If you watch TV on almost any channel, usually in less than half an hour you'll see that intimate relations between unmarried persons, a mortal sin from a religious point of view, are accepted as if they were something perfectly normal. This is why I say that the 'system' is indeed diabolical. But that person had come to say that maybe smoking is good, otherwise the system wouldn't be trying to persuade us to give it up."

"Is that so?" Daniel asked, astonished. "Even smokers know that smoking is bad for their health."

"Yes, he really said this. I think it is very dangerous to totally and indiscriminately oppose a theory, a person, a system or even the devil himself. Yes, even if the system were the devil himself, Christian tradition teaches us to ignore anything coming from him. We should not believe what he's saying, but also we should not come to believe the opposite either. We should simply ignore him completely. Although in such a case we might be tempted to say that the man is motivated by hatred against the system, I think that we should refrain from guessing what his reasons are. Let's try not to judge his inner state, the Lord has told us to judge no one:"

> *«Judge not, that you be not judged. For with what judgment you judge, you will be judged; and with the measure you use, it will be measured back to you.»*[10]

"And we certainly cannot make a right judgment anyway," Michael concluded.

"This is a useful lesson," Daniel said. "When I was a teenager, sometimes I acted exactly contrary to how my parents were advising me, because I was being rebellious. I was not doing the things that I wished to do, but exactly the opposite of the advice I was getting from them. I was even doing things I didn't like, just because they were contrary to my parents' advice."

"I think now you realize that it was just your inner *something* in action."

"Yes, probably."

3.1.5. Vaccines

"OK, let's move on now to something even more controversial, namely vaccines."

---

[10] Matthew 7:1-2.

"Yes," Daniel said, "here we'll probably find even more people who dispute the generally accepted idea that vaccines are good and useful. I too know a few persons who are against vaccination."

"Yes, I told you that we are going to take it step by step. Here we see another kind of a limit of knowledge. Although the human body and the chemical substances are permanently in front of us, it is impossible to determine or to exactly measure a vaccine's effect on a human being. And this is not only because of the complexity of the human body, but also because the research is limited by ethical reasons: it is usually wrong and immoral to perform experiments on people. Modern medicine assures us that vaccines are safe, that they are effective, and urges us to get vaccinated. But the number of people who don't accept this is significantly larger than the number of people who believe that the earth is flat or that the universe is rotating around us."

"What complicates things is that there also are some doctors and scientists who claim that vaccines are not good."

"The effects of a vaccine on the human body cannot be measured as easily as you measure, for example, the width of a building. It is by far not as easy and obvious as some claim, since some side effects can only be detected after a couple of days or even months. Because of this, each person uses, sometimes unconsciously, his inner *something* in order to accept or to reject the arguments of modern medicine. If you study the problem, you will notice that this is actually a battle between arguments. The advocates of vaccines enumerate their benefits, especially preventing and eradicating diseases. Usually, advocates don't seem to know cases of children who suffered serious side effects following vaccination. And when such cases are brought to their attention, they say that it's not the vaccine to blame, that the parents of those children are medically illiterate and they're talking nonsense. The opponents of vaccines enumerate the adverse effects and the fact that in some countries, cases of certain diseases decreased without vaccination about as much as they did in the countries where the population was vaccinated. Usually, opponents don't seem to know cases of children who got sick with some serious diseases because they hadn't been vaccinated. And when such cases are brought to their attention, some of them say that these are lies, that the parents of those children are 'people of the system,' paid to lie, and so on. Sometimes the vaccine opponents talk like the diseases that these vaccines are trying to prevent didn't even exist."

"And yet, most of us are vaccinated, and we're still alive and rather healthy. So where does the idea that they're so harmful come from?"

"Read for example the leaflet of the Hepatitis B vaccine. You'll see there listed a lot of contraindications[11] and possible side effects, some of them very serious. In our country[12], this vaccine is administered to babies in their first day of life. The obvious question is this: Does anyone test the baby to see whether he is vulnerable to any of the conditions listed in the vaccine's leaflet? Usually the answer is no."

"I'm trying to figure out whose side you are on," Daniel said.

"I'm not on either side; I'm only saying that this is an issue that is very difficult to clarify, a limit of knowledge. For example, one of the main accusations against vaccines is that they cause allergies. The pro-vaccine side keeps saying that there is no clear scientific proof that vaccines cause allergies. The anti-vaccine side claims that there is also no clear scientific proof that vaccines have nothing to do with allergies. Both sides should admit that, if there is indeed no proof, then this only means we don't know. That's all, we simply don't know. Lack of proof for a statement doesn't mean that the statement is false, it only means that we don't know whether it is true or false. In November 2001, in the US city of Seattle, scientists debated the hypothesis according to which vaccines cause disorders of the immune system, especially

---

[11] Contraindication: something (such as a symptom or condition) that is a medical reason for not doing or using something (such as a treatment, procedure, or activity). (Merriam-Webster)

[12] Romania.

allergies and autoimmune diseases.[13] The conclusion was that there is no clear proof for or against this accusation.[14] In other words, we cannot know for sure."

"This is the 21st century, how is it possible that we can't know for sure? Haven't so many studies been conducted about this subject?"

"Yes, there have, but the results are not clear, and sometimes they are even contradictory. For example, a certain group of children from Sweden who received fewer vaccines also were found to have fewer allergies. For the moment, it seems there is a connection between vaccines and allergies. But if we look further, we see that those children were also administered fewer antibiotics and that they consumed a larger percentage of organic food. Therefore, the connection is not that clear anymore. It is possible that that group had fewer allergies because of the other two reasons, too, not necessarily because of the lack of vaccines. Science simply cannot determine the true cause or causes. It is beyond science's capabilities and it should admit it."

"Indeed," Daniel said, "when you have two or three possible known causes, there is no way to know which one is the real culprit. Then you think that there could also be other causes, which are unknown at this moment..."

"Here's another study, mentioned very often by the advocates of vaccination. In East Germany, before reunification, vaccination was mandatory. However, allergies were rather rare. After the 1990 reunification, the vaccine advocates say that vaccination rates went down a little, but the number of allergies started to climb. Obviously, as in the case of the Swedish children, all the details need to be clarified: Have new substances been introduced

---

[13] Autoimmune disease: disorder of the immune system in which it attacks the host organism, because the immune system mistakes the organism for external pathogens. An example of an autoimmune disease is psoriasis.

[14] http://www8.nationalacademies.org/onpinews/newsitem.aspx?RecordID=10306

in the vaccines after 1990? Have the procedures for diagnosing and recording allergies changed after 1990? And so on."

"Yes, I begin to understand now why it is so hard to find the truth."

"Recently a new theory emerged, according to which the main culprit for the increase in the number of allergies is excessive hygiene. In other words, too much hygiene is harmful to the immune system, and causes it to start to behave abnormally.[15] Obviously, this theory has not been clearly proven, either. I'm not trying to jump to the defense of one side or the other, I'm only trying to show you that science has reached some limits that are very hard for it to overcome, although it doesn't usually admit this."

"But are vaccines effective in preventing diseases, or not?"

"I think it is clear enough that they are indeed effective, that they prevent the infection in most cases. But it is equally clear that there are also countless adverse effects, some very serious, some less serious. The truth is that their effects vary from person to person, and we should humbly admit that we simply cannot know exactly all the details related to this subject. I know cases of children who were left partially paralyzed following the administration of a vaccine. What is truly sad is that in such cases, the doctors treat the parents like they are idiots, tell them that they don't understand medicine and that actually, the child was left paralyzed for other reasons. What a coincidence, exactly when the vaccine was injected! But I also know the case of a family that, following the advice of the vaccine opponents, did not vaccinate their child against tuberculosis, and the child got sick with this disease at the age of a couple of months and this brought him to the brink of death. Also, very sad, when I tell this story to the anti-vaccine people sometimes I get back replies like 'Are you sure it is so? Maybe they are paid to lie.'"

"This really is outrageous," Daniel complained.

"You see, that's why I'm not on either side. I'm disappointed by both sides. But let's get back to what we are analyzing, that is,

---

[15] https://en.wikipedia.org/wiki/Hygiene_hypothesis

the inner *something* and the impossibility of knowing some things with certainty. During the talk about vaccines I gave you several examples of that *something* in action. I think you were able to detect them, too."

"Yes, I think so," Daniel said. Although I'm not a doctor, I, too, know that vaccines are a little bit controversial. If everything were clear and safe, why would there be an official website financed by the American government for monitoring the negative effects of vaccines?[16] I, too, know that each human body is unique and it reacts differently to different substances. Some may end up with a gastric hemorrhage because of a common aspirin; others can get into anaphylactic shock[17] because of a dose of penicillin. So it is obvious that the substances in the vaccines will cause different reactions in different people, reactions that are impossible to anticipate before the administration of the vaccine. So, I observe that vaccine advocates don't accept the accounts of those who complain of serious secondary reactions after vaccination, although there's no way for them to prove that the vaccine is not the culprit. *Something* inside them makes them believe that other causes are to blame. Similarly, the vaccine opponents blame vaccines without being able to prove in any way that indeed they are the culprit. *Something* inside them assures them that the vaccines are to blame. Here I agree with you: When you have a serious medical situation a few hours or days after vaccination, it is impossible to argue scientifically, clearly and unequivocally, that the vaccine is or is not guilty. It is simply beyond the capabilities of modern medicine. Some will believe that the vaccine is the cause, and others that it isn't, as their inner *something* tells them."

---

[16] https://vaers.hhs.gov/
VAERS: Vaccine Adverse Event Reporting System, a program of two US governmental agencies, CDC (Centers for Disease Control and Prevention) and FDA (Food and Drug Administration).

[17] Anaphylactic shock (or anaphylaxis): an often severe and sometimes fatal systemic reaction in a susceptible individual upon exposure to a specific antigen (as wasp venom or penicillin) after previous sensitization that is characterized especially by respiratory symptoms, fainting, itching, and hives. (Merriam-Webster)

Michael looked gladly at Daniel and said:

"I'm glad that you've come to this conclusion."

"And I think I've also detected something about you, too," Daniel said.

"What exactly?" Michael asked.

"Well, you seemed pretty indignant that some vaccine opponents treated with distrust the parents whose unvaccinated child got sick, suggesting that maybe they are paid to lie. But how well do you know that family? Do you know for sure that they had not been paid to lie? Is it not that *something* inside you that makes you believe they are honest, even though you have no concrete evidence about this?"

"You're making progress," Michael smiled. "Yes, obviously, I have no concrete evidence, but indeed, *something* inside me makes me almost sure that they are honest. You see, as I was telling you, that *something* is present in almost all aspects of our lives. I'm glad you're starting to see it, too."

"Yes, and I hope that eventually I'll also see what this discussion has to do with the evidence about the existence of God. You know, this is actually what I'm interested in the most."

"We're getting there, soon. For now I want to add just two things, one for each belligerent side. First, it is possible that some vaccine advocates are aware of the side effects, but they treat everything like some mere numbers."

"What do you mean?"

"For example, they have to vaccinate 1,000,000 people. Of these, 1,880 show serious side effects after vaccination, and 20 more die. For them this is a success rate of 99.8%, which they may consider to be good. The second problem is that some of the scientists who oppose vaccinations may be doing this for evolutionary reasons. I mean, some of them may be of the opinion that humans who don't have the strength to naturally defeat the disease should be left to die, otherwise we're not letting natural selection do its job right."

"Although I'm still not a believer, it seems very wrong to me to see things that way. However, from an evolutionary standpoint, they are right, only the strongest and most resilient people should survive and reproduce..."

"This is just one of the reasons why I don't believe in the theory of evolution, but we're getting there, soon."

"How is the problem of vaccines seen from a religious point of view?"

"From a religious point of view, nothing ever happens by chance alone. Everything that happens in this world, no matter how insignificant it seems to us, happens either because God directly causes it, or because God allows it to happen:"

«Are not two sparrows sold for a copper coin? And not one of them falls to the ground apart from your Father's will. But the very hairs of your head are all numbered. Do not fear therefore; you are of more value than many sparrows.»[18]

"However," Michael went on, "people have to do their part in order to prevent bad things from happening. For example, when I get behind the wheel, I have to pay attention to the road and the traffic, and not close my eyes and say that God will turn the steering wheel for me. But there is no clear delimitation between our part and God's part; each person sees his part differently, as his inner *something* dictates to him. Therefore, in my opinion, from a religious point of view there are two approaches for the problem of vaccines. First: One can refuse the vaccines and pray to God to protect him from diseases. Second: One can accept the vaccines and pray to God to protect him from the side effects. So this is up to each person's faith and to how convinced he is that vaccines are harmful or not. Some people say that it is our duty to do everything possible to avoid the disease, and therefore we have to get vaccinated. As they see it, if you don't get vaccinated, it is like you yourself are causing your disease, and maybe even your death. Others say exactly the opposite. Opinions are divided."

---

[18] Matthew 10:29-31.

"So there is no safe choice that can certainly keep you from any negative consequences. From a religious point of view, you say, you have to trust that God will protect you from either the disease, or the side effects."

"Maybe some people understand it this way. But I think that putting your trust in God doesn't mean to believe that you won't get sick or that you won't suffer any side effects, but to believe that God takes care primarily of your soul and, even if you do get sick or suffer a side effect, the disease or the side effect is allowed by God for the salvation of the soul."

"You mean to accept the disease or the side effect as something sent by God?"

"Exactly. Bottom line, I think this is about each person's faith. Some people see the vaccine as an insurance policy, and the risk of a side effect like the premium paid for that policy. I remember, however, that Saint Paisios of Mount Athos, a 20th century Greek monk, was telling someone that there is no greater insurance than the trust in God.[19] I don't think he was talking about vaccines, but the idea is the same. And I perfectly agree with him; if I had his faith, I wouldn't insure my car and my home, and I would probably never get vaccinated. But because my faith is way weaker than Saint Paisios' faith, I have optional insurance for both my car and my home. And if in my city very many cases of a serious infectious disease were reported, and the vaccine didn't have a bad reputation, I probably would get vaccinated and I would pray to be kept from side effects. Otherwise, I would probably refuse the vaccine and I would pray to not get sick. Anyway, this is just my opinion and I don't advise anyone to do as I do. Everyone decides for himself. Someone with a stronger faith than mine probably will proceed otherwise, will never get optional insurance policies and will reject the vaccine regardless of the risk."

"They say that soon vaccination will be mandatory."

---

[19] Elder Paisios of Mount Athos, *Spiritual Counsels*, vol. 2 (*Spiritual Awakening*), Holy Monastery "Evangelist John the Theologian," Souroti, Thessaloniki, Greece, 2008, p. 304.

"I really don't agree with this. Although I'm trying to be neutral and I don't advise anyone to either accept or reject the vaccines, I am, however, against making them mandatory. You can't force someone to get a vaccine; it is each person's choice. The government doesn't own our bodies."

3.1.6. Christmas Bonuses

Michael kept quiet for a moment, looked at his watch, then went on:

"Now let us analyze a hypothetical example. Let's say that every year before Christmas, all the employees of the company you work for are expecting a bonus, the Christmas bonus. But in a certain year, the management of the company said that the company had little revenue, so there will be no bonus."

"I've heard of such cases from friends working in other companies."

"What do you think?" Michael asked. "Did everybody react the same way? I mean, did they all believe the official explanation, or did they all refuse to believe it?"

"No, of course not. Some believed that indeed that year there hadn't been enough profit. Others believed that the bosses were lying. Some were very indignant. Others were resigned and tranquil."

"But, save the top management, how many of them really knew what the financial situation of the company was? Did any of them have access to the real numbers, to the proceeds and expenses?"

"Probably not," Daniel said.

"So none of them knew exactly what the truth was," Michael said.

"I see what you're trying to say," Daniel said, "although all of them were in the same boat, that is, they were having only a very vague idea about how the company they were working for was doing, they arrived at very different conclusions. Yes, it is clear, *something* inside them made them either accept or reject the story offered by the management. Or partially accept it. Or partially reject it."

"Although I presented the problem to you in a simplified manner, you understood that actually the situation is not either white or black, but that there could also be many shades of gray. Our inner predisposition can make us accept something, reject something, partially accept something, enthusiastically accept something, partially reject something, categorically reject something, be undecided and try to clarify things, or even decide that we're not at all interested in that subject and that we can forget about it."

3.1.7. Everyday Life

Daniel nodded and Michael went on:

"As I was telling you, that *something* is to be found in almost all aspects of our lives, because it is very often that we have to accept or to reject an argument, or to interpret something and draw a conclusion. Look, for example, at your workplace there is a small argument between two coworkers, let's say between Andrew and George, an argument witnessed by all the others. Do you think everybody will interpret the incident the same way? Some will take Andrew's side, others will take George's side, while still others will reproach both of them that they're noisy and are not letting the others work. And some will say that they're both right, that they're expressing differently the same thing, and that there's nothing to argue about."

"Yes, I've seen situations like this."

"Well, this is another example in which that inner *something* of ours reacts differently even when several persons have seen and have heard exactly the same thing, with their own eyes and with their own ears. Now let's try to find some real examples from your life."

"How exactly?" Daniel asked.

"Try to remember, have you ever been wrongly accused? Have you ever been reproached for doing something that you actually didn't do?"

"Certainly, it has happened many times. Obviously, there was no way for those who accused me to know the truth with certainty, but *something* inside them preferred to believe that I was guilty."

"Let's also look for a positive example. I mean an example in which you did something bad on purpose, but somebody else preferred to believe that you didn't actually do it on purpose."

"Something like this doesn't happen too often, but yes, I remember such an occurrence, too. Once I lied to a friend, and the truth was soon discovered. But my friend did not accuse me of lying to him. He simply thought that I told him things I sincerely believed to be true, although they actually weren't. *Something* inside him preferred to believe that I didn't lie to him on purpose. I remember I felt very guilty…"

"I'm glad you also found an example in which somebody preferred a positive explanation," Michael said.

"Such things happen all the time. For example, you set your phone to silent mode and you forget about it, you miss a few calls, you notice it in the evening, when it is too late to call them back, and some of those who called you draw the conclusion that you did not want to talk to them. Yes, some people are very suspicious; they immediately draw the conclusion that they were lied to. *Something* inside them has a predisposition to this, has something against other people."

"It's possible," Michael said, "but let's not judge people's inner reasons; we'll never know them for sure."

"Meanwhile, some people are very naive, I mean they believe you even when you tell them a lie. I understand what you're trying to say. Neither the naive ones, nor the suspicious ones know the truth, but *something* inside them makes them incline one way or another. And both of them can be wrong; the naive one may believe a lie, and the suspicious one may reject the truth."

"If we look carefully, we'll see that we're confronted very often with situations like this, therefore we have to pay attention to ourselves, to the way we're filtering the information and the arguments that we encounter in day to day life. If in front of this parking lot there were a hundred people and each one of them were asked how many cars are in it, all without exception would answer immediately that there are four cars. And that's because the cars in the parking lot are accessible, right in front of their own eyes, and counting them is extremely easy, and the result of the counting is in no way filtered by anything inside them. But any other more complex thing passes through this filtration process, and the results, as you can see, differ from person to person. And sometimes they differ a lot."

"Yes," Daniel admitted, "I agree."

"God told us not to judge anyone, but instead we have to judge ourselves, we have to pay a lot of attention to that inner *something* of ours and to its inclinations. Let's think about a person we like and trust, and we'll notice that if we hear something good about him, we might be somewhat predisposed to believe that thing without much proof, and if we hear something bad, we might be somewhat predisposed to not believe that thing, even though we're offered some arguments, or it may seem an insignificant thing to us. Then, though it is a sin to hate someone, let's suppose for a moment that there is a person we don't like and whom we don't trust. Let's think about that hypothetical person, and we'll notice that if we hear something good about him, we might be somewhat predisposed to not believe that thing, even though we're offered some arguments, or it may seem an insignificant thing to us, and if we hear something bad, we might be somewhat predisposed to believe that thing without much proof. And, obviously, we can be wrong in all four cases mentioned just before. Therefore, I believe that we have to always be reserved and leave any judgment to God."

"I imagine that an ill-intentioned person can take advantage of these inner predispositions of ours. For example, he can spread negative false rumors about someone."

"He can do something even worse; for example, he can spread positive false rumors. I mean he can say that a certain person, public or not, did a certain good thing, a thing which that person didn't actually do. Maybe this person did other good things, but not that one. But his sympathizers might believe and even spread those rumors, and when they prove to be false, their trust in that person might be seriously affected, because they might think the other good things they have heard about him are false, too. And also the other way around, one might spread negative false rumors about himself, and then he will also clearly prove them to be untrue. Thus, his critics might believe that other negative things they have heard about him are false, too."

"Those would really be some very bad deeds," Daniel said. "Real cases of psychological manipulation."

"Yes, that's true. However, I told you these things not in order to discourage you and to make you not trust anybody or anything anymore, but instead for you to be aware of our limitations. I'll give you two more real life examples told by Saint Paisios of Mount Athos, whom I told you about before. Once he was visited by a child who didn't know him. 'I want to see Father Paisios,' the child said, not knowing that he was talking to him. 'He went to buy cigarettes,' Father Paisios joked. 'It looks like he must have gone to help someone,'[20] the child replied."[21]

"So nice of him; he didn't even think that Father Paisios was the one who needed the cigarettes."

"Obviously, Saint Paisios didn't smoke. And here is the second example. Saint Paisios had just convinced someone to quit smoking, and that person had left the pack of cigarettes in the church, where the discussion had taken place. And the next person who went in saw the pack and drew the conclusion that Saint Paisios used to smoke inside the church."[22]

"Yes, a typical example of a wrong conclusion."

---

[20] In the Romanian translation: "It looks like he went to buy them for someone."

[21] Elder Paisios of Mount Athos, *Spiritual Counsels*, vol. 3 (*Spiritual Struggle*), Holy Monastery "Evangelist John the Theologian," Souroti, Thessaloniki, Greece, 2010, pp. 29-31.

[22] Ibid., pp. 70-73.

3.1.8. Complex Systems

"Now I'll give you another example of things whose knowledge is sometimes uncertain for us, despite the fact that they are things that we ourselves are making. And here I'm talking about the complex mechanical and electronic systems. Although they are created by humans, the very people who made them cannot fully understand the way they function. I'll mention only two examples, namely large airplanes and computer software. Both are extremely complex, are tested by hundreds or even thousands of people before being put on the market, and still, many times, design defects are discovered in them even years after being put to use. Their complexity makes certain defects become visible only in certain conditions. I've seen cases of passenger planes with design or manufacturing defects that caused them to crash several years after being put to use. Here's an example that includes both categories of products: in 2007, six F22 fighter jets, recently put to use, experienced total failure of their onboard computers when they crossed the International Date Line, you know, that imaginary line that runs from North to South through the middle of the Pacific Ocean, the crossing of which implies changing the date.[23] The problem was so serious that the pilots were unable to restart the computers; without computers, electronic navigation was no longer possible, and all six jets had to return to their base following the refueling aircraft that were accompanying them."

"How did such a thing happen to all six of them?" Daniel asked.

"The engineers who had written the program for those computers had not considered all possible scenarios. And when the

---

[23] Crossing that line implies adjusting the calendar date by one day forward for those traveling from East to West, and by one day backward for those traveling from West to East.

http://www.defenseindustrydaily.com/f22-squadron-shot-down-by-the-international-date-line-03087/

http://www.dailytech.com/Lockheeds+F22+Raptor+Gets+Zapped+by+International+Date+Line/article6225.htm planes crossed that line, all of them encountered the same problems because the same program was running on all six onboard computers. The planes could have flown for decades without anyone ever noticing this problem, if they hadn't needed to cross the International Date Line."

"I understand very well what you're trying to say," Daniel confirmed, "I work with computers, too, and I'm perfectly aware of these problems. This is most frustrating when a program doesn't work well on my computer, but it works fine on other computers. In such cases it is very difficult to find and fix the real cause."

"That's true," Michael confirmed. "You probably know that most, or maybe all, computer software licenses clearly state that the companies that produced them assume no responsibility if those products malfunction and cause losses of any kind. And this is so because no matter how well they are tested, nobody, absolutely nobody, can guarantee that the software contains no more errors or security holes that have not yet been discovered. This is due to the unimaginable complexity of these products. In other words, it is another limit of knowledge. I'm not going to give you examples about how our inner *something* reacts when confronted by the uncertainties caused by these complex systems, because you'll probably only encounter them if you work for a company that produces computer software or if you are part of a team that investigates the crash of an airplane. I mentioned them only for us to see how limited is our capability of comprehending even things that are in front of our eyes and which are the products of our work. For comparison, think about the game of chess and the game of tic-tac-toe. The tic-tac-toe game is predictable; if both players are careful, it will always end in a draw. But the game of chess seems to us extremely complex, with billions of billions of ways in which it can unfold, far from being predictable. But it seems to be so only because our minds are incapable of comprehending all possible variants, otherwise chess would be as predictable as the tic-tac-toe game."

"Obviously, and this is why in recent years engineers have built computers capable of defeating famous chess players. Those computers can simply consider more variants than their human opponent. The computer is not smarter than the man, it just can calculate a lot more."

3.2. Limits in Knowing the Future

"OK," Michael said, "so we've seen how difficult it is sometimes to know the present and how often we use, usually without even realizing it, that *something* inside us that filters so much of the information that we receive. Let us move on now and talk briefly about the limits in knowing the future. I say 'briefly,' because there isn't too much to say here. The future is incredibly difficult to predict, almost impossible. Just think about the weather forecast: how many times does it prove to be incorrect? Why do most contracts signed by people, institutions or companies include a cause named *force majeure*[24], which frees them from contractual obligations in the case of uncommon events? Because in the course of history, people have noticed that their plans for the future can be thwarted by totally unpredictable events."

"However," Daniel said, "certain things can be predicted, for example I can accurately predict the time the sun will rise tomorrow."

Michael smiled and replied:

"And I can predict the time the sun will set tomorrow. We can do this because the sunrise and the sunset are events that repeat daily at exact times. But let's see something else, can you predict whether the global economy will completely collapse in the near future, or not?"

"Hmm…" Daniel said. "This is a little harder. Especially because I don't know much about the global economy."

"Let me give you a few details. There is a category of people, not too many, who claim that the world economy will collapse

---

[24] https://en.wikipedia.org/wiki/Force_majeure

soon, totally and irremediably. If you listen to their arguments, everything seems to make sense: People are irresponsibly consuming the resources of the planet, especially oil and underground fresh water, and these resources are going to be exhausted soon, causing a global crisis that will only end with the death, by starvation probably, of the majority of the population of the world."

"What an apocalyptical scenario," Daniel said. "But I think I've heard such predictions before. Are they real?"

"It is obvious to anyone that if you have a bag of potatoes, and you keep taking one or two at a time from it, and you never put others back, eventually the bag will become empty. So it is as clear as it can be that, if things keep going on this way, eventually the world economy will completely collapse. Those resources are already showing signs of depletion in many places in the world."

"Aha, so those are not really exaggerations. Do you think there will be such an economic collapse? And if so, when?"

"Even if it will indeed happen this way, to me it seems impossible to predict when exactly this collapse will take place. It is possible to happen even this year, but it is also possible it will happen only after another 30 years. The mechanisms of an economic collapse are way too complex to be predicted. Another possible scenario is that humankind will cease to consume so many resources, either willingly, or forced by circumstances. Or maybe it will succeed to replace in time the oil with alternative energies, for example with solar and wind energy. In these cases, maybe there will be no major economic collapses during the next 500 years."

"Yes, solar and wind energy are the future," Daniel said.

Michael went on:

"There is also a camp opposed to these apocalyptic guys, a camp that claims there will be no economic collapse and that everything will get increasingly better. Both camps that debate this subject are starting from the same information. The amount of oil produced and consumed annually, the amount of oil estimated to be left underground, the amount of fresh water extracted annually from the natural underground reservoirs[25], the amount of water added annually by rain and rivers to those reservoirs, the exponential growth of sovereign public debts, all this is public information, accessible to everyone. Both camps have access to it and use it as a starting point for their reasoning. And yet they arrive at completely different conclusions."

"*Something* inside them sees things in totally different ways," Daniel noticed.

"Yes, and in both camps there are people extremely well motivated interiorly. Some of them are firmly convinced that the economy will crash this year. Others are firmly convinced that it will not crash during their lifetime. But we must not judge their reasons."

"But I don't understand why the issue is so complicated and unclear, that they arrive at diametrically opposed conclusions. Those numbers, the amounts of oil, for example, aren't they clear enough? To me it looks like a simple mathematical calculation."

"It's not quite like that. The problem is not necessarily that the oil will run out, because it will not run out completely. The problem is that the oil becomes more and more expensive to extract, because the cheap oil has already been extracted long ago.

"But they say there are still enormous underground oil reserves," Daniel said.

"This statement is both true and misleading at the same time. The amount of oil left in the ground is irrelevant. What actually matters is the speed and price at which it can be extracted. Here's a comparison: There's gold in the water of seas and oceans, lots of gold. Enormous amounts of gold. Actually, according to the most recent estimates, the amount of gold in the seawater is 120 times greater than the entire amount of gold extracted during the entire history of humanity.[26] Yet still, that gold is so expensive to

---

[25] Also known as aquifers.

[26] http://oceanservice.noaa.gov/facts/gold.html
http://www.numbersleuth.org/worlds-gold/
http://www.bbc.com/news/magazine-21969100

extract, that at this moment no company extracts it on a large scale."

"I think I'm beginning to understand the problem…"

"Yes, the same thing goes for oil, and for any other resource, finite or renewable. Shale oil, for example, is significantly more expensive than oil extracted in Saudi Arabia. And oil produced from kerogen[27] is even more expensive. There are statistics that show that during the last ten years, the oil industry has spent almost three times more money than during the preceding ten years, and this for extracting about the same amount of oil. This is, I think, a clear proof that cheap oil is almost gone. Other studies say that for extracting a barrel of oil today, we're spending five times more than we were spending 15 years ago. Another clear proof that we're running out of cheap oil."[28]

"But the price of oil has gone down in recent months."

"Prices can also go down due to destruction of demand[29], not only because of an increase in supply. It may seem paradoxical, but a decrease in supply, which initially causes an increase in prices, can cause in the long term the destruction of demand and, inevitably, a fall in prices."

"What about fresh water?"

"We're having water problems, too. In many places in the world, the huge natural underground reservoirs are in decline.

The amount of gold extracted so far is not known with certainty, but it is estimated at 150 - 170 thousand metric tons (116 - 133 times less than the gold in oceans). The largest estimates put it at 2.4 million metric tons, but even this way, the amount of gold in the oceans (20 million metric tons) would still be eight times greater.

[27] Also known as oil shale (not to be confused with shale oil).

[28] http://energypolicy.columbia.edu/events-calendar/global-oil-market-forecasting-main-approaches-key-drivers

http://energypolicy.columbia.edu/sites/default/files/energy/Kopits%20-%20Oil%20and%20Economic%20Growth%20%28SIPA%2C%202014%29%20-%20Presentation%20Version%5B1%5D.pdf

[29] https://en.wikipedia.org/wiki/Demand_destruction

From one of the largest reservoirs in North America, Ogallala[30], the amount of water extracted annually is, in many places, six times larger than the amount added back by rain and rivers. You don't have to be a mathematician to realize that that reservoir will eventually run dry. And at such an extraction rate, it takes, for example, 60 years for the rain and rivers to undo ten years of consumption. The situation of other reservoirs is even worse, because water from rain and rivers doesn't make its way to them, and if these reservoirs run dry, they remain that way. In the American state of California, there are several regions where ground level is sinking a few centimeters[31] or even dozens of centimeters each year, because underground water is being extracted for irrigation. Then, these reservoirs are not uniform. I mean when they run dry, they don't run dry everywhere at the same time. There are places where the water is already gone. The town of Happy in the American state of Texas is a well-known example. It used to be a thriving agricultural community, fueled by the Ogallala reservoir. But the underground water was exhausted a few years ago, and the area around the town of Happy is turning back into an arid, semi-desert one."

"I understand," Daniel said, "this is not a simple mathematic calculation; you can't just divide two numbers and figure out exactly the date the oil will run out or the date the water table will be gone."

"Apart from that, the population of the world is starting to become aware that it is not good to consume so many resources. Meanwhile, solar and wind energy are gaining ground, although there still is a long way till it will be possible to completely replace oil. And even if oil is replaced, this would only fix half of the problem, because only about half of the oil is used to produce

---

[30] Having an area of about 450,000 km² (174,000 square miles), Ogallala is almost twice the size of Romania.
https://en.wikipedia.org/wiki/Ogallala_Aquifer
[31] 1 centimeter (1 cm) ≈ 3/8 inches.
1 inch = 2.54 cm.

fuels; the other half is used to make plastics and many other substances that the modern society is using."

"It seems there are good arguments on both sides and, indeed, it is hard to predict whether the economy will soon collapse or not."

"Another example," Michael said, "of cases in which different people filter the same arguments in totally different ways. I think it is clear now that predicting the future is almost impossible for us. An obvious limit of knowledge, in my opinion. Again, I'm not on either side, I only tried to show to you how difficult it is to predict the future."

"Yes," Daniel approved. "How is this problem seen from a religious point of view?"

"The future is in the hands of God, Who is all-powerful and Who can do anything. If we, the people, sinned less, and if it was beneficial for our souls, then maybe God would give us enough rain so that all our water problems would be solved."

"What about the oil, or the alternatives to oil?"

"Mankind has lived for thousands of years without oil."

3.3. Limits in Knowing the Past

3.3.1. Cars in the Parking Lot

Michael pondered for a few moments, then said:

"Now let's move on and let's talk about knowing the past, something almost as difficult as knowing the future. You see, if I were to ask you how many cars are there in this parking lot, you would immediately reply that there are four of them. But what if I asked you how many cars were there yesterday, at the same time?"

"I see the problem," Daniel said, "I wonder how could one answer this question?"

"The only way you could try to find the answer would be to look around and see whether there are any video surveillance cameras."

"Aha," Daniel mumbled, upset that he hadn't thought of this solution.

"But even if you do find some cameras, and even if their administrators give you access to the recording from this time yesterday, I wonder how could you know whether the recording is authentic or not?"

"Usually these recordings show the date and time in a corner."

"And you think that one cannot make a false recording, that shows a different date or time than the real one? You said you're working with computers. Look, I have a digital camera that can place in the corner of the picture the date and time. But the camera doesn't know what the real date and time are, so if I tell it the year is 2011, the pictures it takes will show the year 2011, despite the fact that the real year is 2015."

"Yes, indeed, it is very easy to make a recording today that shows yesterday's date, or tomorrow's date. But why would someone do something like this?"

"Usually nobody has reasons to forge video recordings from a parking lot. But what if, at some point, detectives are investigating a serious crime and they want to see whether on a certain day, at a certain time, a certain car was in the parking lot or not? For someone, this could be a very serious reason to fake the recording, if he or she has access to it."

"I begin to understand what you're trying to say; it is extremely hard to know for sure how certain events from the past unfolded."

"Yes," Michael said, "and even more, the information we have about the past is not verifiable. The predictions about the future are verifiable: If someone predicts an economic crisis in two years, well, in two years we'll see with our own eyes whether he was right or not. But if someone makes a statement about the past, regardless of how many good arguments he offers, it is impossible for us to go back in time and see with our own eyes whether it was indeed so or not. So even if you do get a video recording of the parking lot showing in a corner yesterday's date, you cannot go back in time and see with your own eyes whether the recording is authentic or not. *Something* inside you will have to either believe, or disbelieve the words of the person or persons or the institution that administers the surveillance camera."

"Yes," Daniel approved, "in the end you still have to trust someone, to take someone's word for it."

"And here's also a logical problem related to the investigation of the past. Let's say tens of thousands of people, equipped as ancient soldiers were equipped, with antique weapons, horses and elephants, successfully cross the Alps dozens of times, back and forth. Is this scientific proof of the fact that Hannibal and his army did the same 2,200 years ago? Obviously not; this is only a proof that they *could have* done the same, not that they actually did it. Of course, nobody doubts the crossing of the Alps by the Carthaginian army, all I want to say is that events from the past cannot be proven scientifically, they can only be believed, or not, based on the accounts of those who lived in those times."

3.3.2. The Trip to the Moon

After a short silence, Michael said:

"Daniel, are you ready now to analyze together a very famous and controversial example?"

"Which one?"

"The moon landing."

"Oh, yes, this one certainly is a controversial issue. I myself know many people who think that everything was a setup."

"Many things have been said about this. Documentary films were produced that try to prove everything was a farce. Other documentary films were also produced that try to prove everything was real. Arguments were presented that those pictures and shootings are not real. Other arguments were also presented that those pictures and shootings are real. It was also said that the foot-tracks and the traces left behind by the astronauts on the moon were photographed several times by various satellites and drones, belonging to several countries. And so on."

"Although I'm not sure, I'm inclined to believe the official account," Daniel said.

"I'm inclined to believe the official account, too. However, now I'm not trying to take either side, but only to point out to you that it is impossible for us to truly know what happened then. This is the truth: With the exception of a few dozen people directly involved, nobody knows absolutely for sure, because nobody else was there to see with their own eyes. The rest of us have no other choice but to believe. And *something* inside us will make us believe either that NASA[32] is telling the truth, or that NASA is lying. In my case, *something* inside me is also telling me that I have to admit, although my pride may oppose this, that I simply cannot know the truth for certain and that I have to resign myself to this. Anyway, this is not an issue as important as the existence of God, or the true religion, so I don't think it's worth it to find the truth at all costs."

"I was once attracted by this debate, and I'm thinking, wouldn't it be possible to find a way to definitively prove which account is the true one?"

"Well, let's think about a few scenarios. If indeed there was no trip to the moon, and one of those directly involved decides to publicly admit this, but NASA keeps lying, contradicting his testimony, whom are we going to believe? Or, if the trip to the moon did indeed take place, what if one of those directly involved now gets into a difficult financial situation and he decides to 'admit' that everything was a lie? This way he becomes famous and earns a lot of money. Obviously, NASA will deny his 'confession.' Whom are you going to believe this time? How will you differentiate the first scenario from the second one?"

"Indeed, in the end I still have to appeal to *something* inside me to tell me whom to believe."

---

[32] NASA: National Aeronautics and Space Administration, the American governmental agency that runs the civilian space program.

"Further: If you get to the moon yourself and see with your own eyes the flag, the foot-tracks and the remains of the modules, will you believe that NASA told the truth? How will you know that the remains have not been placed there much later, say a year or two before you got there? But what if you get to the moon and you find no tracks there, but NASA keeps claiming that it told the truth and that astronauts from another country have erased its tracks, in order to discredit them? It would be difficult to erase those tracks, but not impossible. So in this case, whom would you believe?"

"My head aches," Daniel complained, "is there really no way to know for sure?"

"Only if NASA is indeed lying, and at some point all those involved decide to publicly admit this. I don't see any other way. You have to admit it: Truth or lie, it happened in the past and you were not there to see it with your own eyes. So there's no way for you to know for certain; you can only believe those involved or those who contradict them. Our abilities to 'see' the past are extremely limited."

3.3.3. Forensic Investigations

"I think I'm beginning to see where you're taking me. Religion is based on past events, too."

"You're seeing well, and we're getting closer to that. Let's take a look now at other issues from the past that some people are confronted with very often, namely the forensic investigations. Such an investigation almost always involves the deciphering of some past events, events that usually took place only a few days or a few weeks ago."

"I always liked detective movies and books," Daniel said.

"Success rates for these investigations vary a lot, from country to country and from one kind of crime to another. Any cop can tell you that the solving rate for cases of scratched cars is almost zero, while the solving rate for murders is rather high. But the cases that police and the prosecution consider solved are not necessarily so. I think we've all heard of people who were sentenced, who spent a few years in prison, and then they were found to be not guilty. But what nobody knows is how many innocent people are still in prisons. Will their innocence ever be discovered?"

"So forensic science and the justice system are getting it wrong sometimes," Daniel noticed.

"The law says that the suspect is considered innocent until proven guilty. Thus, very many suspects, some of them probably guilty, are acquitted for lack of evidence. However, sometimes it happens the other way around; I mean, innocent people are sometimes found guilty. In America there is a national organization called The Innocence Project that investigates cases of jailed people who claim that they are not guilty.[33] Hundreds of such cases have been uncovered so far, and those people have been released."

"I'm wondering," Daniel said, "couldn't mistakes have also been made in the process of discovering the wrongly convicted inmates? Haven't some truly guilty people also been released this way?"

"This is also very possible," Michael said, "what is impossible is to know for certain."

"Why does the justice system get it wrong? Why does it convict innocent people?"

"Because the events being investigated took place in the past, and the judge and the jurors weren't there to witness them. At first sight it would seem that, if there are eyewitnesses or if the suspect admits to committing the crime, the case is solved. But things are not always that simple. There were many cases in which the suspect was identified by an eyewitness, or even by more than one eyewitness, was convicted, spent many years in jail, and then

---

[33] http://www.innocenceproject.org/

it was proven that he was not guilty—the eyewitness or eyewitnesses had been wrong.[34] The Innocence Project claims that eyewitness misidentification is the main cause for mistaken convictions, playing a role in over 70% of uncovered cases."

"This is truly shocking," Daniel said, "I didn't know that eyewitnesses can be wrong so often."

"And even when the suspect admits guilt, you still cannot be sure that he is indeed guilty. In most countries, a suspect who confesses gets a significantly reduced sentence, and he can also be conditionally released sooner. In some of the cases mentioned before, the suspects did not admit to the accusations, and because of this, the true culprit was eventually caught. But maybe many other people, in their place, seeing themselves identified by several eyewitnesses, would have thought that they had no chance of being acquitted and would have 'admitted' that they were guilty, although they weren't, in order to get a reduced sentence."

"To me," Daniel said, "the most difficult cases seem to be those where it is someone's word against someone else's word, and there are very few other clues. They seem almost impossible to be solved correctly; in the end, the judge or the jury will simply have to believe one of them. And sometimes it happens that even those few clues are not clear and are subject to interpretation. I know what you're about to say, the decision is taken by that inner *something.*"

"Yes, that's correct. Here's an example: A few years ago, in Italy a murder was committed that made headlines around the world. The victim was a student from the United Kingdom, and two of the main suspects were a student from America and one from Italy. Well, the two suspects were put on trial several times, were sentenced, were put on trial again, were released for lack of evidence, and then the case was opened again. Modern science simply cannot determine who the real culprit is. The murder took place in the past, the judges were not there to see it with their

---

[34] See, for example, the cases of Herman Arkins, Ray Krone, Ronald Cotton and Alan Crotzer, the latter having been "recognized" by five victims.

own eyes, the suspects deny the accusations, and so nobody can know what really happened there. It is possible that the two of them are totally innocent, victims of the judicial system. But it is also possible that the two of them are cold-blooded killers, who premeditatedly murdered the British student. Is there any way for us to find out the truth? I don't think so, modern science is powerless in this regard."

"I thought that nowadays DNA can help solve this kind of problems."

"If a trace of somebody's DNA, say person X, is found on the handle of a knife, what exactly does it prove? It only proves that person X held that knife in his hand at some point. But what if later person Y came along, with gloves, and used that knife to kill person Z? I wonder, has all of person X's DNA been removed from the knife? What if person X and person Z were enemies and hated each other, will the judge or the jury consider that person X had a reason to kill person Z? Will person X be convicted of murder? If he is sure that he will be convicted, will person X 'admit' to the guilt in order to get a reduced sentence? Did I say that a trace of DNA could prove that person X once held the knife in his hand? But what if person W wanted to frame person X and somehow obtained a sample of his DNA, say from another object that person X has indeed touched, or from some of person X's clothes, and placed that DNA on the murder weapon? Does it seem impossible to you? All that is needed is a drop of sweat, which contains enough DNA to make a connection between a man and a weapon."

"I am scared by these cases," Daniel said. "To me it seems absurd, in the 21st century, to be convicted of something that you haven't done."

"I have told you all this about the judicial errors in order for you to better understand what we're up against when we try to decipher the past with the help of science. And now a final example: In 2005, the famous American singer Michael Jackson had problems with the justice system again, being accused of indecent behavior toward minors. While the trial was unfolding, a poll was conducted to see whether ordinary people considered him guilty or not. Something that immediately stood out in the poll results was that 70% of the white population thought he was guilty, compared to only 30% of the African-American population."[35]

"A very large margin," Daniel noticed.

"Both whites and blacks had access to the same information about him, mainly from the TV. Neither group had been present for those events to see with their own eyes what Michael Jackson had done."

"Yes," Daniel said. "But *something* inside them was inclined to either consider him guilty, or to consider him not guilty. But the justice system found him not guilty. If the jury was right, then 70% of the whites and 30% of the blacks were wrong. I understand the problem. It is wrong to consider someone guilty just because of his color. But it is equally wrong to consider him not guilty also just because of his color."

3.3.4. Ancient History

Michael thought for a few seconds, looked at his watch again, then went on:

"If investigation of the recent past can sometimes be so problematic, how are we going to decipher the distant past, the events that took place hundreds or thousands of years ago? All we have at our disposal for scientific investigation are the ruins of the old civilizations, the objects left from them and many, very many manuscripts. All these help us form an image, more or less detailed, about what the distant past was like. But we cannot go back in time and see with our own eyes whether the image we're forming is true or not. Of course, in this process, too, our inner *something* filters and interprets all these sources of information about the past. For example, many researchers reject from the beginning any written source, any manuscript that tells of supernatural events or events that look inconceivable to them. Did they

---

[35] http://www.prnewswire.com/news-releases/differing-percep-tions-of-the-guilt-or-innocence-of-michael-jackson-kobe-bryant-and-martha-stewart-according-to-harris-interactive-survey-58977412.html

witness those events? No, but *something* inside them makes them consider them fairy tales."

"Little by little you're getting closer to religion," Daniel noticed.

"Yes, and here's an example: The Bible talks about an ancient empire called Assyria. But until the 19th century, with the exception of the Bible, there were no other important historical sources that mentioned it, so some unbelievers doubted that it had ever existed. But around the middle of the 19th century, archaeologists unearthed the ruins of the city of Nineveh, the capital of this empire. Bible critics were forced to admit that they were wrong."

"So far, the main character of your story was the inner *something*," Daniel noticed.

"Yes," Michael replied, "I had to begin with this before discussing the arguments for religion and the arguments against the theory of evolution. I think I've shown you clearly enough how limited are our abilities to investigate the present, the future and the past. I think it is now obvious that each one of us has that inner *something*, which is present in all aspects of our lives and it affects the way we perceive everything that is going on around us, the way we see our friends, the way we see the present, the way we imagine the future and the past."

"OK, I agree," Daniel said, showing some signs of impatience. "Let's now get back to my initial question, what makes you think that there is a God?"

"Take a look at this car that is now passing by in front of us. It was designed by engineers and built by workers inside a factory, right? But what if I were to tell you that actually it was not built by humans, but by the rain, the wind and other elements of nature, which assembled, by chance, the components and the result was a car? You would say that I'm not in my right mind, wouldn't you? Well, what about a living being, thousands or millions of times more complex than a car? Doesn't it also need an Engineer to design it? But look, modern science comes and says something else. It says that actually there is no need for a Creator and that everything happened by itself, during billions of years of time."

"The Big Bang and evolution."

"Well," Michael said, "let's now take these arguments of science and analyze them one by one."

"Finally."

3.3.5. An Extremely Absurd Theory

"However, before analyzing the arguments about the age of the universe, I want to briefly mention an absurd theory. It was proposed by evolutionists as a joke, as a way of making fun of believers, but it can very well be used against them, too."

"Which theory?" Daniel asked curiously.

"Get ready to hear the most absurd scenario you have ever heard: The universe is just a few hours old. It was created this morning, and so were we."

"I remember pretty well what I did yesterday," Daniel said, smiling.

"Let's say that all our lifetime memories were created this morning and implanted in our minds. This whole process lasted a few hundredths of a second. God is all-powerful and He could do this, too, if He wanted to. This theory was first proposed, as a joke and in a slightly different form, by Bertrand Russell, an atheist philosopher. Then it was developed by others under the name 'Last Thursdayism,' because the final phrasing says that 'the world was created last Thursday.'"

Daniel laughed.

"OK... If you yourself are saying that it is an absurd theory, why do you mention it?"

"Because I want you to truly understand how limited are the abilities of science to investigate the past. I wonder, how could science ever prove that this theory is false? Or if it were true, how could science ever determine this? If all scientists and all laboratories in the world would concentrate only on this problem, could they ever come up with the slightest scientific argument, either for or against?"

"OK, and what kind of arguments do you have against it?" Daniel asked.

"I have no scientific arguments," Michael replied, "because it is not possible to argue that way. I'm only telling you that *something* inside me is absolutely sure that this theory is false."

"I can't believe that there are really no arguments against it. For example, if the theory were true, your God would be a liar, because He has implanted in your mind false information."

"This is a very good argument, but it is not a scientific one. This is a theological or moral argument. Besides, even if God did give us false information, I don't see a serious problem here. Sometimes we also give false information to our little children, when they are not the necessary age to understand the truth. For example, we tell them that babies are brought by the stork."[36]

"OK, but this theory is extremely improbable."

"Improbable?" Michael asked. "And how exactly did you calculate the probability? What mathematical formula did you use? When you cast the die you know that the probability of getting any side is 1/6, because you have the die in front of your eyes and you can see that it is symmetrical and balanced. But tell me, please, how do you calculate the probability that God created the universe this morning? Do you know the mind of God, so you can deduce how likely or unlikely it is for Him to do something like that? Isn't it that *something* inside you that *feels* that the probability is zero?"

"Yes, maybe…"

"Here we have a funny and interesting paradox. Although we cannot argue logically and scientifically that the universe was not created this morning, we can, however, deduce logically and scientifically the fact that we cannot argue logically and scientifically against this absurd theory."

"Yes… Maybe it is indeed so. But if you start to reason this way, you can't be sure of anything anymore."

---

[36] In Romania, when little children ask where babies are coming from, (sometimes) they are told that it is the stork that brings them.

"That's true, from a scientific point of view you cannot be absolutely sure of anything. And if we reject this reasoning, all we do is lie to ourselves that science could offer us absolutely certain answers. No, science cannot determine such things. Think carefully about this absurd theory and you'll have a revelation. You'll discover how powerless science is, and more exactly, how weak, how non-existent is man's capability of knowing things only by his own means. Man cannot even *know* that there was a yesterday, man can only *believe* and nothing more. And at the same time, you'll discover how powerful is man's capability to believe: Although there is absolutely no logical or scientific argument against this theory, we're all absolutely certain that it is wrong. *Something* inside us is absolutely sure of that, without having any tangible proof."

Daniel thought for a few moments. It was hard for him to accept that he simply could not find any rational, scientific argument against such an absurd theory. Eventually he said:

"I don't see why I should think about arguments against this absurd theory. According to the same atheist philosopher you mentioned, namely Bertrand Russell, if one makes statements that are impossible to investigate scientifically, then it is his obligation to offer proof for them. For example, Russell was saying, if he were to assert, without offering any proof, that between the earth and Mars there is a teapot that also orbits around the sun, he could not expect people to believe him just because his statement cannot be proven to be false."

"This problem has two sides," Michael answered, "and since you mentioned it, let's look at both of them. First, unlike Russell's teapot, for which there is no proof, for the existence of God and the divine creation, there are countless tangible arguments, as we'll see further on. Second, the fact that his statement about the teapot can be neither invalidated, nor confirmed scientifically, means neither that the teapot exists, nor that it doesn't exist. It only means that, from a scientific point of view, we don't know. And third, that hypothetical teapot has no importance for us; it affects in no way either this life of ours, or the eternal one. But the existence of God, of the soul and of the eternal life are of the greatest importance for us. Russell probably wanted to say that we don't have to accept to believe in God solely because we cannot prove scientifically, tangibly, that He does not exist. But someone else might say, on the contrary, that we should not reject the belief in God solely because He cannot be analyzed scientifically in a lab as we use to analyze matter. As I was saying, the problem can be looked at from both sides."

"Yes, it seems so. But tell me, please, you've heard about Occam's razor, haven't you? It is a principle according to which, among multiple hypotheses, we should choose the simplest one, the one that implies the fewest assumptions."

"Of course I've heard about it. But you do realize that Occam's razor cannot be proven mathematically or scientifically in any way, it is only a principle adopted by some people."

"Yes, that's true," Daniel admitted.

"Well then, let's now apply Occam's razor to the theory that the universe was created this morning. Which explanation is the simplest one? Which explanation involves the fewest assumptions? Do you see the problem? There is no law of physics and no mathematical formula with which you could calculate how 'simple' such a hypothesis is. There is no law of physics and no mathematical formula with which you could evaluate the assumptions involved so that you could compare them to the assumptions involved by the other explanations as you compare, for example, two numbers."

"Yes, I understand what you mean."

"Is the number 1 greater than the number 2? No, obviously, this statement is clearly false. But is the hypothesis that the universe was created this morning 'simpler' than the hypothesis that it was created seven or eight thousand years ago? How do you express the 'simplicities' of these two hypotheses in digits, so that you can compare them as you compare the number 1 to the number 2? I think that the 'simplicity' of such a hypothesis is something *totally* subjective, and it cannot be measured or calculated in any way."

"Yes," Daniel admitted, "I give up. Indeed, *something* inside me *feels* which hypothesis is 'simpler' and accepts it. It is impossible to argue scientifically, one way or another. But what if I ask you now what the nature of that inner *something* is?"

"I believe that it is the soul, the spiritual component of the human being, which, depending on its free will, is either helped by the grace of God, or influenced by the lies of the devil. And a nonbeliever probably believes that it is just something in man's brain, some chemical reactions. I don't believe science can determine who is right. And if you try to use Occam's razor, you will encounter the same problem: How do you determine which option is 'simpler'?"

"The option that does not imply a soul...?"

"Are you sure? How did you calculate that? Why do people have brains? Aren't people without a brain 'simpler'? Why do cars need a steering wheel? Aren't cars with no steering wheel 'simpler'? Why do we have to eat in order to survive? Wouldn't it have been 'simpler' if we could live without eating? Do you understand the problem? A human body with no soul may be, indeed, 'simpler' than one with a soul, but that does not mean that it would also be functional. A body without a soul is just a corpse."

"Yes, you're right," Daniel admitted, "many times the simpler alternative is not functional. Besides, a brain capable of such things would not be at all simpler than a brain that is only an intermediary between soul and body, so religion's alternative would be simpler... But I think this problem has to be phrased differently: Imagine, for example, a brain as a nonbeliever sees it, that is, a brain capable of many things that believers attribute to the soul, like the capability to believe or not to believe something. Wouldn't such a brain be simpler than the soul that you're talking about?"

"Science cannot answer this question at all. Science can't even understand the brain well, let alone the soul, which it cannot analyze in any way. Therefore, *something* inside you will *feel* which alternative is 'simpler' and will choose that one."

"Therefore, the nature of that inner *something*..."

"Cannot be determined scientifically. However, that inner *something* can *feel* what its own nature is. I know, this is circular reasoning, but it is unavoidable in this situation."

4. Billions of Years?

4.1. Some Basic Things

4.1.1. Can the Universe Be Eternal?

Michael waited for a few seconds, then went on:

"Let's look at the arguments now. Some time ago, nonbelievers used to say that the universe was eternal, that it has always existed and, thus, there is no need for a Creator to explain the existence of the material world."

"I've thought of this, too," Daniel said. "Isn't it possible that the universe has always existed?"

"One of the laws of physics, namely the second law of thermodynamics, does not allow something like this. This law says that in an isolated system, the entropy[1] can only increase or remain constant. Therefore, if our universe is an isolated system, its entropy will keep increasing till it gets to a state called 'heat

---

[1] Entropy: a measure of the unavailable energy in a closed thermodynamic system that is also usually considered to be a measure of the system's disorder, that is a property of the system's state, and that varies directly with any reversible change in heat in the system and inversely with the temperature of the system; broadly: the degree of disorder or uncertainty in a system.

The degradation of the matter and energy in the universe to an ultimate state of inert uniformity. (Merriam-Webster)

death."[2] It is not going to affect us, because there's a very long time until then, billions of billions of billions of years[3], but because of this law, we know that the universe cannot exist forever only by its own means. And obviously, it couldn't have always existed, because it would have suffered a heat death by now."

"Is this process an irreversible one?"

"It is irreversible from the point of view of the laws of physics. God, however, can break or even change the laws of physics, He can make it reversible, or He can simply terminate it."

"The end of the world?"

"Exactly, God can conclude the existence of this material world at any moment. Otherwise, without divine interventions, the universe will get to the state of heat death anyway, but in an extremely long period of time."

"I got it," Daniel said, "it couldn't have existed forever. Now I understand why scientists don't support such a theory, either. But tell me, please, how do you know these things? You said you take care of the church when the priest is missing..."

"That's true, sometimes in my spare time, I take care of the church. But my main job is that of engineer. I graduated from a technical university, and I spent many years studying the arguments for and against the theories of the Big Bang and evolution. I'm not a scientist with a PhD and, with some exceptions, I won't be offering you my own ideas about these scientific aspects. Instead, I will quote real life scientists, with many academic studies and PhDs. This way, generally you won't feel that you have to trust an unimportant person like me, but the scientists whom I will mention further on. Besides, you don't need to be a scientist in order to realize that the Big Bang and evolution theories are so flawed, the same way you don't need to be a doctor with a PhD in order to tell someone is missing a leg or an arm. And these theories are missing both legs, both arms and they have no heads, either."

---

[2] https://en.wikipedia.org/wiki/Heat_death_of_the_universe

[3] There is no clear calculation, but it is estimated that the time period is a minimum of 10^{100} or $10^{1,000}$ years.

4.1.2. Science's Account

"First let's see science's account of events," Michael said. "Sometime, about 14 billion years ago, there was a great explosion, called the Big Bang. It is not known what exactly was the thing that exploded, but the result was, scientists say, the universe we're living in and in which the stars and planets have formed. Our planet, they say, formed itself about 4.5 billion years ago. Then, on this planet, about three to four billion years ago, the first living organism was formed—also by itself, they say. This later evolved and diversified, giving birth to all living beings we see today. The key element in this story is time. The theory of the Big Bang and the theory of evolution have a desperate need of time—billions of years."

"Obviously, without billions of years we can't even think about evolution."

"The most important question about the so-called Big Bang is what exactly caused it? Everything happens with a certain cause, a car slows down because the driver pushes the brake pedal, an apple falls from the tree because its stem dries up, nothing happens all by itself. So what caused this Big Bang? Modern science says that before that explosion there was no space and no time. It seems obvious to me that something or Someone from outside space and time is needed in order to make them exist, right?"

"I thought Stephen Hawking[4] has solved this problem…"

"He has only solved it for those whose inner *something* is desperately looking for a solution that doesn't involve a Creator. Stephen Hawking employed a mathematical artifice; he converted the time from a linear variable into a complex one, that is, with two components, a real one and an imaginary one, if you remember complex numbers from mathematics. Obviously, there is absolutely no proof that time is bidimensional, as Hawking suggests.

---

[4] Stephen Hawking: well-known British physicist, author of the book *A Brief History of Time* in which he supports the idea of "imaginary time," which would eliminate the need for a cause for the Big Bang.

In the same way, I could express the strength of my muscles by complex numbers and I could write some equations from which it would result that I could lift ten metric tons[5] with a single finger. But that would be a real absurdity, wouldn't it?"

"And one more thing, you said that every effect must also have a cause, but some researchers in quantum physics have said that they have discovered at the atomic level events that happen with no cause."

"I can't understand," Michael said, "how such educated people, with so many university degrees can say such stupid things. The fact that they are unable to determine the cause does not mean that it does not exist, does it?"

"In a way, this is true," Daniel admitted, "at the atomic level, you can't see with your eyes everything that's going on there, even though those atoms are right in front of you."

4.2. Age of the Universe

"Have you ever wondered," Michael went on, "how some people come to believe that the universe is billions of years old? Not one of them witnessed the alleged explosion; not one of them saw our planet forming itself out of the so-called cosmic dust; not one of them saw the first cell forming itself out of the inanimate matter; not one of them saw that cell evolving into mammals and other complex organisms."

"Just a second," Daniel interrupted him, "did the believers witness the creation of the world in six days by God?"

"No, they didn't. Not even Moses, the author of the first book of the Bible, where these events are related, not even he was there. This time, too, everything is up to our inner predisposition. *Something* inside the believers makes them accept the account of

---

[5] 1 metric ton = 2,204.6 pounds (1,000 kilograms (kg)).

the six day creation. And *something* inside the atheists makes them accept the Big Bang story."

4.2.1. The Laws of Physics

"Wait a second," Daniel said, "I thought there were some clear scientific arguments for this theory."

"Don't forget that each argument is filtered by our inner *something*. Let's take them one by one. The first thing I want to mention here is that modern science relies on the fact that the laws of physics are the same everywhere in the universe. That is, the gravitational force works the same way everywhere, the speed of light is the same in all corners of the universe, all electrons in the universe have the same mass and electric charge, and so on. Obviously, this base assumption cannot be verified scientifically. However, some people will say that if the laws of physics were even very slightly different in other places, then the universe couldn't have existed for so many billions of years, the galaxies couldn't have formed, and so on. But this argument of theirs starts from the assumption that the universe is billions of years old and that the stars have formed themselves, without any divine intervention. And that assumption is wrong."

"Do you have any reason to believe that the laws of physics are different in other areas of the universe?" Daniel asked.

"I have no reason to believe that, and maybe they are not different. But I want you to be aware of the fact that if they were indeed different, I don't think we would be able to detect that from here, from Earth."

Michael stopped for a few seconds, but Daniel didn't say anything.

4.2.2. Distance to the Stars

"Let's move on," Michael said. "The next question is how do scientists know how old the universe is? Stars and planets don't have labels with the manufacturing date on them."

"And even if they had, how would you know that the labels are telling the truth?" Daniel asked, smiling ironically.

"Well, from an evolutionist point of view, the universe *must* be a colossal age. This is the starting point for their reasoning. All the other arguments derive from the study of galaxies and of distant space, or better said, the study of light and other electromagnetic radiation that we receive from them."

"Obviously," Daniel said, smiling, "you cannot hold a galaxy in your hand and closely analyze it."

"If I may suggest a comparison," Michael said, "imagine that I'm looking through a set of binoculars at a stranger two or three kilometers[6] away, and then I start telling you what kindergarten he went to when he was a little child and whether he uses to write poetry."

"It doesn't seem to be a good comparison."

"Why wouldn't it be a good comparison? A scientist looks through the telescope at a galaxy and says that it took the galaxy two to three billion years to 'create' itself. But what exactly makes him think that it did create itself? How does he know that it was not created by Someone, in a much shorter period of time? But let's get back. You have probably heard of the Doppler effect."

"Yes, when a car passes by you at a very high speed, the sound you hear when it is moving away from you is different than the sound you hear when it is moving toward you. This is due to the fact that the source of the sound, that is the car, is moving, and the sound waves in front of it have a shorter wavelength than the sound waves behind it. I mean, the sound waves in front of the car are compressed, while those behind it are dilated."

"That's correct," Michael approved. "The same thing seems to be happening with light, too, only it is harder to detect with the naked eye. Namely, the faster an object moves away from us, the redder we see the light emitted by it; and the faster it moves toward us, the bluer we see its light."

---

[6] 1 kilometer (km) = 0.622 miles; 2-3 km = 1.24 - 1.87 miles.

"Yes, I've heard of this phenomenon, it is called redshift[7]."

"Well, the majority of scientific conclusions about the size and the age of the universe were arrived at by studying the values of this redshift for various galaxies and cosmic objects. While analyzing the light coming from distant galaxies, scientists noticed that it was redder than it was supposed to be, sometimes way too red."

"Just a moment," Daniel interrupted him, "how do the astronomers know what the starlight is supposed to look like?"

"They don't know, of course," Michael replied, "they only assume, but it is a reasonable assumption, I think. You see, there are various chemical and physical reactions that produce light, for example, the reaction between hydrogen and oxygen, that is, burning, nuclear fusion and many others. To the naked eye, the light coming from these reactions can seem to be somewhat the same, but if we look through a spectrometer, we see that the light has different compositions. A spectrometer disperses the light into its component colors, more exactly into the component frequencies. Have you ever looked through a glass prism?"

"Yes, I did such experiments in school; the spectrometer disperses white light into a multitude of colors."

"The rainbow is a very good example. In this case, the atmosphere acts as a giant natural spectrometer. Well, looking this way at the light coming from chemical and physical reactions, it was observed that it is not homogenous, that is, it does not contain all possible colors, from red to violet. Some of them are missing, depending on the kind of reaction and on the chemical elements involved. For example, the burning of hydrogen produces one set of colors, and the burning of magnesium another set of colors. Each reaction has its own pattern of shades, its own specter of colors, which looks, for example, like a measuring tape on which someone made a few scratches, for example at positions 17 mm, 105 mm, 254 mm and 847 mm.[8] The scratches represent

---

[7] Redshift: shift toward red. The shift toward blue is called "blueshift," but usually it is referred to as "negative redshift."

[8] 1 inch (1") = 25.4 millimeters (mm).

the shades that are missing from the specter, and usually there are many more missing than in my example. This is how the astronomers know what starlight is supposed to look like. And what they have seen is that the set of colors emitted by distant stars looks a lot like the set of colors emitted by nearby stars, only all shades are shifted a little bit to the red side. Like the scratches on the measuring tape in my example were at positions 14 mm, 102 mm, 251 mm and 844 mm, that is, each scratch being 3 millimeters closer to the end."

"Isn't it possible, though, that this is how starlight naturally looks, and there is no redshift involved?"

"It is possible, but pretty unlikely. In a way, it is like finding two people with identical fingerprints."

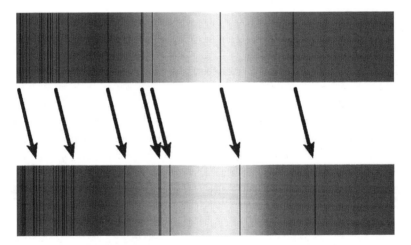

Comparison between the light of the sun (up)
and the light of a distant galaxy (down).
(source: https://en.wikipedia.org/)

"I see," Daniel said. "We can go back to the redshift of galaxies."

"The farther away the galaxy seemed to be, the greater the redshift was. It seemed that all galaxies were moving away from us at great speed, or at least they were moving away when the light we see today was emitted. And the farther away they were, the greater their speed was. This led to the formulation of the theory that the universe is, or at least it used to be, expanding at an enormous speed. Then astronomers tried to calculate for how long this expansion has been going on, and thus they came to the age of about 14 billion years that they assigned to the universe. But their first calculations did not produce the results they were expecting, so they said that the expansion of the universe has not always been going at the same speed. More exactly, immediately after the so-called Big Bang, they say there was a rather special expansion, at an extremely high speed, far greater than the speed of light, which only lasted for about 10^{-32} seconds.[9] Obviously, there is no way this statement can be proven."

4.2.3. Dark Energy

"I didn't know all these details," Daniel said. "What exactly caused or is still causing this expansion?"

"Astronomers were unable to explain what exactly caused the expansion. Not finding any plausible explanations, explanations that would have employed the laws of known physics, they coined the term 'dark energy.' This is the name they have given to that invisible and inexplicable force that has expanded the universe. But so far, this hypothetical energy has not yet been observed in any lab, and by its own definition, it is undetectable."

"The name sounds a little occult, like something from the paranormal realm," Daniel noticed, unwillingly.

"Yes, it's true. If I were an astronomer, I would have felt ashamed to come up with such a name. I wonder, how do they

---

[9] The theory is described in detail here:

https://en.wikipedia.org/wiki/Inflation_(cosmology)

As can be seen from the article, not all scientists accepted the theory.

About the (alleged) expansion of space that takes place in the present, see this article:

https://en.wikipedia.org/wiki/Metric_expansion_of_space

know that what they call dark energy isn't actually the Hand of God that has dilated the universe? Many of the advocates of the six day creation, also known as creationists, do not dispute the expansion of space or the calculated distances to the most remote galaxies, despite the fact that these calculations are based only on speculative interpretations of redshift values. Usually, creationists only dispute the period of time that these events took place in and especially their cause. The Bible speaks in a few places about the fact that God *«stretches out the heavens,»* so it is possible that those biblical verses are referring to the expansion of space. But it is sad that astronomers do not admit that God is the cause of it, and are calling that invisible force "dark energy." Here are some of the verses:"

> *«It is He who stretches out heaven like a vault, and spreads them out like a tent to dwell in.»*[10]

> *«Thus says God the LORD, Who created the heavens and stretched them out, Who spread forth the earth and that which comes from it, Who gives breath to the people on it, and spirit to those who walk on it: [...]»*[11]

> *«I have made the earth, and created man on it. I–My hands–stretched out the heavens, and all their host I have commanded.»*[12]

> *«Indeed My hand has laid the foundation of the earth, and My right hand has stretched out the heavens; [...]»*[13]

---

[10] Isaiah 40:22.

[11] Isaiah 42:5 (NKJV).

This quote and the next two are taken from the NKJV translation, because the OSB one (used almost everywhere else) has replaced the verb "stretched out" with the verb "established." However, both the NKJV Bible (translated from the Masoretic Text) and the Romanian Orthodox Bible (translated from the Septuagint) use the verb "stretched out."

[12] Isaiah 45:12 (NKJV).

[13] Isaiah 48:13 (NKJV).

«The Lord–who made the earth in His strength, who restores the in-habited world in His wisdom and discernment–stretched out heaven, [...]»[14]

«He who alone stretches out heaven; He who walks on the sea as on firm ground; [...]»[15]

«Thus says the Lord, Who stretches out the heavens, who lays the foun-dation of the earth and forms the spirit of man within him: [...]»[16]

Michael went on:

"So it is possible that these verses are actually speaking about the expansion of space, but this is not a dogma of any church, it is only a possibility and a personal opinion. The expansion of space is not a certainty; it is only a supposition. And there's one more question: this expansion of space, if it really did take place, was it uniform? I mean, did the space expand by the same amount in all regions of the universe? Did it have any effects on matter and on the laws of physics? Did it change the speed of light? Did it increase or decrease the distances between atoms and mole-cules? Obviously, nobody can answer these questions, because nobody has ever dilated or contracted space in a lab to see what effects it has on matter and light."

4.2.4. Background Radiation

"I see," Daniel said. "What about the cosmic background radiation[17]? What do you think about it? It is considered to be proof of the Big Bang."

"To me this looks like a joke. This is just radiation that seems to be coming from everywhere in space, from all directions. But how exactly could this prove that the universe is billions of years old? Imagine that I enter an empty room and I measure the air

---

[14] Jeremiah 10:8.

[15] Job 9:8.

[16] Zechariah 12:1.

[17] CBR (Cosmic Background Radiation) and CMBR (Cosmic Mi-crowave Background Radiation).

temperature in all corners of that room, then the temperature of the walls and of all the objects in there. After that I draw the conclusion that in that room, a week ago, there was a heated discussion among several persons. Doesn't this sound a little bit absurd?"

"Actually, it does," Daniel admitted.

4.2.5. Dark Matter

"Another interesting thing noticed by astronomers is the fact that galaxies are rotating around their centers, and many of them are spiral shaped, with the arms of the spiral clearly visible. However, something is not right here. If the galaxies were indeed billions of years old, then the rotation around their centers for such a long period of time should have turned them into almost homogenous disks, and it wouldn't be possible for us to clearly see the spiral arms, as we do. Another problem observed is that the speed of stars on the outer edge of galaxies is way too high. In billions of years, the galaxies would surely break apart. In other words, galaxies look as if they were rotating for only several thousand years, not for billions of years. What do you think, has science accepted what it was seeing with its own eyes, namely the fact that the galaxies look to be much younger?"

"It seems it hasn't," Daniel said.

"Indeed, *something* inside some people was much too strong for this argument. So they said that maybe inside those galaxies there are enormous amounts of what they called 'dark matter,' which kept the galaxies intact and made them keep their spiral shape for billions of years. This dark matter, by the definition assigned to it by astronomers, is an invisible matter and it is impossible to be detected in any way. Its existence is 'proven' mainly by the fact that the galaxies are still intact and still look like a spiral after so many alleged billions of years. And you shouldn't think that scientists needed to add only a small amount of dark matter into the equation; no, they say that there is more than five times more dark matter than the visible matter that we can see with the naked eye or through the telescope. And, in case you're wondering how this dark matter, about which they say it exists in so large amounts, does not collide with the visible matter, well, science's answer is that dark matter can pass through visible matter without touching it and without affecting it in any way, the same way a spirit can go from one room to another by passing through the wall. This, I think, raises a few questions: How is this dark matter distributed? Is it homogenously distributed? Does it only exist in some regions of space? About how much dark matter is there in our solar system? If there indeed is such a thing, did it affect the way we calculated the strength of the gravitational force, which is considered to be constant everywhere in the universe?"

"Are there other explanations besides this invisible matter?" Daniel asked.

"Yes, for example, the law of gravity could be acting differently in other regions of space. Or maybe their way of calculating the speed of a star based on the value of the redshift is completely wrong. Or maybe the universe is only a few thousand years old. Or maybe all of the above. To me, dark matter seems to be the worst possible explanation. Scientists have been looking for it in the lab for over 40 years and still haven't even found a tiny bit of it."

Daniel thought about this for a few seconds, but didn't say anything.

4.2.6. Comets

"Let's move on," Michael said. "Studying the comets that visit us from time to time, astronomers noticed that every time the comets pass by the sun, they lose a part of their tail and of their gas shell. This observation led to a worrying conclusion for the advocates of billions of years. Comets, which scientists suppose were formed at the same time the solar system was, four to five billion years ago, have a maximum lifespan of 10,000 to 15,000 years, after which the entire gas shell would be gone. Therefore, all comets still visible today cannot be more than 15,000 years old. What do you think, has science accepted what it was seeing with its own eyes, namely the fact that our solar system is not that old?"

"This time, too, it seems it hasn't," Daniel said.

"Indeed, *something* inside some people was much too strong for this argument. So they said that maybe somewhere near the solar system there is a warehouse of fresh comets, with intact gas shells. As existing comets wear out and disappear, they are replaced by brand new ones from that warehouse, called 'Oort's cloud.'"

"And why wouldn't this be a good explanation?" Daniel asked.

"No one has ever seen that cloud.[18] No one has ever seen a comet getting out of there and starting to rotate on an orbit visible to us. It seems to be just a creation of the minds of those who don't want to accept that our solar system cannot be more than 15,000 years old."

"And the astronomers have no arguments for its existence?"

"Their best 'argument' is the fact that without it, the solar system could not be the age they say it is. Apart from that, every time they notice a stranded object wandering through space, *something* inside them assures them that it is clear proof for the existence of the Oort's cloud and that that object was once a part of it. This is like finding in the woods a large uprooted tree, and then drawing the conclusion that in that forest there are gigantic bears, weighing more than ten metric tons each."

4.2.7. Starlight and Time

"There's one more problem," Daniel said. "If the universe isn't billions of years old, how would it be possible for us to see the light of stars at so many billions of light-years away? That light needed billions of years to get here, so how can we see it? And how did those stars get so far away from us in such a short period

---

[18] As the secular Wikipedia article says, "no confirmed direct observations of the Oort cloud have been made."

https://en.wikipedia.org/wiki/Oort_cloud

of time? The laws of physics say that the speed of light cannot be exceeded, so, after biblical chronology, the most remote visible star should be at a maximum distance of seven or eight thousand light-years from Earth."

"Firstly, using classical geometric methods we can only measure distances of several hundred light-years, or a maximum of a few thousand light-years, if you don't care that much about precision. Distances of billions of light-years are just speculative interpretations of the redshift values of those galaxies."

"Why do you say they are speculative?"

"Because nobody has ever dilated space in a lab to see how light reacts to this dilation. So if those distances were a hundred times shorter, or a hundred times longer, there would be no way for us to know it. Anyway, I don't dispute those interpretations, let's say they are correct. There are numerous other alternative explanations for the fact that we can see the light from galaxies so far away in such a short period of time. But these explanations are speculative, too, because those who proposed them were not there to see what really happened, they only presume things they cannot know. These explanations include the possibility that the speed of light was different in the past, the theory of relativity and other things.[19] My opinion is that some long time ago those galaxies used to be much closer to us and that their light was visible from the earth even from the day they were created. I don't think God created something that was going to become visible only

---

[19] For example, one such theory says that, although the entire universe, and everything it contains, was created less than ten thousand years ago, **now** the distant galaxies are indeed billions of years old, because, due to the expansion of space, time went significantly faster on the outer edges of the universe. The author of this book neither accepts, nor rejects such explanations, but only considers them speculative and completely beyond our means to investigate. However, it may also be worth mentioning that if the conclusions of the theory of relativity about time dilation are indeed correct, then the word "now" emphasized above may not mean exactly the same thing in all corners of the universe.

https://en.wikipedia.org/wiki/Time_dilation

after thousands of years, and then only through very powerful telescopes. Well, maybe the expansion of space brought them to where they are now, and this expansion has also dilated the light that was then traveling from them to our planet, and it is that light that we're seeing now so much redshifted. It is just an opinion; I don't claim that it is mine or that it is correct."

"I understand," Daniel said. "Indeed, I see that the only differences between the Big Bang theory and the version I hear from you is the period of time and the cause of the expansion. The atheist astronomers say that it was caused by the dark energy; you say that it was caused by God."

"Oh, there are other differences, too. The Big Bang theory says that stars and planets formed by themselves, without divine intervention, and so on. Another observation that I want to make is that the Big Bang version has a problem with the speed of light as well. The estimated diameter of the universe is about 92 or 93 billion light-years. But the laws of physics say that the speed of light cannot be exceeded, at least not by classical matter, which has mass. So how did some celestial bodies come to be separated by such a distance in just 14 billion years?"

"Interesting, I didn't know of this problem. What is the official explanation?"

"The expansion of space. It seems dark energy, scientists say, has the power to override the laws of physics. Obviously, God has this power, too."

4.2.8. Natural and Supernatural Explanations

"I noticed," Daniel said, "that you mix physical explanations with supernatural ones. For example, you say that the light was indeed 'dilated' because of the expansion of space, but you also say that this expansion was done by God. Why don't you instead say that there are no distant galaxies, and that God only created the light that seems to be coming from them? And this only during the past few decades, since we have powerful telescopes. Or maybe there is no universe, maybe all there is is an enormous 'screen' around our solar system on which God projects the image of some galaxies."

"It is obvious that there is no way to prove scientifically that it is or that it isn't so. As with the absurd theory of Last Thursdayism, which I mentioned earlier, it is just *something* inside us that believes that it isn't so. As for the mixing of the scientific explanations with the supernatural ones, I don't see why it would be a problem. I noticed that many times God acts upon the material world by means of the matter itself. I'm thinking about the biblical flood. God told Noah to build an ark, and this took a rather long period of time. Then God gathered the animal pairs and made water fall from the sky till it covered the entire earth. I wonder, couldn't God simply have taken the souls of all the people, leaving only Noah and his family alive? Yes, of course He could have done this in less than a second and there would have been no need for a flood. But, for reasons beyond our power of understanding, God chose to do this by means of the water and of Noah's Ark. And this flood left traces: all over the world we can find very thick sediment layers in which there are buried billions of fossils of the creatures that died during the flood. Also, after the Resurrection of Christ, couldn't God have appeared in a vision separately to each human being on the face of the earth and preached the Gospel to him? Of course He could have, He is all-powerful, and He can be in many places at the same time. But for reasons beyond our power of understanding, God chose to send the 12 Apostles to preach the Gospel to the world. The 12 Apostles have also left 'traces,' especially the Gospels and the Epistles written by them, that is, the New Testament, the second part of the Bible. This is why scientific explanations seem to be mixed with the supernatural ones. The redshift of distant galaxies, the cosmic background radiation and other such 'proof' for the Big Bang could be just 'traces' of God's action upon the universe. There were two important events that completely changed the material world. The first one was the sin of Adam and Eve, following which God drove them away from heaven and then He changed the laws of nature in the entire creation. And the second one was the flood, which only Noah and his family survived. So it is possible that these two events also left other 'traces' in the universe besides the sediment layers that we can see all over the earth."

"So you're trying to say that science is wrongly interpreting the traces left by God's actions upon the world?"

"Yes, of course. We have to differentiate between values that are measured and values that are deduced from the interpretation of some measured values. The shifting of light toward red is a value that has been measured countless times by very many astronomers. But the expansion, the size and the age of the universe are not measured values, they are only interpretations of the redshift of light. There is no way for us to find out for sure whether these interpretations are correct or not; there is no way for us to effectively measure the expansion, the size and the age of the universe."

"I understand what you mean; if the interpretations were wrong, nobody would know this for sure."

"Obviously. Modern science has crossed in many areas the boundaries of what can be known for sure, by experiment, and has entered the realm of speculations and suppositions. This has happened on the macroscopic level, regarding the study of the universe, as well as on the microscopic level, regarding the study of the atomic and sub-atomic particles. Personally, I don't claim that I *know* with certainty why the starlight is shifted toward red, I'm only saying that *maybe* it is this way because *maybe* the expansion of space really took place. There is no way for us to know how God created the world, or what laws of physics He used and changed during the biblical flood. And maybe it is also a sin to try to explain these things scientifically, as some Protestant creationists are trying to. All that I claim is that the theories of the Big Bang and evolution are wrong, and there is no need at all to replace them with other detailed scientific explanations. Those who ask for something like this probably start from the wrong assumption that such explanations must exist. No, the only thing that we can explain scientifically, logically and rationally, is that the theories of the Big Bang and evolution are wrong, that's all.

The alternative is the divine, supernatural creation, and its details cannot be explained scientifically."

"Why can't they?" Daniel asked.

"I don't know, maybe because they cannot be comprehended by the limited human mind. For this reason, I so often use words like 'maybe' and 'possible,' because there is no way for us to know details that God has not uncovered for us. I can't explain scientifically God's miracles, and I believe that it's a sin to try to explain them this way; I only want to show you that there are also other alternatives, besides the explanations offered by the atheist scientists. And those alternatives, for which we can only have an extremely vague understanding, have a supernatural cause."

"Many people have a problem with the supernatural explanations."

"What does the word 'supernatural' mean? It means something that is beyond our capability of comprehension, and which, usually, is not situated in the material world that we can see. For us, an angel is a supernatural being, but this seems so only because of our limitations. I think that in the afterlife, the angels will seem to us like perfectly 'natural' beings, because we'll also be situated in the same world with them. Only God will remain forever a supernatural being for all the others, because His inner nature is totally inaccessible even to the highest angels."

4.2.9. The Sub-Atomic Universe

Michael paused for a few seconds, then went on:

"Because we're going to discuss the dating of rocks by radioactive isotopes, I'm going to tell you a bit about the sub-atomic universe, the world of tiny particles, protons, neutrons, electrons, photons and so on."

"I thought that at the microscopic level things were pretty clear," Daniel said.

"Down to a certain level they are rather clear. However, the more science has tried to advance in this direction, the weirder and harder to investigate were the phenomena it encountered. You have probably heard of the double-slit experiment[20], right?"

"Yes, I did that experiment in school, in physics class, and I observed the interference of light. This proves that light exhibits the characteristics of waves as well, not just of particles."

"Well, light is not the only one with these characteristics. The experiment was repeated with electrons and even with some small molecules, and it was observed that these particles have wave characteristics, too. Therefore, a beam of electrons going through the two slits also produces interference fringes on the other side."

"This is a little bit weird," Daniel remarked.

"A truly weird observation was made only when researchers replaced the beam of electrons with isolated electrons, launched one by one, from time to time. Even this way, interference was still observed on the other side of the slits. Classical physics couldn't explain something like this; it was like each electron was passing through both slits at the same time, and then was interfering with itself on the other side."

"Yes, this is truly weird."

"From the point of view of macroscopic reality, something like this is outright absurd; it is like one would enter a car through two doors at the same time, and then he would bump into himself inside that car. But this is not all. Something even weirder happened when the researchers tried to use a particle detector to see which slit each electron was actually going through. Then the electrons stopped behaving like waves and started to behave like classical particles. The interference fringes didn't form on the other side anymore. This happened even when the particle detectors were placed behind the slits, and were encountered by the

---

[20] https://en.wikipedia.org/wiki/Double-slit_experiment

Broadly, the experiment involves an opaque plate in which two slits were cut, two very small openings close to each other, with sizes comparable to the wavelength of the particles being analyzed. A beam of light or a jet of elementary particles, electrons, atoms or even small molecules is sent toward these two slits. On the other side, at a certain distance, there is a solid screen, with no openings. The interference fringes are formed on this screen.

electrons after they 'decided' to behave either like waves, and pass through both slits, or like classical particles, and pass through a single slit. This made some scientists think about retro-causality, that is, they suggested that the electrons go back in time and reverse their decision when they 'realize' that they are being watched by us. However, I am inclined to believe that this explanation is wrong; there are also alternatives that do not require time travel."

"Very weird... Like the electrons were somehow able to tell that they were being watched and they were changing their behavior... This 'observation' was probably not entirely passive, but it was interacting with them somehow."

"Yes, something like that. But the research of elementary particles encountered even stranger phenomena. The most famous of these phenomena is the one named quantum entanglement[21], a phenomenon so weird that Einstein called it 'spooky action at a distance.'[22] In simple words, the researchers noticed that in certain conditions some elementary particles become 'linked' to one another, and the change of the state of one of them almost immediately affects the other one, although physically they may be separated by arbitrary distances, of several meters[23] or even more. Einstein couldn't believe that such a thing was possible, so he proposed some alternative explanations, but it seems later experiments didn't prove him right."

"Indeed, it sounds very weird. What is the explanation?"

"This phenomenon is totally and completely contrary to the principles of classical physics. There is no logical explanation, the researchers only say that it exists and that's it, they can't explain it. Nobody can perform a detailed analysis of the photons, electrons or atoms involved in such experiments and see in what way they are linked to one another and how they communicate among themselves. And this is not all, it seems that this communication

---

[21] https://en.wikipedia.org/wiki/Quantum_entanglement

[22] *Spukhafte Fernwirkung* was the expression used by Albert Einstein in 1947.

[23] 1 meter (1 m) = 3.281 feet (3' 3 3/8").

between particles only takes place when one of them is observed, I mean when one of its properties is being measured."

"Very weird, very, very weird," Daniel repeated. "How is it possible for a photon to 'know' that it is observed and to 'tell' this to another photon several meters away?"

"From such experiments we learn that at the sub-atomic level matter seems to be much more complicated and harder to understand than it was thought to be at the beginning of the 20th century. Sub-atomic particles cannot be seen through the microscope; they are way too small for this. You cannot immobilize an electron and then study it on all sides, see what shape it is and so on. And if you cannot do this to an electron, then you especially can't do it to a smaller particle, such as a photon or a boson."

"Then how do the scientists know so many things about sub-atomic particles? Quantum physics has been studying them for so many years."

"A large part of the things that are 'known' are actually interpretations[24] of some observations. Some of these interpretations could be correct, and others could be wrong, but nobody can know for certain which ones. Some of these particles are hypothetical, which means that their existence is only supposed, not proven. An example of such a hypothetical particle is the graviton, the alleged particle of gravity. In the case of the double-slit experiment, you can't see with your own eyes the electron passing through both slits at the same time. All you can see are the interference fringes, the rest are just suppositions. Obviously, there are also alternative interpretations that have emerged: Some people say that the electron is actually only passing through a single slit, and the interference fringes are formed because of a wave that accompanies the moving particle. This explanation makes us wonder what exactly is that wave? Does it have anything to do

---

[24] The most widespread interpretation is named the "Copenhagen interpretation," and it was developed (mainly) between the years 1925 and 1927 by Niels Bohr and Werner Heisenberg. The term "Copenhagen interpretation" only began to be used during the 1950s.
https://en.wikipedia.org/wiki/Copenhagen_interpretation

with the luminiferous aether, a theory abandoned about a century ago? In the case of the entangled particles, that link between them is not visible; they are not connected through a wire that can be seen with our eyes, as the washing machine is connected to the power grid. That connection is only deduced from the interpretation of the results of some experiments. At this moment, those interpretations seem to us to be correct, but it's also possible that we are wrong. At the quantum level, matter cannot be observed and studied as easily as it can be studied at the macroscopic level."

"You're trying to say that these are nothing but interpretations of some observations, in the same way that the expansion and the size of the universe are nothing but interpretations of the redshifts of distant galaxies?"

"Yes, exactly like that; they are just interpretations. This is why there are many unclear issues. For example, there are some aspects in which quantum physics contradicts the theory of general relativity or other theories related to astronomy. And I think they have gotten here because these two branches of physics have crossed the boundaries of what can be directly observed and measured, and have entered the realm of speculations and of suppositions that cannot be verified with certainty. Search the Internet for 'conflicts between quantum mechanics and general relativity' and you'll find many scientific articles that explain why the two theories are at odds in certain respects."

"I'll remember this," Daniel said, "I really am curious to find out more."

"The best example of such a conflict is, in my opinion, the problem of the cosmological constant, a conflict which is also called 'the vacuum catastrophe.'[25] In simple words: The astronomers and the physicists who study outer space have calculated a certain value for the cosmological constant and the energy density of the vacuum of space, and that value is related to the alleged

---

[25] https://en.wikipedia.org/wiki/Cosmological_constant#Quantum_field_theory

https://en.wikipedia.org/wiki/Cosmological_constant_problem
https://en.wikipedia.org/wiki/Vacuum_catastrophe

expansion of the universe. But most of the quantum physics theories propose a totally different value for the same thing. To be more exact, the value proposed by quantum physics is 10^{120} times greater. Not 120 times greater, but 10^{120} times greater, that is 120 orders of magnitude more. The first value would have to be multiplied by a 1 followed by 120 zeros in order to get the second one, although the two values should be the same. This can't be a small calculation error, something is fundamentally wrong here. At least one of the two branches of physics has gone in a fundamentally wrong direction. Of course, it is also possible that both branches have gone in wrong directions."

"I didn't know physics had such big problems," Daniel said.

"Physics has no problems when it calculates the water pressure at the bottom of the ocean, or when it calculates the lift generated by the wing of an airplane. Physics runs into problems when it ventures into areas that are way beyond its means and, instead of admitting this, it starts to make wrong assumptions. And from a religious point of view, quantum physics and many other branches of science are nothing more than a monumental and monstrous waste of time. The purpose of our existence is the salvation of the soul, not the detailed study of elementary particles. What good will it be for us to know all the characteristics of the electron, if we lose our souls? God has warned us:"

> «For what will it profit a man if he gains the whole world, and loses his own soul? Or what will a man give in exchange for his soul?»[26]

"And obviously," Michael went on, "if it's absurd to lose your soul in order to gain the whole world, then it's even more absurd to lose it in order to gain something of much smaller importance."

"Well then, if scientific research is useless from a religious point of view, how do you know all these things? Why have you studied these issues?"

---

[26] Mark 8:36-37.

"Maybe I studied some of them before becoming a believer... Besides, maybe they are useful for arguing that the theories of the Big Bang and evolution are wrong."

4.3. Age of the Earth

Michael waited for a few moments, then said:
"Let's move on now, and see how modern science calculates the age of the earth."

4.3.1. Radiometric Dating

"With the help of radioactive isotopes," Daniel said.

"At first glance, the procedure seems simple. Certain isotopes of some chemical elements are unstable, and sometimes they undergo radioactive decay, giving birth to lighter elements. For example, most carbon atoms have the atomic mass 12, that is, they have six protons and six neutrons. This isotope is called carbon-12 and it is stable and does not undergo radioactive decay. But there is also the carbon-14 isotope, which has six protons and eight neutrons. This isotope is unstable and it undergoes radioactive decay and gives birth to a nitrogen-14 atom, an electron that is emitted as beta radiation, and an antineutrino, which is a much smaller particle. It was observed that each isotope has its own rate of radioactive decay, also known as a half-life. For C-14, the measured half-life is 5,730 years. This means that if you have 2,000,000 C-14 atoms, after 5,730 years you'll have about 1,000,000. And after another 5,730 years you'll be left with only 500,000, and so on."

"Yes," Daniel said, "I know the process. And by knowing the initial amount of radioactive isotopes and by measuring the current amount, one can calculate how much time has elapsed."

"Yes, it looks easy, but the first problem is that there's no way for you to know the initial amount. You were not there to measure it, so all you can do is to presume it. And you cannot go back in time to see whether you presumed it right or not. This is a serious problem for the radiometric dating methods. You don't know the amount of that isotope that was there in the beginning."

"But there is also a radiometric dating method for which there is no need to know the initial amount of the radioactive isotope."

"Yes, it is called the isochron method[27]. It involves several isotopes and it does not rely on knowing the initial amounts, but instead on the ratio between them and on the fact that that ratio changes over time. But even this method is far from fixing all the problems of radioactive dating, and this is why: It is possible to apply the isochron method on the same sample several times, using different groups of isotopes. For example, you can calculate the age of a rock using the Rb/Sr isochron, then using the U/Pb isochron, and then using the Pb/Pb isochron. Well, the problem is that many times the ages calculated this way are very different, way over the error margin. If you get an age of 1.2 billion years with method 1, with an error margin of ±5%, and an age of 2.3 billion years with method 2, with an error margin of ±4%, then something is clearly wrong. There are very many cases like this, a simple search on the Internet will make it clear for you. The specialists claim that the isochron method can detect the situations in which the sample being analyzed has been contaminated, meaning that a certain amount of isotope has been added to it, or a part of that isotope has been lost by other means; for example, it was washed away by water. But when the result comes in with an error margin of only ±5%, it is obvious that there was no contamination detected. Therefore, how is it possible for the second age to be 92% more than the first one, when the error margin was calculated to be just 4% or 5%, and there was no contamination detected?"

---

[27] https://en.wikipedia.org/wiki/Isochron_dating
And from the creationist perspective:
http://creationwiki.org/Isochron_dating

"And what exactly is wrong? Where are the differences coming from?"

"Their problem is that they consider the radioactive decay rates to be constant. Well, in present times, the radioactive decay rates have been measured countless times and they indeed seem to be approximately constant. But have they always been constant?"

"Do you have any reasons to believe that the half-lives of radioactive isotopes used to be different and that this leads to erroneous calculations for the ages of the rocks?"

"First, let's see exactly what the radioactive decay is. There are countless radiometric dating methods, both classical ones and isochron ones. However, although scientists say that there are so many methods, all of them are based on the same phenomenon, namely radioactive decay. And though this decay has been observed and measured countless times, its exact causes have not yet been determined. It was observed, for example, that out of a large number of carbon-14 atoms, in 5,730 years about half of them decay. But nobody has yet determined what exactly is causing this decay for each particular atom. Why do some atoms decay now, a few seconds after being formed, others after 100 days, others after 100 years, and others after 3,000 years? Are all atoms identical? Do the atoms have an invisible 'fuse' that causes the decay when it is done 'burning'? Or are there some forces or particles that we have not detected yet, and which are acting upon the unstable atoms, causing their decay?"

"There are still no answers for these questions," Daniel admitted.

"Well then, since we don't know exactly what makes each individual atom decay, is it OK to assume that the half-lives have always been constant? What if they were different at some point, could we know this today? Let's use an analogy: Imagine a large basketball hall with a very smooth floor. This morning, tens of thousands of pencil cores were placed upright on that floor. Let's say they are carpenter pencil cores, which are somewhat thicker. Obviously, the pencil cores are standing in unstable equilibrium, somehow similar to the radioactive atoms, which are also unstable. From time to time, pretty rarely, one of them falls down, either because of an air current, or because of a little tremor. But what if there is a small earthquake, won't the majority of them fall down?"

"Sure enough, yes."

"Well then, five minutes later, a person who hasn't felt the earthquake walks in, sees that three quarters of the pencil cores are down and he observes that, on average, one more of them is falling every hour. He calculates and draws the conclusion that the pencil cores were placed there three or four years ago."

"Yes, I understand what you mean. If there ever was such a radioactive quake, all ages calculated by radiometric methods are totally wrong."

"And there is also something else in support of this theory. I said before that the radioactive decay rates have been observed to be *approximately* constant. I used the word *approximately* because small variations have also been reported. More exactly, it was observed that certain isotopes decay a little bit faster during winter.[28] It is not a large variation, but it does raise an important problem: the half-lives are not fixed values, they are not laws of physics, they can be altered by external causes."

"Interesting, I didn't know this," Daniel said.

"Then, an extraordinary example is the rhenium-187 isotope, which usually has a half-life of more than 41 billion years. But when it is completely ionized, the half-life decreases to just 33 years. That is 1.24 billion times shorter. Another unusual example is the dysprosium-163 isotope. Although usually stable, in completely ionized form it becomes unstable with a half-life of 47 days."

"Indeed, two completely unusual examples."

---

[28] http://news.stanford.edu/news/2010/august/sun-082310.html

In short, the variation seems to be synchronized with the rotation of the sun's core, which has a period of 33 days.

"And now let me tell you a bit about the famous carbon dating method. First, due to the rather short half-life, under 6,000 years, radioactive carbon dating can calculate ages of a maximum of several tens of thousands of years; for ages of one hundred thousand years, the error margin is already way too large. The physical process goes like this: Our atmosphere contains about 70% nitrogen. The upper layers of the atmosphere are hit by solar radiation and thus some of the nitrogen atoms are turned into unstable carbon-14 atoms. This carbon reacts with the oxygen and gives birth to the carbon dioxide. The atmosphere only contains 0.04% carbon dioxide. And most carbon dioxide molecules contain stable carbon-12 atoms, and only 0.000000000001% of them contain unstable carbon-14 atoms. So out of a trillion carbon dioxide molecules, only one contains C-14. Living beings assimilate the carbon dioxide from the atmosphere. Plants absorb it directly, by photosynthesis, then they are eaten by herbivores, which in turn are eaten by carnivores. Therefore, both the atmosphere and living beings contain an extremely small, but approximately constant, percentage of radioactive carbon. When the creature dies, absorption of C-14 ceases, but its radioactive decay goes on. So if we find a piece of very old wood or bone, all we have to do is measure how much C-14 is left in it and thus we can calculate how long it has been since that creature died."

"Looks like a pretty straightforward procedure," Daniel said.

"Yes, but there are two serious problems with it. First, the method assumes that the planet Earth has existed for at least a few hundred thousand years, otherwise there would have been no time for the radioactive carbon to accumulate in the atmosphere. But what if the atmosphere was created with no radioactive carbon at all? If one had done such a test with an organism a few years after creation, he would have found an extremely small amount of carbon-14 and he would have drawn the conclusion that the organism had died tens of thousands of years before. Obviously, a wrong conclusion. This explains very well, I think, why certain fossils dated with C-14 seem to show ages of over 10,000 to 15,000 years. The percentage of C-14 in the atmosphere was much smaller back then than it is today."

"And the second problem?"

"This is the second problem: Only an extremely small percentage of all carbon in living beings is radioactive. Because of the relatively short half-life, under 6,000 years, a few million years after the death of an organism, its remains should not contain detectable traces of carbon-14 anymore. Yet still, many times, traces of carbon-14 were found in fossils presumed to be hundreds of millions of years old, and even in samples of coal and diamond."

"Isn't it possible that they were contaminated, I mean that that carbon-14 got there from other sources?"

"There are many articles and books on this subject and they can give a detailed answer to your question. Contamination is pretty unlikely, especially in the case of diamonds. But *something* inside some people is firmly convinced that all those samples have somehow been contaminated, otherwise the age of the earth couldn't possibly be in the order of billions of years."

"How do they date the fossils that are estimated to be billions of years old?"

"Methods that yield ages in the range of millions or billions of years can usually only be applied to metamorphic rocks, that is rocks that at some point have been in a melted state. Volcanic rocks are a good example of metamorphic rocks. But fossils are not found buried in such rocks, but in sedimentary layers, and the dating of those layers is extremely difficult. Therefore, the age of most fossils is not even 'calculated' by radiometric methods, it is only estimated."

"I see," Daniel said.

"Besides, radiometric dating methods very often yield totally wrong dates for known historical events. For example, many times volcanic eruptions from the past two or three hundred years were radiometrically dated to be millions or even billions of years old. Even the famous isochron method fails shamefully many times, sometimes even yielding dates in the future, which is outright absurd."

"And all these because, you say, the radioactive decay rates used to be different in the past, for a short period of time?"

"Not only because of this, there are numerous factors that make these methods absolutely unreliable. You can find a lot of specialty literature on the Internet; you can read, for example, the paper *The Radiometric Dating Game*[29], by David Plaisted, and the paper *Isochron Dating*[30], by Paul Giem."

4.3.2. Equilibrium of Radioactive Isotopes

"Are there other dating methods besides the radiometric one?" Daniel asked curiously.

"Yes, there are many more, but they do not give an exact age for the planet, only a maximum age. Since we just finished talking about the radiometric dating, I want to continue by talking about the problem of the equilibrium of the radioactive isotopes. In nature we find the so-called radioactive decay chains or decay sequences. For example, isotope I1 decays into I2, I2 decays into I3, and I3 into I4, which is stable. Each isotope, except I4, has its own half-life. A simple mathematical analysis will show you that after a certain period of time, regardless of the initial amounts, the ratio between the amounts of I2 and I3 becomes constant. This is the equilibrium I was telling you about. Depending on the half-lives, it can take anywhere from a few thousand years to a few hundred million years for this equilibrium to be reached. But many rocks, estimated to be billions of years old, were found in which the equilibrium still hasn't been reached, although it should have been reached in a few million or tens of millions of years."

"But isn't this method, too, affected by the possibility that the radioactive decay rates were different in the past?"

"Yes, it is. But, as I was telling you, these methods do not give us an exact age of the earth. They only prove to us that radiometric dating is completely unreliable."

---

[29] https://www.trueorigin.org/dating.php
[30] http://www.scientifictheology.com/Articles/IsoD/IsoD.html

4.3.3. Helium in Zircon Crystals

"Are there any other methods?" Daniel asked.

"There are over one hundred geologic 'clocks' that show us that our planet cannot be billions of years old. The most well-studied and documented of them is the process of the diffusion of helium from zircon crystals."[31, 32]

"One second," Daniel interrupted him, "helium is an inert gas, so how did it get into those crystals?"

"Zircon crystals contain various minerals, among which there are also some radioactive elements. Their radioactive decay produces, among other things, helium atoms. This is how this inert gas 'gets into' the crystals. But the helium atom is relatively small and it does not remain inside the crystal for a long time; gradually, little by little, it gets out, and this process is called diffusion. But while analyzing many such crystals, it was observed that they still contain way too much helium. If those rocks were billions of years old, all helium produced during this time should have escaped long ago from inside the crystals, the diffusion rate being relatively high."

"Isn't it possible that the helium was there from the beginning, or that it got there from other sources? I mean, isn't it possible that the crystals were contaminated?"

---

[31] Zircon: a tetragonal mineral consisting of a silicate of zirconium and occurring usually in brown or grayish square prisms of adamantine luster or sometimes in transparent forms which are used as gems. (Merriam-Webster)

Zirconium: a steel-gray hard ductile metallic element with a high melting point that occurs widely in combined form (as in zircon), is highly resistant to corrosion, and is used especially in alloys and in refractories and ceramics. (Merriam-Webster)

Zirconium's chemical symbol is Zr and its atomic number is 40. Zircon's chemical formula is $ZrSiO_4$.

[32] An exhaustive study of this process can be found in *Radioisotopes and the Age of the Earth* (RATE), by Andrew A. Snelling, Eugene F. Chaffin and Larry Vardiman (Institute for Creation Research, 2000, 2005).

"Even if all the helium was there from the beginning of the existence of the crystal, there should have been enough time for all of it to get out, if those samples were indeed billions of years old. Also, contamination was excluded, because no potential sources were identified nearby.[33] Helium concentration in the surrounding rock is about 200 times lower than the one inside the crystal. As Dr. Russell Humphreys says, 'that means, according to the laws of diffusion, that the helium is presently leaking *out* of the zircons *into* the biotite[34], not the other way around.'[35]"

"But is the helium diffusion rate constant?" Daniel asked.

"It is not constant, of course," Michael replied. "But researchers investigated many potential factors that could affect this rate, especially temperature, and they noticed that it does not vary too much. You see, if the earth were billions of years old, the helium diffusion rate should have been, for all this time, hundreds of thousands of times lower than it is today."

"In the end," Daniel said, "I think it's still our inner *something* that has the last word on this issue; none of us has watched those crystals for their entire existence, to see exactly why they still contain so much helium. Some accept an argument; others accept the opposing argument. To each one it seems that his argument is realistic and that his conclusion is obvious."

"Yes, this is how it is," Michael said. "But this process of helium diffusion is particularly important for creationists for two reasons. First, it seems to indicate a maximum age of ten thousand years for our planet. And second, the mere presence of such large amounts of helium inside the crystals supports the theory according to which, in the past, for a certain period of time, the radioactive decay rates were much higher than they are today.

---

[33] http://creationwiki.org/Criticism_of_RATE%E2%80%99s_helium_diffusion_data

http://www.trueorigin.org/helium01.php

http://www.trueorigin.org/helium02.php

[34] Biotite: a generally black or dark green form of mica that is a constituent of crystalline rocks and consists of a silicate of iron, magnesium, potassium, and aluminum. (Merriam-Webster)

[35] http://www.trueorigin.org/helium01.php

Otherwise, the helium would have escaped from the crystal as it was being produced by the decay of the unstable isotopes."

"If the radioactive decay rates could have been much higher in the past, couldn't the helium diffusion rate also have been much lower?"

"Think for a second about the example with the tens of thousands of pencil cores placed upright on a smooth floor. The pencil cores, the atoms of the radioactive isotopes, the helium in the zircons, these are all examples of systems that are in unstable equilibrium. A very little impulse can make them leave that state and get into a more stable one. The pencil cores fall down, radioactive atoms decay, and helium atoms move one more step to the edge of the crystal. Of course, the little tremors that can cause the fall of the pencil cores will have no effect on the radioactive isotopes, so there is not a single type of impulse that can affect all three unstable systems enumerated before. Helium atoms have their own share of little impulses, more exactly the movement of surrounding atoms, caused by the thermal agitation and by the small variations in temperature, which is what makes them advance step by step toward the exit. Well then, this process couldn't have been much slower unless the temperature of the zircons had been much lower for their entire existence. Not even the evolutionists claim something like this; the zircons were extracted from great depths, hundreds or even thousands of meters[36], where the temperature is high."

"So what is the difference?"

"The difference is that if the radioactive decay rates had been much greater for a short period of time, then all ages calculated by radiometric dating are completely wrong. But the age of several thousand years calculated from the helium diffusion rate could be wrong only if that diffusion rate had been millions of times slower for billions of years, that is, for about the entire existence of those rocks."

---

[36] 100 meters (100 m) = 328 feet.
1,000 meters (1 km) = 0.622 miles.

4.3.4. Sodium in Seas and Oceans

Both men kept quiet for a few seconds. Then Michael resumed the conversation:

"Another carefully studied and analyzed process is the accumulation of sodium in the oceans. I'll only describe it briefly. The rivers that flow into the seas and the oceans of the world carry along small amounts of sodium. This sodium accumulates over time, and a simple calculation will show us that all the sodium now present in the oceans wouldn't have needed more than 60 or 70 million years to accumulate there. And this is only if the oceans contained no sodium at all in the beginning of their existence. But the oceans have probably always had a certain concentration of sodium, so we're actually talking about a much shorter period of time."

"But is this process going on at a constant speed?" Daniel asked. "How can you know that it went on at the same speed for the entire existence of the oceans?"

"We don't know, of course, this is just an estimate. But that sodium usually comes from the rocks and minerals that water erodes and dissolves on its way to the ocean. If the earth were indeed billions of years old, then during all this time the process of erosion should have been hundreds of times slower than it is today. But this is impossible; it is like the planet had, during all these alleged billions of years, hundreds of times less rain and rivers than it has today. But not even atheist geologists claim something like this."

"I'm curious to know what the arguments of the long-agers are," Daniel said.

"So far I haven't seen a single serious counterargument. Someone mentioned at some point the forming of a mineral named albite in the waters of the oceans, a process that consumes a lot of sodium and that, he said, could explain why the oceans contain much less sodium than they should after billions of years. But the creationists reminded him that when the temperature changes, the newly formed albite decomposes and releases all the sodium it had previously consumed back into the ocean. Therefore, the evidence still points to a young ocean. And this is not all, the amount of river runoff spilled yearly into the oceans also points to a period of time significantly shorter than the 'official' one. For example, a researcher has calculated that, at the present rate of runoff, the Gulf of Mexico would be filled in just six million years.[37] Therefore, this gulf cannot be 300 million years old, as 'official' geology says it is."

"These are some topics that are worth investigating more… Other 'clocks'?"

4.3.5. Recorded History

"I'll only mention two more. The first one is about the recorded history of mankind. The oldest civilizations to leave us written information began their existence only a few thousand years ago. This time frame fits perfectly within the biblical age of the earth."

"I think I once heard that there was a problem with the biblical chronology; the Egyptian writings place a few dynasties in other periods of time than those deduced from the Bible."

"This is not exactly like that," Daniel said. "First, most ancient writings, not only the Egyptian ones, are not very explicit and do not mention exact reign periods for the rulers of those times, like we use to say today that a certain president was in office from 2010 till 2014. Usually historical sources only mention some rulers and the number of years each of them reigned. Some historians thought they had to add those years, but others, after a more careful analysis, concluded that a part of those reigning periods overlap. This could be true for other ancient civilizations, too. Several Christian archaeologists have studied this problem and have come to the conclusion that all ancient chronologies, the Egyptian one, the Assyrian one, the Babylonian one, and the

---

[37] Harold G. Coffin, Robert H. Brown, R. James Gibson, *Origin by Design*, Review and Herald® Publishing Association, Hagerstown, Maryland, U.S.A., 2005, p. 370.

Greek one, when correctly interpreted, match quite well the biblical chronology."

"What do you mean by overlapping dynasties, were there two pharaohs at the same time?"

"In the history of the world we can find several situations in which a state had two or three leaders at the same time; for example, the Romans had the triumvirate, that is, they had three rulers at the same time.[38] In the Roman Empire we can also find many examples of emperors whose reign periods overlap, usually one of them being considered co-emperor. For example, Valerian and Gallienus, or Diocletian and Maximian. So why wouldn't it be possible for other ancient dynasties to overlap as well?"

"And how do we know which interpretation of the Egyptian hieroglyphs is the correct one?"

"None of us were there to see exactly what those scribes had in mind when they wrote about those dynasties. But, as you're probably already realizing, *something* inside us makes us accept either one version or the other."

"Yes, that *something*, present everywhere… And the second 'clock'?"

4.3.6. Dendrochronology

"Have you ever heard the term dendrochronology?"

"Dendro… Does it have anything to do with trees?"

"Yes, it is about measuring time by counting the tree rings."

"This should be easy," Daniel said, "there is one ring for each year."

"Not always," Michael replied, "there are also situations in which a tree can grow two rings during a single year, and there are also situations in which a tree can grow no rings for one or more years."

---

[38] A complete description, as well as other examples, can be found here:

https://en.wikipedia.org/wiki/Triumvirate

"OK, and how does dendrochronology help us determine the age of the earth?" Daniel asked curiously.

"Here, too, we have a few clues. The oldest living tree is approximately 5,065 years old,[39] which is a time period almost equal to the time elapsed from the biblical flood till today. A coincidence? *Something* inside you will help you figure out whether it is so or not. That tree is old, indeed, but it shows no signs of being close to death, so certainly it can live longer. Then why can't we find even older trees, say 10,000 or 15,000 years old?"

"I'm curious, how did they count the rings if the tree is still alive?" Daniel asked.

"There are two ways of doing this. First, they can extract a cylinder a few millimeters[40] thick that goes all the way to the center of the tree. Second, they can do a magnetic resonance test, the same way it is done to people with joint diseases. This test is similar to the medical MRI[41]."

"MRI for a tree! I have to remember that."

"And now an observation related to the tree rings. Those rings are not identical, some are thicker, some are thinner, and some are a different color, depending on how the weather was during that year."

"Doesn't it also depend on the quality of the soil?" Daniel asked. "I'm thinking that as the root system expands, it can encounter more fertile or less fertile soil."

"Yes, it may depend on this, too. But usually, in a limited geographical area, if you cut down several trees of the same species, you notice that the ring patterns are almost the same for very many of them. For example, if you notice in a tree's rings three

---

[39] https://en.wikipedia.org/wiki/Methuselah_(tree)

Actually, Methuselah is the name of another tree from the same area, which is 4,846 years old. The 5,065-year-old tree, discovered in 2012, doesn't seem to have a name or an article dedicated to it, but it is mentioned in the article about Methuselah indicated above. Germination date is 3051 BC (estimated).

[40] 1 millimeter (1 mm) = 0.0394 inches.

1 inch = 25.4 mm.

[41] MRI: Magnetic Resonance Imaging.

rainy years followed by two dry ones, then another rainy one and again a dry one, then you'll also notice the same pattern in the rings of most trees in that area."

"Obviously," Daniel said, "when there's a drought over here, there's a drought 200 meters away, too. Of course, with some exceptions, maybe the roots of some trees have made it to the water table, and the roots of others haven't."

"Well then," Michael said, "by this method a connection can be established between a living tree and a tree that died hundreds or thousands of years ago. You can observe, for example, that the pattern from the beginning of the living tree's life matches perfectly the pattern from the end of the dead tree's life, and this way you can calculate, approximately, when the dead tree germinated, and when it died. Then you can establish a connection between the dead tree and another much older tree, and so on."

"That's an interesting procedure," Daniel said. "What is it used for?"

"The most reliable unbroken chronology established this way takes us back a maximum of 11,000[42] years. If the billions of years really did exist, why can't we find trees at least a few hundred thousand years old, using this method?"

"But isn't a time span of 11,000 years longer than the biblical chronology?"

"It does seem to be a little longer, but maybe in the time before the flood it was the norm for a tree to grow two or even three rings a year. Something like this still happens nowadays, but not very often. But there were documented cases in which certain trees grew even five rings during a single year.[43] Other researchers, making several questionable assumptions, came up with a

---

[42] Bernd Becker and Bernd Kromer, *The continental tree-ring record – absolute chronology, ^{14}C calibration and climatic change at 11 ka*, Palaeogeography, Palaeoclimatology, Palaeoecology, vol. 103, 1993, pp. 67-71.

[43] http://www.icr.org/article/tree-ring-dating/
http://creation.com/tree-ring-dating-dendrochronology
Eugene A. Vaganov, Malcolm K. Hughes, Alexander V. Shashkin, *Growth Dynamics of Conifer Tree Rings: Images of Past and Future Environments (Ecological Studies)*, Springer-Verlag, Berlin, 2006, p. 232.

time span of 13,000 years.[44] But this result is rather uncertain, because it involves the combination of a couple of separate chronologies."

"13,000 years is even more than the biblical age of the earth," Daniel noticed. "But if it is indeed possible for a tree to sometimes grow two or three rings a year, then it can fit. But isn't it possible for the rings from the end of a tree's life to only seem to be matching the rings from the beginning of another tree's life, without the two trees being indeed from the same historical period?"

"It is possible, it is not an infallible method, so obviously this can happen from time to time. Here I should also mention the fact that when there are multiple sequences that match, many times researchers reject the one that matches the best and choose the one that better suits the C-14 dating.[45, 46] The C-14 age can be wrong, for the reasons discussed before, and this can make the ages calculated by dendrochronology even greater than they really are."

"Anyway, we cannot go back in time and see with our own eyes whether it was so or not."

"Now here is something else related to trees: In some places in Yellowstone National Park, in the United States of America, there are multiple layers of petrified trees, buried upright, one on top of the other. At Specimen Ridge there are about 27 layers, while at Specimen Creek there are about 50 layers, amounting to a thickness of about a thousand meters[47]. This discovery did cause some stir, because it was presumed that the layers were from different periods of time, and the sum of the ages was well above the age of the earth that could be deduced from the Bible. It was

---

[44] Stuiver, Minze et al., *Radiocarbon age calibration back to 13,300 years BP and the ^{14}C age matching of the German oak and US bristlecone pine chronologies*, Radiocarbon, vol. 28, 1986, pp. 969-979.

[45] David K. Yamaguchi, *Interpretation of cross-correlation between tree-ring series*, Tree Ring Bulletin, 46:47-54, 1986.

[46] Bernard Newgrosh, *Living with radiocarbon dates: a response to Mike Baillie*, Journal of the Ancient Chronology Forum 5:59-67, 1992.

[47] 1,000 meters (1 km) = 3,281 feet (0.622 miles).

being estimated that about 40,000 years had been required for the formation of the entire series at Specimen Creek. But the story with the tens of thousands of years had some problems. First, the trees had almost no roots at all. This suggested that they had actually grown someplace else, then they had been uprooted and transported, probably by a water current, to the place where they were buried. Then someone had the curiosity to analyze in detail the rings of those trees, and thus he observed two interesting things: the ring patterns were repeating in almost all layers, and, with a few exceptions, most of them had died together, during the same year. This could only mean one thing: those trees had all grown during the same period of time and had been buried together by a gigantic cataclysm. The tree layers had been deposited during the same period, not hundreds of years apart."[48]

4.3.7. Ice Layers

"Speaking of tree rings," Daniel said, "I want to ask you a question. Snowfall in Greenland and Antarctica also builds up, year after year, into layers that over time turn into ice, and those ice layers can be counted, the same way you count the rings of a tree. I read somewhere that one can count about 110,000 such layers, each layer representing a single year."

"Depending on the weather conditions, it is possible for more than one layer to be deposited each year. The snow is not like the trunk of a tree, which cannot exceed a certain rate of growth. For example, we have abundant snowfall for an entire month almost with no interruptions, and during this time interval the air currents bring five different times certain amounts of fine dust, or volcanic ash, or something else into that area. How is that snow going to look like after several years, when it has turned into ice? I think it is pretty obvious, we'll see one layer of clean ice, followed by a layer of ice mixed with dust or ash, then another layer of clean ice, and so on. One could interpret those layers as

---

[48] http://creation.com/the-yellowstone-petrified-forests
http://www.icr.org/article/yellowstone-petrified-forests/

representing a period of five, six, or even ten or eleven years. But in reality, the time period is just one month."

"Indeed," Daniel said, "a tree cannot get 30 centimeters thicker in a year, but snow can, depending on how much it snows."

"The real problem of this dating method is that nobody has ever counted those hundreds of thousands of yearly layers of ice. Actually they didn't count anything, they only estimated the oscillations of the ratio of two oxygen isotopes, oxygen-16 and oxygen-18, and they supposed that each oscillation represents a single year."

"And what is wrong with this approach?" Daniel asked.

"This approach presumes that all the ice comes from snow that was deposited uniformly, year after year, for hundreds of thousands of years. But what if some of that ice comes from an iceberg or from a frozen lake? What if in the past, exceptional events took place, something that caused snowfall hundreds or thousands of times more than the yearly average we see today? What if during those snowfalls there were thousands or tens of thousands of variations of that isotope ratio annually, and this for dozens or hundreds of years?"

"What kind of extraordinary events do you have in mind?"

"For example, a glaciation that could have happened in some areas, probably after the biblical flood. This is a possibility that has to be taken into account, those enormous amounts of ice must have been caused by something."[49]

"It is obvious that there is no way for you to know something like that for sure," Daniel said.

"Nobody can know for sure, none of us was there to see how it happened. These are all just theories and arguments that *something* inside us will either accept or reject. All I did was briefly present some of the arguments against the theory that the universe and our planet are billions of years old. On TV and in

[49] http://creation.com/do-greenland-ice-cores-show-over-one-hundred-thousand-years-of-annual-layers

http://creation.com/ice-cores-vs-the-flood

schools they deceivingly say that this theory has been scientifically and unequivocally proven, and that it is not a theory anymore, but a fact. This is one of the greatest lies ever told. It is just a theory, an extremely weak one, and 'proven' only for those who desperately want to believe it."

Daniel didn't say anything. Michael waited for a few moments, then said:

"At the end of our discussion about the age of the universe and the earth, I'll briefly quote, from memory, a parable called the parable of the candle:"

> Chris and Lucy enter a building, looking for Manuel. On the table they find a lit candle and a note that reads:
>
> 'I left at 2 PM to run some errands. I'll be back soon. By the way, the electricity is out, so I lit a candle for you.'
>
> Lucy doesn't believe the note and begins to calculate how long ago Manuel left, by measuring how fast the candle is burning and the rate at which the wax is dripping on the table, and she draws the conclusion that the one they're looking for has been away for at least 24 hours. Then Manuel shows up and tells them:
>
> 'I lit the candle at 2 PM, as I wrote in the note. But the candle isn't burning as brightly as when I first lit it. Then, I didn't light a new candle, but a used one. And I lit it using another candle, so the wax from that candle spilled all over this one. And I didn't mean to deceive you by this; I told you clearly at what time I lit it. It is your fault you didn't believe me and you began conducting silly experiments, like measuring the amount of wax.'[50]

"Yes, I get the point," Daniel said.

"This is all I have to say about the alleged billions of years. If you still have patience to listen to me further, I'll also tell you about the alleged evolution of living beings."

---

[50] The parable was written by the creationist Garth Wiebe, and the full version can be found here:
http://creation.com/the-parable-of-the-candle

Daniel thought for a few seconds, then replied:

"Since I have listened to you so far, I'll listen to you till the end."

5. Can Living Beings Evolve?

After thinking for a few moments, Michael resumed the conversation:

"This is what the theory of evolution claims: Sometime, about three or four billion years ago, in the oceans of this planet, somehow, without any kind of divine intervention, there appeared some organic substances. Later, also without any kind of divine intervention, those substances combined and gave birth to the first living organism. That organism, evolutionists suppose, was a pretty simple one, probably made up of a single cell, but it was capable of reproducing itself. Then, also without any kind of divine intervention, that organism evolved into the life forms we can see today: plants, animals and humans."

"Yes," Daniel said, "and we can see the 'traces' of this evolutionary process at the museum. I mean, the fossils of dinosaurs, and many more."

"We'll get to the fossils in a few minutes. Now, the first question being raised is whether life can appear out of the blue, whether it can create itself. For a religious person, the question is incorrectly phrased, because by life he means both the soul and the body. But for the moment we're only talking about the material side of life."

"I'll interrupt you for just a second; I thought that religion considered that only humans have a soul."

"Only humans have an immortal soul. However, both animals and plants have a spiritual component, too, but I cannot call it a soul, because it is way inferior to the human soul, and it does not survive the death of the body. When an animal dies, its 'soul' also dies."

"Sorry about the interruption; you can return to the evolution of the living beings."

"The first problem for evolution is that it didn't have time to unfold. However, let us see how likely or unlikely evolution would be if it had at its disposal those billions of years that never existed."

"I'm listening," Daniel said.

5.1. Complexity of Life

5.1.1. Complexity of Cell Machines

"A big problem for the theory of evolution is that even the 'simplest' life forms we can see today, bacteria, are extremely complex. I think that anyone who has ever opened a molecular biology textbook[1] was downright shocked by the unimaginable complexity of the 'simple' unicellular creatures. The cell is like a real industrial platform, with countless factories that produce all kinds of things. Tiny little robots[2] are milling everywhere, accomplishing various tasks. Some of these little robots are made up of just a couple of thousands of atoms. Others are a little bit bigger. These little robots, too, are built atom by atom, molecule by molecule inside the 'factories' of the cell. Have you ever heard of the mitochondria and the ribosomes?"

---

[1] An example of such a book: Bruce Alberts, Dennis Bray, et al., *Essential Cell Biology*, Garland Science, 3rd edition, 2009 (a textbook for American students).

Although such books usually exhibit a pro-evolution bias, they help us understand how complex a 'simple' cell is.

[2] In scientific language they are called enzymes or proteins. Most enzymes are proteins, but there are also some exceptions.

"Yes, I think I learned about them in school, but I didn't really like biology, so I don't remember much."

"Well, these ribosomes and mitochondria are truly miniature factories. Mitochondria produce the fuel for these little robots that are milling everywhere in the cell. The same way a car runs on gasoline or diesel, the little robots need a substance shortly called ATP[3]. At almost every step they make, they consume a molecule of ATP. And the ribosomes are the factories that produce all the types of robots that exist inside a cell."

"How are the little robots manufactured?"

"The procedure for manufacturing such a robot is pretty complex. In the nucleus of the cell there is a gigantic molecule named DNA[4], which you have surely heard of. Some robots walk along this molecule, step by step, and stop at a certain position. Then they copy a small portion of the DNA molecule, a portion that is also called a gene, thus creating a smaller molecule named RNA[5]. The DNA contains thousands or tens of thousands of genes, but this small copy only contains the information from a single gene. Then the little robots carry this new molecule inside a ribosome. The RNA molecule, the copy of a DNA gene, contains instructions for building a new robot, or another component that is needed by the cell, a component that is usually called a protein or an enzyme. Inside the ribosome there are countless other tiny little robots that interpret the instructions from the RNA molecule and, following them step by step, build a new robot or a new component."

"This is incredible," Daniel said, "I never imagined that the 'simple' cell is actually so complex."

"It is very complex, indeed. If you want to, when you get in front of a computer, search the Internet for movie clips titled 'molecular machinery.' You'll really see things that cannot be expressed in words. But this is not all. Think that all those tiny little robots are following a certain choreography; they don't move

---

[3] ATP: Adenosine triphosphate.
[4] DNA: Deoxyribonucleic acid.
[5] RNA: Ribonucleic acid.

chaotically, at random. One of the most complicated events in the life of a cell is the reproduction, that is, the cellular division. All cells reproduce themselves by division, even human cells. Although humans and other multicellular creatures do not reproduce by division, the cells we're made of do reproduce themselves by the same process, namely the controlled 'breaking' of a cell in two other identical, or almost identical cells. Cellular division is extremely complex. It requires, first, the duplication of the nucleus and of the DNA. There is a little robot that walks the entire DNA chain and makes an almost exact copy of it. He does make a few mistakes, here and there; for some creatures it was estimated that this robot makes one mistake at every ten million steps. Behind him there comes another little robot that looks for the errors left behind by his predecessor, and fixes approximately 99% of them."

"Aha," Daniel said, "so the mechanism is not perfect."

"No," Michael confirmed, "nothing is perfect in this ephemeral world. Then, after an almost identical copy of the DNA molecule is made, the cell divides in two. I presented the process in an extremely simplified way, but please keep in mind that for each of these steps briefly described, there are books of hundreds of pages that describe it in great detail. I think I am not mistaken if I say that a cell is much more complex than a modern automobile. Also, keep in mind that the cellular division in multicellular organisms does not happen chaotically. Each cell knows for how long it has to divide itself and when it has to stop, otherwise our internal organs would grow at random and uncontrollably. Even more, during the development of the embryo, each cell knows not only when it has to divide itself, but also what it has to transform itself into. Some turn into muscles, others turn into bones, others into liver cells, and so on. The entire process is truly unimaginably complex and it is not even by far completely understood by science."

Daniel had already pulled the phone from his pocket and was looking on the Internet for the movie clips that Michael had told him about.

"I can't understand," Daniel eventually said, "how do these tiny robots know where to go and what to do? I built a small robot when I was in college, but it was very complex. It had a video camera so it could see where it was going, and a computer with memory, so it could know what it had to do. Where do all these fit into just a few thousand, or tens of thousands of atoms?"

"Science cannot yet unlock all the secrets of the cell. The way these little robots work is only a part of the problem. First, the cell needs to know when to make a certain robot and especially how many copies of it. When a certain robot is needed, the cell knows exactly where in the DNA to find the instructions for building it, and it copies those instructions and sends them to the ribosome. Then, some of the newly built robots need to be transported to certain places in the cell, otherwise they would be useless. It may seem surprising, but those little robots contain a short sequence of amino acids that specify their place in the cell. That sequence has the same role as the address on an envelope sent by mail. Some special robots, called chaperons, carry the newly built robots to the right 'address.'"

"Amazing. So, do the little robots move by themselves, or are they transported by others to their designated place?"

"Some move by themselves, others are carried by the chaperons."

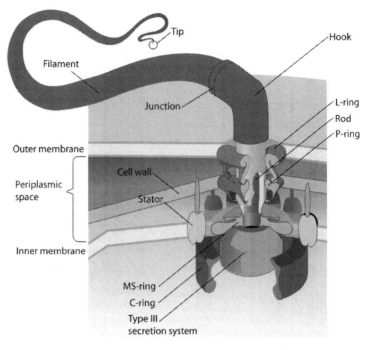

(source: https://en.wikipedia.org/)

The bacterial flagellum, similar in some aspects to an electric motor, is an example of a complex cellular mechanism. The rotor alone can rotate at speeds of up to 6,000 - 17,000 revolutions per minute (rpm), but with the filament attached, only at 200 - 1,000 rpm. The direction of rotation can be switched almost instantaneously. The diameter of the filament is about 20 nanometers, that is about 140 carbon atoms or 70 water molecules side by side.

The flagellum is powered by protons (H^+), and sometimes by sodium ions (Na^+). It is very efficient and consumes very little energy.

5.1.2. Protein Folding

Michael went on:

"But maybe the most amazing aspect is the one called 'protein folding.' Following the instructions copied from the DNA, the ribosome produces a long sequence of a few hundred amino acids, tied to one another like the links of a chain. But the links of this molecular chain are not identical like the links of a real chain. There are 20 types of amino acids, so there are also 20 types of links, and their chaining forms robots with various functions, the same as the chaining of the 31 letters of the alphabet[6] forms words and sentences. But this is not all. The amino acid chain is not rigid, but it can change its shape; it can be bent, folded, the same as a real chain can. Moreover, besides those links adjacent to it, through folding, a link can become tied to other links, too. For example, link number 124 is initially tied only to link 123 and to link 125. But following the bending of the chain, link 124 gets into the vicinity of link 200 and it connects to it through a chemical bond (without breaking off with links 123 and 125). This process repeats itself dozens or hundreds of times, and the end result is a very complex three-dimensional shape, called the native state of the protein. The proteins, the cell's tiny robots, need to be brought into this state in order to function correctly."

"Interesting," Daniel said. "There are probably millions of ways a chain of amino acids can be folded."

"The total number of combinations is astronomical. Cyrus Levinthal, an American molecular biologist, calculated in 1969 that such a chain could be folded in 10^{143} different ways, a number with 143 zeros. And yet, the proteins fold in the same way almost every single time. Errors are rare, and when they happen the protein is not only non-functional, but it can also be toxic. Two great questions need to be raised here. First, how does the protein know which shape is the right one? Second, how can the protein fold into the right shape so quickly? If it tried all combinations till

---

[6] The Romanian alphabet has 31 letters, the standard 26 Latin/English letters plus 5 additional ones: Ă, Î, Â, Ș and Ț.

it got to the right one, it would need trillions of trillions of years. However, most proteins are folded into the right shape in less than a few seconds, and some of them in a few microseconds, that is, a few millionths of a second."

"You make me curious. How?"

"Science could not come up with a full answer for this question. In my opinion, this is also because science is only looking for materialistic explanations and it excludes any supernatural alternative. In simple terms, science presumes that the proteins fold in the right shape so quickly because there is a natural predisposition for the links to bind to one another in a specific way. In other words, link 124 is predisposed to bind to link 200, in the same way hydrogen is predisposed to 'connect' to oxygen and form water molecules."

"And what is wrong with this theory?" Daniel asked.

"Link 124 will not connect to link 200 unless it gets close to it. Two hydrogen atoms won't connect to an oxygen atom unless it gets close to them. So, first of all, the theory does not explain why link 124 gets close to link 200 in order to bind to it. Then, it is obvious that any link is predisposed to bind to other links, because almost any chemical substance is predisposed to react, to bind to other chemical substances. Therefore, link 124 is predisposed to connect to dozens or hundreds of other links, not only with link 200, and it will connect to the first of them that it encounters. Two hydrogen atoms will combine with the first oxygen atom they come in contact with. The theory does not explain why the links almost always come in contact with each other in the right order."

"Although link 124 is predisposed to connect to hundreds of other links, maybe it has a stronger predisposition for link 200."

"I understand what you mean, but there are two problems with your statement."

"What problems?" Daniel asked.

"The predisposition to connect to a certain link is given by their chemical composition, in other words, by the laws of physics that are obeyed by the atoms that form chemical bonds. And those laws are always the same, for all atoms on this planet, and maybe even for all the atoms in the universe. It seems impossible to me that for each protein type, each link has the maximum predisposition to bind exactly to the right link in order to give birth exactly to the native state of that protein, because the blind laws of physics do not give birth to functional complex structures."

"It's hard for me to understand why…"

"Let's suppose that we have some magnetic digits, from 0 to 9. Let's suppose that, due to the laws of physics and to the shape of the digits, digit 2 has a maximum predisposition to connect to digit 0, 0 with 1 and 1 with 5. Therefore, if we mix in a bowl the digits 0, 1, 2 and 5, we will always get the number 2015. But what if we throw in digit 8? We'll get 82015 or 20158. Will we ever get the number 20815? No, because 0 is more predisposed to connect to 1 than to 8. Do you understand the problem now?"

"Yes, now it's a little more clear," Daniel said.

"There are 20 types of links in the amino acid chain that is called a protein. If links of type 1 have a maximum predisposition to connect to links of type 5, then a protein for which it is required that a type 1 link connects to a type 8 link, but which also contains a type 5 link, will never fold correctly, because the link of type 1 will always connect only to the link of type 5, and never with the one of type 8."

"Yes, that's right. Now I understand the problem."

"If, due to the laws of physics, the water of the rivers shaped the stones on the bottom to look like cars, then on the bottom of all rivers in the world we would find stones shaped like cars, not like cows or like flowers. The laws of physics act the same way everywhere, they are blind and devoid of reason and intelligence. If somehow, by chance, the laws of physics produced a complex structure, then they would always produce *only* that structure and nothing else."

"Yes, I understand," Daniel said. "And the second problem?"

"A link in the chain is just a molecule that cannot see, so it cannot know how many other links are there in the chain. Therefore, it will connect to the first link it encounters and for which it has any kind of predisposition. But, as I have already told you, for reasons that science cannot explain, during the protein folding process, the links encounter each other almost always in the right order."

"Indeed, this is something that is hard to explain."

"Yes, sometimes it does happen that wrong bonds are established, and specialized proteins called chaperons detect and break some of them. But the establishment of these incorrect bonds is an exception, not a rule, otherwise the folding of a single protein would take very many years, because there is only one correct combination and an astronomical number of wrong ones. And once a bond is broken, a new bond will be established with the first link encountered, even if it is not the right one. Besides, it is possible that the right link never gets close to the one it is supposed to connect to if one of them, or one of their neighbors, has already connected to another link. Let's not forget, the links are still part of a chain and they do not have absolute freedom of movement. To conclude, the protein folding process cannot be a random process, in which the right combination is arrived at by multiple tries or as an inevitable consequence of the laws of physics."

"Yes, I understand," Daniel said.

"Imagine that you have 20 kinds of magnetic geometric shapes and about 200 items of each kind. Then imagine that you're forming chains with 200 or 300 such shapes, of different types. Then you throw such a chain into a bathtub full of water, to see how the links bind to one another. You also cause some horizontal and vertical water currents, to make the links move around. Obviously, being magnetic, many of them will bind together, and some will be more attracted to certain links than to others, that is, they will be more 'predisposed' to connect to some than with others. But what do you think, will you ever get a complex shape with a specific functionality? A toy car, for example? Obviously not. But this is not all. Throw the same magnetic chain into the water a few dozen times and you'll see that every time you get a different result. But in the case of proteins, something totally contrary happens: they fold in exactly the same configuration almost every single time."

"After they are manufactured by the ribosome, do the proteins fold by themselves, or are they folded by other little molecular 'robots'?"

"Some fold by themselves. Others are assisted by the specialized proteins called chaperons. The whole process is of an unimaginable complexity, and it is hard to understand how some molecules that are devoid of intelligence, made up of a few thousands or tens of thousands of atoms, can do something like this. If human engineers were to build a device capable of detecting incorrectly folded proteins, try to imagine how complex and smart that device would have to be."

"I understand the problems," Daniel said. "And in your opinion, what is the explanation for this miracle of life?"

5.1.3. The Soul Quickens the Body

"I believe, as the Church that I belong to teaches, that a living being is made up of a material part, called the body, and a spiritual one, called the soul in the case of humans. Don't you find it interesting that hundreds of years before the invention of the microscope, certain saints were saying that the soul is present in all parts of the body and that it gives life to that body? More exactly, that the body without the soul is dead? This explains very well why science cannot find all the answers regarding the functioning of the cell and the development of the embryo."

"You mean that that spiritual component of life, which you think exists, is the directing force behind all these tiny components found in every cell?"

"Yes, this is what I believe. According to the Christian tradition, the human soul has three components: a vegetal component, also found in plants and animals; an animal component, also found only in animals; and the actual soul, or the spirit, which is what makes us human and differentiates us from animals. This third component is the one that survives the death of the body. The vegetal and animal components do not survive; that's why when a plant or an animal dies, it is dead forever. And the vegetal component probably takes care, among other things, of the functioning of the cells."

"I remember that in the description of the Christian heaven there were plants and animals, too," Daniel said.

"Yes, but probably new plants and animals, ones created by God. The plants and animals of this world don't have immortal souls, but it is possible that the animals in heaven will be immortal. However, if they will also have a spiritual component—I cannot call it a soul—it will be way inferior to the human one."

"If the soul takes care of the functioning of the body, then why do mistakes happen when the DNA is being copied? I mean, why are there genetic mutations? Why is the mechanism not perfect?"

"We live in a fallen world, corrupted by the sin of Adam and Eve. In this world even our souls are sick, not just our bodies. We'll talk later about this topic."

"And you think that there is such a close connection between the body and the soul?"

"Yes, this is what I believe. Here's another hint. You have probably heard that they say that the human DNA and chimpanzee DNA are 98.8% identical?"

"Yes."

"Well then, first of all, this percentage is pretty controversial; some researchers say that actually it is only 80% or 86%. But let's suppose that the former are right and the percentage is indeed 98.8%. If there is no soul, if the DNA is the only blueprint of material life, how is it possible then that the man and the chimpanzee are so different when they have almost identical DNA? Even though it can be said that, from an anatomical point of view, the human organism is somewhat similar to the chimpanzee one, from an intellectual point of view, the distance between the two beings is enormous. How could a DNA difference of only 1.2% produce such different beings? The scientific explanation seems absurd to me."

"And what is your explanation?"

"The soul quickens the body, but this is not all. The soul is present even from the moment of conception, when the body is made up of a single cell, and it directs all of the body's development. This is what I believe. Obviously, I cannot prove it scientifically, but neither can those who believe the contrary. So you cannot *know* for certain what the truth is. You can only *believe*. *Something* inside you will be attracted to one of these two explanations, and you will accept it and believe it."

5.1.4. The Soul and the Heart Transplant

Michael went on:

"Let me tell you something else about the connection between the body and the soul. The first heart transplant was carried out in the year 1967. Since then, tens of thousands of such transplants have been performed, and now the yearly average is about 3,500. But very many patients who have received someone else's heart have reported a strange phenomenon, namely that they have acquired something from the personality of the donor. More exactly, some patients started to have desires that they didn't have before, or to be attracted to things they previously weren't interested in. They later found out that the donor of the heart had the same desires and attractions. For example, a person who never liked motorcycles started to feel a strong desire to ride such a vehicle after receiving the heart of a motorcyclist who was killed in an accident. Someone who has never liked classical music started all of a sudden to like it, after receiving the heart of a violinist."

"Very strange, indeed. What do the scientists have to say about this?"

"The phenomenon is way too big, with hundreds, maybe thousands of real cases reported around the world, and could not be ignored by all of them. Too bad though, many of the scientists who took these cases seriously do not believe in the existence of the soul, and they came up with a scientific 'explanation.'"

"What explanation can you find for something like this?" Daniel asked.

"The explanation is called 'cellular memory,' and its advocates claim that nerve cells inside the heart have memory, that is, they store information, which is then transplanted together with the heart."

"Honestly, to me this seems to be an absurd explanation."

"It is an absurd explanation, indeed. From a scientific and materialistic point of view, something like this is impossible. The only explanation that I can see is based on the existence of the soul."

"And what is that explanation?"

"The soul is closely connected to the body. When the body dies, the vegetal and animal components of the soul also die, and the spirit, the actual soul, departs from this world to a place where it awaits the resurrection of the dead and the Last Judgment. The introduction of heart transplants, however, has brought in something new. Most of the donor's body dies, but one part, or a few parts, continue to live on. What happens then to the three components of the donor's soul? Do any of them stick around and somehow influence the soul of the one who receives the organs? This is a question we cannot answer, either from a scientific point of view, or from a religious point of view. But we surely see, however, that the receiver also gets 'something else' along with the heart. And I'll also say that transplants performed while the donor is brain dead are very controversial and condemned by many voices inside the Church."

"Really? Why? They save lives, don't they?"

"From the Church's point of view, a man is dead when his heart stops beating, the body gets cold and the immortal soul departs to God. But modern medicine uses another definition, and pronounces the man brain dead a lot sooner, in a moment when it is possible for the soul to still be inside the body. For this reason, this kind of transplant is seen by some as murder."

"Have these phenomena been observed only for heart transplants?"

"Most of them, yes. Probably because the heart is the dwelling place of the spirit, as the Christian tradition says. But a few similar phenomena have also been reported after liver or other kinds of transplants."

5.1.5. The Right Explanation

"I noticed," Daniel said, "that in many cases there are two totally opposite explanations, the scientific explanation and the religious explanation. For example, in the recently discussed case of protein folding, science says that it is something that happens by itself, and you say that it is something directed by that creature's soul. How can you find out which explanation is the correct one?"

"You cannot find out for certain by scientific means. But *something* inside you will be attracted to one of the two explanations and you will end up believing that one."

"Why can't you find out for certain?"

"Because this is something that exceeds our capabilities of knowing. The folding of a protein is not a simple thing, like the reaction of hydrogen with oxygen for the formation of water. The folding of a protein is something way more complex, which can happen in 10^{143} different ways. The theory according to which this happens by itself, because of the blind laws of physics, is just a supposition, impossible to prove at this moment. More than 50 years after the discovery of protein folding, researchers are still talking about what is causing it. So it is pretty obvious that it is not something simple, as clear and easy to study as the reaction of hydrogen with oxygen."

"But there is, however, a scientific explanation," Daniel said.

"What is, actually, an explanation? An explanation, scientific or not, is nothing more than somebody's opinion. Here's an example: do you see that car moving away from us? What do you say, is there a human driver inside of it or not?"

"Of course there is a driver inside," Daniel smiled, "it is moving."

"Well, I can explain the movement of that car without any need of a driver. You have certainly heard of cars that are being driven by a computer, right? So there is no real need for that car to have a driver. What do you say about my explanation?"

"I say that it is wrong."

"Unlike the scientific explanations about the origin and functioning of life, my explanation is pretty realistic, it does not require anything out of the ordinary. The technology for driverless cars has existed for a few years. However, as you yourself are saying, my explanation is wrong. Certainly that car does have a driver."

"I think I begin to understand what you mean. Even though an explanation seems to be realistic, however, that does not mean that it is also true. This is a matter of logic."

"Exactly. And much less when it is about totally unrealistic explanations, like the scientific explanations for the origin and functioning of life. Science has an explanation for everything, but its explanations are nothing more than aberrant opinions. Let's say I'm looking at a car from a certain diagonal angle and through the window I can see the upper part of the steering wheel. But I cannot see the driver—the back windows are tinted and he is keeping his hands on the lower part of the wheel. Then I notice that the car's wheels are slowly turning to the left. I look carefully and I see that the steering wheel is also rotating to the left, though I still can't see the driver's hands. What conclusion do I draw? Is the steering wheel the one that's driving the car? Thus also are science's explanations about the functioning of the material life. Science sees the steering wheel moving, it does not see the driver, and it draws the conclusion that there is no driver and that the steering wheel is the one that's driving the car. Obviously, an absurd conclusion."

"In your opinion, the steering wheel represents the proteins or the molecular robots, and the driver is the soul?"

"Yes," Michael replied.

5.2. Origin of Life

5.2.1. Spontaneous Generation?

"Let's get back to our subject," Daniel said. "Now that you've explained to me how complicated a cell is, I begin to understand this problem of the theory of evolution. How could something so complex appear out of the blue? Isn't it possible that it emerged in several steps?"

"Very many people have asked themselves this question. Indeed, nobody dares to suggest that such a complex system as the cell could have appeared out of the blue. The evolutionists claim that the first cell formed in stages, starting with something much simpler. But not even they know what exactly was that much more simple organism, which nobody has ever seen and which exists only in their imagination. Their problem is that even that simple organism must have been able to reproduce itself, otherwise it couldn't have evolved into anything. And reproduction is one of the most complicated functions of a cell."

"What about viruses? I thought these organisms are much more simple than a cell."

"Viruses are not real living organisms, they cannot reproduce themselves. A virus reproduces when it infects a cell and it is copied by the reproductive system of that cell. Otherwise, the virus disappears."

"But I've heard that many kinds of experiments were conducted in the laboratory in order to try to create artificial life."

"In gigantic factories, engineers and technicians build passenger planes. Is this in any way proof that passenger planes could also appear out of the blue, that they could also be 'built' by the blind forces of nature, for example by the wind and by the lightning, without the intervention of human intelligence? Obviously not. The same is also true about the hypothetical artificial life created in the lab. Even if they ever succeed at such a thing, this does not prove that it could also happen by itself."

"I was thinking about the experiments that try to produce simple organisms only by mixing together some substances, as it is presumed that life has emerged on this planet."

"Here, too, we have a logical problem. Even if they succeeded in producing what they're dreaming about, this would not prove that it also happened in the real history of the planet, it would only prove that *it could have* happened, that's all. But these experiments are extremely far from accomplishing such a thing. Probably what you have in mind is the famous Stanley-Miller experiment."

"Yes, yes, that's the experiment I was thinking about. They said that they mixed certain substances in water, then they introduced electric shocks or discharges and they got the building blocks of life."

"This is a very vague phrasing," Michael said. "At the lowest level, the main building blocks of the material life are carbon, hydrogen, oxygen and nitrogen. Look, if I have a piece of coal and a glass half-full of water, I can say that I have the main building blocks of the material life, and this without conducting any experiments with electric discharges. What they actually got were some amino acids, which are substances a little bit more complex than water and carbon, and which indeed are the base of the material life, at a level superior to simple water and carbon. But from those amino acids to a living organism there is an extremely long way to go. Imagine that I have a million letters cut from newspapers, all of them thrown in and mixed in a large bowl. If I keep mixing them, what are my chances of getting a coherent text, dozens of pages long, some beautiful poems, for example? This is how huge is the distance between the amino acids made by Stanley and Miller and the DNA of a living organism. Besides, they didn't get all of the necessary amino acids, only some of them."

"Well, I knew it was not a perfect experiment, but I thought they proved something important."

"The most important component of the material life are not the amino acids or other substances, but the *information*, I mean the arrangement of the amino acids in a certain order, an order that has a certain meaning. Otherwise it is like you had millions of letters cut from newspapers and mixed together. The DNA is, in fact, an enormous chain, with tens of millions or even billions of 'links,' which in scientific language are called nucleotides or base pairs. For humans, the number of links is about three billion. Each link can have four distinct 'values,' named A, T, C or G, after the names of the four nucleotide types.[7] Three such neighboring links represent the code of an amino acid. There are 20 amino acids and 64 possible combinations of the four values A, T, C and G taken in groups of three.[8] So for each amino acid there are several ways in which it can be coded. A special combination, also made up of three links, tells the robot that the gene is over, and that it has to stop copying and take the newly built RNA to the ribosome. From the information in that RNA, a new little robot or another component is built. During that building process, a single amino acid is produced from the information encoded in each group of three links. This is the most important component of the material life, the 'blueprint' written in the DNA, from which the ribosomes build all the little robots and all the other components of the cell, which accomplish all the complicated tasks that I briefly described just before. The DNA is like a sequence of letters, but its base alphabet only has four symbols, the four nucleotide types. And the alphabet on the next level has 20 symbols, that is, the 20 amino acid types. These letters make up instructions for the functioning of the cell and of the organism, and without these instructions, the cell and the organism couldn't live. The information in the DNA is like the program for a computer. If you remove all programs from your computer, will it still know how to do anything?"

"It won't know anything, obviously," Daniel admitted.

"That's why I, too, say that information is the most important component of the material life. A book that addresses this topic very well is *In the Beginning Was Information*[9], written by

---

[7] Adenine, thymine, cytosine and guanine.

[8] $4^3 = 64$.

[9] Dr. Werner Gitt, *In the Beginning Was Information*, Master Books (A Division of New Leaf Publishing Group), 2006.

the German creationist Dr. Werner Gitt, who used to be Head of the Department of Information Technology at the German Federal Institute of Physics and Technology. Dr. Gitt explains to the reader step by step what information is and why it is impossible for it to appear out of the blue. Therefore, the information in our DNA has to be syntactically correct, that is, the nucleotides have to be arranged after certain rules. Then, information has to be semantically correct, that is, it has to make sense. Then there is the pragmatic level, and that means that every piece of information copied by the proteins from the DNA has a certain purpose, it transmits a certain message to the ribosome, a message that the ribosome knows how to interpret. And finally, the whole system in which this information exists has a purpose for its existence, and for DNA, the purpose is to support the material life of the creatures."[10]

5.2.2. Maximum Number of Tries

"OK," Daniel said, "but if I have the letters, isn't it possible, after a couple of tries, to also generate a meaningful text?"

"You can, if you handpick the letters yourself and place them in a certain order. But it is absolutely impossible for something like this to happen all by itself. Let's do a simple calculation, to see what is the maximum number of tries that could be done. The total number of atoms in the entire universe is estimated to be 10^{80}, that is a 1 followed by 80 zeros. It is a colossal number. Let's suppose there are a million times more atoms, I mean 10^{86}. And let's suppose that each group of one million atoms in the universe does a billion billion tries a second to organize itself into something meaningful for the material life, a piece of DNA, for example. Let's also suppose, against all reason, that the universe is indeed 14 billion years old. How many tries do you think could be done in total during this time interval? The total number of possible tries would be 10^{115}, that is a 1 followed by 115 zeros. It seems to be a huge number, right?"

---

[10] Dr. Gitt calls this final level "apobetics."

"Yes, it is a huge number," Daniel confirmed.

"OK, now let's see how this number looks when it is compared to the probability of getting coherent information by random tries. How many tries do you think are needed in order to get a certain text made up of 329 letters? I said 329 letters because I meant it to be comparable to a medium sized gene, which contains about the same amount of information."

"I don't have the slightest idea," Daniel said. "A few billion billion tries?"

"If we use only the English alphabet, 26 letters plus space, with no other punctuation and without differentiating between uppercase and lowercase letters, then we would need 27^{329} or 10^{470} tries[11] to get through all possibilities of generating groups of 329 letters. This is a number that has 355 zeros more than the maximum number of tries that could have, theoretically, been done. It is hard to express this in words, the number is ten billion billion billion billion billion billion…, and so on. I should say 'billion' about 39 times only to express how many times it is greater than the total number of tries that could have been done if the universe were indeed 14 billion years old and all the atoms in it had tried continuously for all this time period to form a piece of DNA."

"This is discouraging, indeed," Daniel admitted, "there is no chance to get that text by random tries. But I think you're a little bit wrong here. I don't want to get a certain text, I would be happy with just any text that was correct from a grammatical point of view."

"I have thought of this, too. However, the first cell would have needed exactly some genes that would have made reproduction possible; any other genes, though functional, would have been totally useless. But let's talk a bit about what you just said, I mean about the likelihood of getting just any correct text. Have you ever had a computer generate random letters in order for you to see how many of them happen to form correct sentences?"

"No, have you?"

---

[11] Because $\log_X 27 / \log_X 10 \approx 1.4314$, $27^X \approx 10^{X * 1.4314}$ and $10^X \approx 27^{X / 1.4314}$ $(27^{X * 0.6986})$.

"Yes," Michael said. "But the computer didn't know whether a sentence was grammatically correct or not, so it considered correct any sentence made up of correct words. For example, the sentence 'goat plane green from' was considered to be correct, even though it is just a nonsensical sequence of words. Obviously, the real number of correct sentences was much smaller than the number found by the computer."

"OK," Daniel said impatiently, "and what did you find out? What percentage of the total combinations of letters are actually correct sentences?"

"One more thing: the simulation allowed a sentence to also contain one or two isolated letters. For example, the sentence 'Today w is a y beautiful spring day' would have been considered to be correct, the letters 'w' and 'y' being ignored."

"I got it, you did it this way in order to also leave room for small errors."

"Yes, exactly. And then, after I set all these rules, I tried to see how many letter combinations were also correct sentences."

"Probably very many," Daniel said.

"Not really," Michael replied. "As the total number of letter combinations is an exponential function, so the calculated, or estimated, number of correct sentences is also an exponential function, but with a significantly smaller exponent. For example, if I try to generate 20-letter sentences, I have a total of 27^{20} or $10^{28.6}$ combinations. Out of these, my test was finding about 10^{14} correct sentences. The same for tests with 15 or 25 letters, the number of correct results was an exponential function, too, but the exponent was about half the value of the exponent of the total number of combinations. In reality, the number would have been much smaller, but my test considered to be correct a lot of sentences that actually weren't."

"However, there are very many correct ones," Daniel observed.

"There seems to be a lot of them, but let's see how these numbers look when scaled against the probability of creating a single gene through multiple tries. The total number of possibilities is 10^{470}. Let's suppose that 10^{235} of them are correct, I mean they make sense from the point of view of the DNA's language, and they describe a functional gene. Well, even this way we still have 10^{235} invalid combinations for each valid one. Anyone who has studied the theory of probabilities in school can tell you that 10^{115} tries are not even by far enough to find at least one of those valid combinations, whatever that one may be. You need 10^{236} tries in order to say that you have good chances of guessing a single valid combination. You need a number of tries that has 121 more zeros than the total, presumed, number of available tries."

"Yes, I understand," Daniel said, "not a chance..."

"And this is not all. As I have told you before, for the first living organism, it's not enough to have just any functional gene, it needs exactly the genes that would make reproduction possible. Even though a few hundred perfectly functional genes, similar to the genes that help cows produce milk, would appear out of the blue, these genes would be totally useless for an organism that cannot reproduce itself. And reproduction needs more than one gene; it was estimated that in order for the cellular division to be possible, a bacterium requires at least a few dozen genes. If the probability of getting a single gene is one in 10^{470}, then the probability of getting 20 genes is one in $10^{9,400}$. A number with 9,400 zeros. Even if there were a billion universes full to the brim with matter that tried to organize itself in order to create these 20 genes, it still has absolutely no chance of creating a single one."

"OK," Daniel said, "we've seen how things are with letters and sentences. But is it the same with genes?"

"An ordinary computer can test in one second between 8 and 14 million sentences, according to the rules mentioned before. So about 29 to 50 billion per hour. But in the case of genes, things are more complicated, because it is much more difficult to have a computer test whether a gene is functional or not, that is, whether it does something useful for the cell or not. However, I believe that the number of functional genes is much smaller than the number of correct sentences, for the same total number of possibilities. *Something* inside me feels this. But I cannot prove it by an experiment. And if one believes the opposite, he can't prove it by experiment either. But let's consider another analogy.

Have you ever drawn lines at random, on paper, with your eyes closed? Has the final drawing ever come close to representing the blueprint of a real world device, like a children's tricycle or a windmill? Have you ever had a computer draw lines at random on the screen? Have those lines ever come close to representing something coherent?"

"But what do you think about the lottery? Although it is hard to guess the numbers, there are winners almost every month."

"In the lottery, any combination drawn becomes the winning combination. In the case of letters and genes, the vast majority of possible combinations are not winning. With the lottery there are between several million and several hundreds of millions of possibilities, which is about the total number of combinations that can be made with five or six letters. Compare this to the size of a medium gene, namely 329 letters."

5.2.3. Chirality

Daniel didn't say anything. Michael waited for a few seconds, then went on:

"And I'll add something else here. There are certain objects that exhibit a property called chirality[12], that is, they are asymmetric compared to their mirror image. A pair of gloves makes a very good example. Or a pair of shoes. Also some types of car tires exhibit this asymmetry, that is, one can only be installed on the right side of the car, the other only on the left side. Well then, a lot of the molecules that make up the material life have this property, too; that is, they can be either right-handed, or left-handed. Chemically, they have the same properties. But, for reasons we still don't know, all nucleotides that make up the DNA molecule are left-handed, and all those that make up the RNA molecules are right-handed."

---

[12] Chiral: of or relating to a molecule that is not superimposable on its mirror image. (Merriam-Webster)

The term was introduced in 1883 by Lord Kelvin.

"Interesting," Daniel said, "so the little robots that build the DNA and RNA molecules know how to tell them apart."

"Yes, but the question is what exactly told them apart the first time these molecules were formed? The chemical reactions that transform non-chiral substances into chiral ones always produce almost equal quantities of each, that is, half of the resulting molecules are right-handed and half are left-handed. The two halves have identical chemical properties, so when they participate in a chemical reaction, both halves participate in approximately equal proportions. The Stanley-Miller experiment we talked about before produced both right-handed and left-handed amino acids, in equal proportions."

"Is there no way to separate them?" Daniel asked.

"They can be separated in the lab, but so far nobody has discovered the natural phenomenon that is presumed to have separated them when, evolutionists say, the first DNA and RNA molecules were formed. The medium-sized gene mentioned before is made up of about 1,086 chained nucleotides. If the gene was formed by chance alone, then we have a probability of one in $2^{1,085}$ or one in 10^{327} for all the nucleotides to be of the same orientation.[13] Remember the maximum number of tries we discussed before, namely 10^{115}."

"I didn't know about this problem," Daniel said. "I did learn a couple of new things today."

5.2.4. The Monkeys and the Typewriter

"And now one last issue related to these probabilities. Some time ago, someone said that if you provide a couple of monkeys with typewriters, and you also give them enough time, in the end, one of them will eventually type, by chance of course, one of Shakespeare's theatrical works. Later on, some people thought about putting this experiment into practice and they provided some monkeys from a zoo with a computer keyboard, connected

---

[13] Because $\log_x 10 / \log_x 2 \approx 3.3219$, $10^X \approx 2^{X * 3.3219}$ and $2^X \approx 10^X / 3.3219$ $(10^{X * 0.301})$.

to a radio emitter. The monkeys had the keyboard at their disposal for a month."[14]

"It's obvious that those people didn't bother to calculate the probabilities first," Daniel said.

"Those people were lecturers and students from a British university. Anyway, the experiment revealed something interesting. The monkeys were not typing letters at random and they were not trying to reproduce a theatrical work of Shakespeare. In total they produced only five pages, consisting largely of the letter 'S' and some other letters here and there. Besides this, they bashed the keyboard with a stone, and they also did to it some other nasty things that I'm not going to describe to you now."

"What a surprise," Daniel said, laughing ironically.

"Well, the same thing happens in nature, too. The atoms and the molecules do not try to combine themselves in the hope of creating a gene. The atoms and the molecules react with each other based on their chemical properties and, after such a reaction, if they got into a stable state, they remain in that state for an indefinite period of time, till an external factor disturbs them. And besides, even if matter did try repeatedly to create a functional gene, it wouldn't know when to stop. Once the correct gene was created, it would be immediately destroyed in order to try other combinations. Matter has no way of knowing that it got to where it was supposed to get and that it has to stop. Matter does not reason."

"Yes, that's an interesting observation," Daniel said.

"Not even the evolutionists dare to suggest that the few dozen genes needed by a bacterium for reproduction were formed by themselves, by chance. Instead, they claim that first a large molecule was formed, which was capable of reproducing itself. Then this molecule underwent mutations, from one gener-

---

[14] A brief description of the experiment (which was done with the help of a £2,000 grant) is available here:

https://en.wikipedia.org/wiki/Infinite_monkey_theorem#Real_monkeys

ation to the next and created itself a membrane, ribosomes, mitochondria and all the other components, and eventually became a real cell. But this is just a fairy tale produced by evolutionists' imaginations. Nobody has ever seen that initial molecule or the intermediate steps. Nobody has ever succeeded in reproducing these stages in a lab. Nobody can even imagine how these intermediate stages looked. And even if they ever succeed in creating all the stages in the lab, we have to calculate the likelihood of the initial molecule to have formed by itself, and then the probability of moving from one stage to the next in a single generation, only through random changes. It should be noted that each stage would have to be perfectly functional, in order to be able to reproduce. For the moment, both the primordial molecule and the other stages that separate it from being a real cell are nothing but illusions. But *something* inside them is firmly convinced that they existed."

"Indeed," Daniel said, "I see that eventually everything comes down to one's inner predisposition to believe one version or another."

"You'll find on the Internet people who claim that they have written a computer program that has generated so far over 50% or 90% of Shakespeare's works. It is a great deception; all that program does is randomly generate small groups of a few letters, which it then compares against the works of Shakespeare, and if they match, it keeps them, otherwise it generates another group of letters, and so on."

"I don't see what the problem is…"

"The problems are these: First, the experiment is an example of 'evolution' guided by an intelligent being. Someone knows where the computer is supposed to get and he guides it step by step in that direction. Second, the intermediate stages in this process are not functional—I mean they are not a correct and meaningful English text. Imagine a die with 26 sides, having one letter on each side. You roll the die till you get the letter S, which you then write down on a piece of paper. Then you roll the die till you get the letter H, and you write it down, too. Then the letters A, K, E and so on, till you complete the word SHAKESPEARE.

You need about 286 tries in total. Compare this against the over three million billion, that is 3×10^{15} tries needed if you used 11 dice and you generated 11 random letters every time."

"Why is there such a big difference? Why is it so easy to get correct words if you only generate one letter at a time?"

"Because you know from the beginning where you're trying to get. It is not a totally random process, but a process guided letter by letter by an intelligent being. But the theory of evolution claims that there is no intelligence that guides this process. Besides, the experiment ignores the fact that 'S,' 'SH,' 'SHA,' 'SHAK' and so on, are not correct English words. In other words, the intermediate stages are totally nonfunctional. In nature, such an 'evolutionary' process wouldn't stand a chance, because each intermediate stage would have to be fully functional in order for it to be able to reproduce itself."

"I understand," Daniel said.

"One of the experiments I previously mentioned generates four letters and punctuation marks at every step, that is about one million distinct possibilities, because it takes into consideration 26 letters, space and four punctuation marks, or 31 symbols in total. For example, the computer tries about a million times till it happens to generate the sequence 'WILL,' then another million tries to get to the sequence 'WILLIAM ' and so on till it gets to 'WILLIAM SHAKESPEARE.' It is a much slower process than generating a single letter at each step."

"I understand," Daniel said. "If it tried to generate eight letters at each step it would need about a thousand billion tries, and if it tried to generate a full sentence at each step, it wouldn't be able to get a single one in 14 billion years, even if the entire universe were full to the brim with computers that would be continuously trying only this. It is obvious now."

"Exactly the same is true for the information in the DNA. Blind nature cannot create a gene step by step, adding one or two nucleotides at a time. First, because it does not know in advance the end result that it is supposed to get to. And then, because the intermediate stages are not functional, they are just meaningless sequences. This is about all I have to say about the possibility of life arising by itself. Now let's see whether living organisms can evolve, that is, whether they can, over time, turn into different kinds of creatures; for example, whether a reptile can become a bird."

5.3. Can Living Beings Evolve into Different Life Forms?

After thinking for a few moments, Daniel said:

"As far as I know, small scale evolution of creatures has been observed many times. It has been used for thousands of years by animal breeders, who select the best traits and get new breeds this way."

"The word 'evolution' is pretty vague and it can mean a lot of things. For example, we can talk about the evolution of technology, the evolution of literature, and so on. From a biological standpoint, we can talk about two kinds of evolution. Micro-evolution, which is what you have just mentioned, means small changes in living beings from one generation to the next, changes that are being closely monitored and selected by animal breeders and farmers. And macro-evolution, which is the alleged transformation, over time, of some animal and vegetal species into totally new and different species. Something like this has never happened."

5.3.1. Genetic Recombination

"Why do you talk about micro-evolution and macro-evolution as about two different things? If micro-evolution goes on for several millions of years, won't it give birth to new, totally different species?"

"Let's see what the sources are for the changes that occur in living beings. First, small changes can occur because of the environment in which the organism is living. I once knew twin brothers, who at the age of 25 were almost impossible to tell apart. Then one of them moved to another country and, after a year, a clear difference between them became visible: the one who left had gained a significant amount of weight and now they could be easily told apart. However, this type of change is not genetically transmitted to the descendants. But there are also genetically transmissible changes, and they can come from two different sources. Unlike unicellular organisms, which reproduce by cell division, more complex organisms reproduce themselves through a more complicated process, which requires a male and a female. The DNA of all these organisms contains two copies of each gene, one from each parent, and for this reason, it is called a diploid DNA. In other words, the entire DNA chain exists in two copies, which are not perfectly identical. Each cell in the living organisms contains these two copies, which the cell duplicates when it divides."

"I think this division is called mitosis," Daniel recalled.

"Yes, classical cell division is called mitosis. But there is also a special type of division, called meiosis, which is only found in sexual cells: sperm and eggs. These cells are formed from normal cells, but they involve an entirely different process, called genetic recombination. The source cell has two copies of DNA, one from the mother and one from the father. During the process of genetic recombination, between the two copies of the DNA, an information exchange takes place, some portions being interchanged. For example, genes number 7,123 from both copies are interchanged. This process takes place several times, at several locations, and eventually none of the two copies are identical anymore to any of the original copies inherited from the parents. Once this process is completed, the cell division takes place, and the resulting cells, sperm or egg, contain only one copy of the DNA. In other words, they have only half the number of chromosomes of a normal cell. I presented the process in a simplified manner; in reality it involves three cellular divisions, and in the end, four sexual cells are produced."

"A very complicated process," Daniel noticed. "But what's the purpose of it?"

"It is believed that genetic recombination never occurs the same way twice, that the interchanged portions are always different. Thus, all sperm cells and all eggs are different from one another. Therefore, no two offspring of a male and a female will have the same DNA, regardless of their species, even if the couple has thousands of offspring. So the purpose of this mechanism is probably to create genetic diversity."

"What about identical twins?"

"Identical twins, also known as monozygotic twins, come from a single sperm and a single egg, which gave birth to a single fertilized cell, also known as a zygote. That cell was duplicated by classical cell division and the two resulting cells were separated, and thus two zygotes resulted, out of which two separated embryos were developed. Identical twins have the same DNA, that's why they resemble each other so much. On the other hand, fraternal twins come from two sperm cells and two eggs, which gave birth to two different embryos. Their DNA is not identical, that's why they don't resemble each other perfectly, and it is even possible that they are of different genders."

"And isn't it possible for this genetic recombination to produce new, different species?"

"Genetic recombination will never produce something new and totally different, because all it does is rearrange information that already exists in the DNA. Genetic recombination can make a lizard somewhat smaller or bigger, somewhat greener or grayer, but it will never make a lizard with feathers and wings. For this to happen, many new genes are required, with new information, information that the lizard's DNA simply doesn't have, regardless of the way it is recombined. The lizard's DNA has no genetic information for feathers and wings, and that genetic information cannot arise by rearranging the genes."

"Yes, I understand," Daniel said.

"Here's an analogy: Let's say you have at your disposal water, flour, oil, sugar, eggs, cocoa and vanilla. How many kinds of cookies can you make with these ingredients?"

"I'm not good at cooking, but probably there are hundreds, or thousands of different combinations."

"I agree. But will you ever be able to make a steak, or a bean soup out of these ingredients?"

"Obviously not. I have no meat and no beans."

"That's exactly why genetic recombination will never produce new, totally different life forms. The required information is missing."

5.3.2. Genetic Mutations

"I see," Daniel said. "You said there are two causes that lead to genetic changes. What is the second one?"

"As you remember from the description of the cell, sometimes it happens that the little robots that copy the DNA make some mistakes. Behind them come other little robots that fix most of these errors, but not quite all of them. You remember that there are 64 possible combinations for each group of three nucleotides from the DNA chain and 20 amino acids, so there are several ways to code an amino acid. For this reason, some of these errors have almost no immediate effect on the organism.[15] Besides these, other mistakes can also happen, for example, a gene can be copied twice, or it can be moved someplace else, or it can be completely deleted. The system is extremely complex and it is not yet totally understood. A few years ago, scientists

---

[15] For example, for the amino acid cysteine, there are two ways of coding it, TGT and TGC; for the amino acids arginine, leucine and serine there are six codes, and for the amino acids methionine and tryptophan, only one. Nucleotide sequences TAA, TGA and TAG are called stop sequences, and encountering any of them signals to the enzyme that the gene is over. A copying error that changes a TGT sequence into a TGC one has no immediate effect on the organism, because both sequences have the same meaning.

used to believe that only a maximum of 10% of the DNA contained useful genes, the rest being useless[16], made up only of vestiges of the process of evolution. But lately it was discovered that a big part of this DNA has its purpose, too, and the amount considered useless has decreased from 90% to about 70%, or even to about 20%, depending on which scientist you ask. But I believe that in the end it will be proven that most of the DNA is useful. The appendix, too, was once considered to be a vestigial[17] organ, but recently it was discovered that it has, however, a well-defined purpose."

"These changes that you're talking about are actually the genetic mutations, aren't they?"

"Yes, that's correct, changes from this second category are called genetic mutations. Changes from the first category, those caused by genetic recombination, are never going to be able to turn a species into something entirely different. But evolutionists claim that changes from the second category, namely the genetic mutations, are capable, over time, of adding new information to the DNA and of producing new, totally different species. Thus, the theory says, in each generation the descendants will have a few mutations more than their parents. If one of those mutations has made one of them somewhat better than the others, then that organism has better chances of surviving and reproducing, thus passing on the mutation to its offspring."

"Well, you said it yourself, sometimes some genes are copied twice, by mistake. Isn't this new information?"

"No, the duplication of a gene cannot be considered to be addition of new information. No, the duplication of a gene can-

---

[16] Also known as "junk DNA."

[17] Vestigial: [an organ] reduced to a rudimentary state in the organism, which indicates a state of involution. (Great Dictionary of Neologisms, 2000 (in Romanian))

It is noteworthy that even in the dictionary the vestigial organs are seen as a consequence of involution, too, not of evolution.

not be considered to be addition of new information. I pronounced the previous statement twice, did I say anything new the second time?"

"No," Daniel admitted. "Now I see what you're trying to say."

"The same goes for the accidental duplication of genes. However, evolutionists claim that gene duplication is the basis for the process of adding new information. More exactly, once duplicated, one of the copies can start to undergo mutations without affecting the other, its original, in any way. And this, they say, can lead eventually to the development of a new trait for the organism."

"It seems to be easy," Daniel said. "The original keeps doing its job, while the copy is being changed step by step till it comes to do something completely new."

5.3.3. Irreducible Complexity

"Theoretically, it seems to be easy, but here, too, there are a few problems. The first problem is that usually genes don't work alone, but in groups. For example, there are probably hundreds of genes involved in the development and functioning of the eye. There are dozens of genes involved in cellular division, and all of them work in sync with one another. Even more, it is possible for a gene to be part of multiple groups at the same time, and that means that a change in that gene affects multiple systems and functions of the organism. Duplication of a single gene and then the changing of its copy does not add anything new to that living being. An entire group of genes should be duplicated, and then they should be changed in parallel. This problem of the synchronized evolution of several genes or internal organs is known as the problem of the irreducible complexity. For example, the eye would be completely useless without the nerve that connects it to the brain; the stomach would be useless without the intestines and without the mouth through which it is fed. All these systems would have had to evolve together, very well synchronized with one another. American biochemist Michael Behe[18] provides a few such examples of extremely complex and interconnected systems, which involve dozens or hundreds of genes and little robots in order to work properly. If a single one of these components is missing or stops working correctly, the entire system ceases its activity. Out of the systems enumerated by Behe, I especially remember the human immune system and the system of cellular transport."

"That's interesting," Daniel said. "I have never thought of this, though now it seems obvious that it is so. I'm curious to know what counterarguments the evolutionists have."

"There were some people who disputed Behe's examples, saying that in nature there are also simpler systems, which are working fine with only a part of those components. Yes, but those are systems that have been designed from the start to be simple and to work with fewer components, also providing fewer functions. You know, they also make three-wheeled cars, don't they? Reliant Robin for example. But if we remove a wheel from a classical, four-wheeled car, what do we get? Do we get a functional three-wheeled car by any chance? Obviously not, we get a classical car that is not functional anymore. Or if we cut a classical car in two, do we get two motorcycles? No, we get just two halves that can only be used as scrap metal. The same is true for the complex biological systems, very many of them simply need absolutely all components in order to function properly, and if a component is removed or it is changed so that it doesn't fit the others any more, the entire system fails. What would happen if we installed on a car a wheel slightly larger than the other three?"

"Yes," Daniel said, "I understand. In a car, in a plane, in a computer, in a cell, and in any other system, the components must perfectly fit with each other for the system to work."

"There are also, indeed, some systems that contain one or two components that are not absolutely necessary and the systems can keep on working, in a limited way, without them. But

---

[18] Michael J. Behe, *Darwin's Black Box: The Biochemical Challenge to Evolution*, Free Press, 1996 (second edition: 2006).

even those systems have a minimum set of components that are absolutely necessary. To that minimum set of components refers the irreducible complexity. A good example is the human body. We can keep on living with only one kidney, or without the spleen, or without the appendix, or without an arm, or without a leg, but we cannot live without the heart or without the liver. Or without the brain."

"This is true," Daniel admitted. "And the second problem?"

5.3.4. Are There Any Beneficial Mutations?

"Let's think for a second about how the theory of evolution claims this process works. A few mutations appear every time the DNA is copied. Thus, at each generation, those mutations are passed on to the descendants. Here I'm only talking about the mutations that occur at the division of sexual cells; the mutations that occur at the division of muscle cells, for example, are not passed on genetically. Because of these mutations, most of the descendants are inferior to their parents, but a small percentage of them will inherit beneficial mutations. The evolutionists say these descendants will be superior both to their parents and to their siblings, and will have better chances to survive and to re-produce, thus passing on the 'beneficial' mutations."

"Yes, this is the official explanation. What exactly is wrong with it?"

"Those mutations, even if they were indeed beneficial, have no chance of turning a species into something entirely different. It is possible for them to make an animal a little bit faster or stronger, but this only within certain limits.[19] Then you need to

---

[19] A pretty good article about these limits is *The Kentucky Derby Limit*, available online here:

http://www.ScienceAgainstEvolution.org/v3i9f.htm

Briefly, the author of the article analyzes the results achieved by the fastest horses in the competition known as the Kentucky Derby. Looking at the data from 1896 till today, we notice that, despite all the know that a mutation that is considered beneficial is not necessarily a mutation that gives a new functionality to the organism. The great majority of the mutations that are considered to be beneficial are actually mutations that cause defects to the organism, but those defects, in certain circumstances, are beneficial."

"I don't get it, how is it possible for a defect to be beneficial?" Daniel asked.

"Let's take a look at some examples. There is a hereditary disease called, in medical terms, sickle-cell anemia, caused by a malformation of the hemoglobin molecule, which in turn causes a malformation of the red blood cells. If one inherits the defective gene from only one parent, he can lead a relatively normal life, because the disease does not manifest itself too much. But if he inherits the defective gene from both parents, then his life expectancy can be seriously affected. However, people with this genetic defect are much more resistant to malaria. Therefore, in countries where malaria is commonplace, there are also very many people with this mutation, because they can survive it better than the others. Here is another example. Some time ago, the majority of sheep used to have horns. But sometime, probably due to some genetic errors, hornless sheep were also born, and this genetic defect was considered to be beneficial by the sheep breeders, who then used those animals to create hornless breeds. But most examples of defects with beneficial effects are from the world of bacteria. More exactly, this is about the bacterial resistance to antibiotics."

"Yes," Daniel said, "this is considered to be a very good proof for the theory of evolution."

---

efforts of the horse breeders, the winning times have reached a level that hasn't been exceeded since 1973:

http://www.ScienceAgainstEvolution.org/KentuckyDerby-Data.pdf

But the main cause for the improvement of the performances of racehorses is probably the genetic recombination, not the DNA copying errors, whose role should be very limited.

"Antibiotic resistance can have many causes; for almost every species of bacteria and for every antibiotic there is a separate explanation. I'll only give you a few examples. In some cases, the bacterial population already contains individuals who exhibit natural resistance to antibiotics. In the presence of the antibiotic, the non-resistant ones die, and only the resistant ones are left and multiply. No evolution here. In support of this information, I'll also tell you that bacteria were discovered that had been frozen for thousands of years in the permafrost and that are resistant to some antibiotics.[20] So they had this resistance from ancient times. Then there is the resistance passed from one bacterium to another. In later years it was discovered that, although the bacteria multiply asexually, there are still situations in which they transfer genetic material from one to another. Antibiotic resistance can also be acquired this way."

"That's an interesting explanation," Daniel said. "I didn't know that bacteria, too, can exchange genetic material."

"And lastly, we have the antibiotic resistance acquired as a consequence of some genetic defects. For example, a defect in the genes that control the absorption of food through the membrane is not fatal, but it is harmful to the bacteria since it cannot feed properly. But this defect also comes with an advantage: The bacteria also cannot properly absorb the antibiotic through the membrane, and thus the bacteria survive. Here's another explanation: There is a substance called penicillinase, which cancels out the effect of penicillin. This substance is being naturally produced by some bacteria, but in small amounts, not enough to resist a treatment with penicillin. But a defect or a deactivation of the mechanism that controls the production can cause a bacterium to produce much larger amounts of penicillinase, and thus to become immune to penicillin."

"This is very interesting," Daniel said, "I didn't know all these things. But why do you call them defects?"

---

[20] http://www.nature.com/nature/journal/v477/n7365/full/nature10388.html

"Because they all involve a disorder in the normal function of some genes or their complete deactivation. It is impossible for a bacterium that keeps on losing genes to ever become a mammal. The best proof that these mutations are actually defects is that antibiotic resistant bacteria, when moved to their natural environment, are inferior to the other bacteria that do not exhibit this resistance. They are only superior in the presence of antibiotics, which is why the best place you can find them is inside hospitals. Outside the environments dominated by antibiotics, the resistant bacteria cannot compete against the normal bacteria and they die off. A bacterium that uncontrollably produces enormous amounts of penicillinase is wasting its internal resources and it doesn't stand a chance when faced with one that doesn't do this."

"Yes, now I can see why."

"There is also a procedure for treating digestive tract infections that have become resistant to antibiotics. The doctors take a small sample from the contents of the digestive tract of a healthy person, I mean partially digested food, which also contains a lot of bacteria that we all have inside our intestines, and they introduce it into the digestive tract of the sick person. It seems disgusting, but it saves the life of the patient. And the explanation is simple: The antibiotic resistant bacteria from the sick man's intestines cannot resist the transplanted bacteria, and they die pretty soon.[21] There are also many cases of patients discharged from hospitals with antibiotic resistant infections, which were healed a few days later with no other medicine. The explanation is simple: In the natural, wild environment, the antibiotic resistant bacteria cannot withstand the competition from the non-resistant ones."

5.3.5. The Problem of the Intermediate Stages

"OK, but isn't it possible that there are also truly beneficial mutations? I mean, mutations that really add something new and functional to the organism?"

---

[21] http://edition.cnn.com/2012/09/26/health/fecal-transplant/

"It is *possible* that there are, but they are so *unlikely*, that I don't think we'll ever see one. Is it possible for a pig's DNA to undergo such a multiple mutation, that it will grow wings? Even an evolutionist will tell you that it is possible, but it is so unlikely, that it will surely never happen. The theory of evolution, in order to be credible, needs billions of billions of such beneficial mutations. Is it possible to transform a correct sentence into another correct, but completely different sentence, in a few hundred steps, doing only a small change at every step? Maybe you will be tempted to say yes, but keep in mind that each intermediate step must also be correct. Even if this transition were theoretically possible, think that it should happen through totally random mutations. My example with the sentences had some very relaxed rules, any sequence of correct words was also considered correct. But in reality things are not like this. Not any chain of DNA sequences makes up a functional gene. Actually, the vast majority of them do not."

"To me, too, this seems to be the greatest problem," Daniel said, "that each intermediate step has to be perfectly functional, otherwise that creature wouldn't be better than its parents and it also wouldn't be able to survive and reproduce."

"Obviously," Michael approved. "What's the use of a quarter of a wing, or a half of an eye? If the eye has evolved from zero, then each intermediate step must have been functional and must have been doing something useful for that creature."

"Yes, that's true."

"And not only that. Each intermediate stage must be obtained from the previous one only through a few DNA copying errors, that is, only with a few different nucleotides."

"So once you have a valid gene, how difficult is it to transform it into another valid gene?"

"If we remember the simulation we discussed before, for each valid text there were 10^{235} invalid texts. The text contained about the same amount of information as a single medium-sized gene. Therefore, it is not that easy to go from one valid gene to another."

"However, your simulation allowed for the existence of some stray letters. If you change such a letter you get another valid text by doing a single 'mutation.'"

"Yes, but that's only because that letter was being ignored, otherwise it wouldn't have been possible any more. And if you change any other letter, you usually get an invalid text. In the case of genes, too, it is possible to find two or three amino acids that can be changed without affecting too much the functionality of the resulting protein, but that's about it. If you modify other amino acids, the protein no longer works correctly, and this disturbs or even stops the activity of the entire system that it is a part of."

"So it is not possible to transform a functional gene into another functional, but totally different gene, changing only one or two amino acids at every step?"

"It is impossible to prove scientifically that something like this is not possible. But the evolutionists have been looking for these series of mutations for decades and so far they haven't found a single one. These hypothetical transformations only exist in their imaginations. And even if they ever find such a series of mutations, the probability of them occurring naturally is comparable to the probability that the gene appeared by itself. Keep in mind that the protein that resulted from that gene has to be perfectly functional at each step, but the functionality changes from one step to another, I mean the protein, though perfectly functional, will do a different thing for every modification. Therefore, even if the resulting protein were functional, it won't fit anymore in the system that it is a part of. Think about the sentences in a book. Every sentence has to be grammatically correct. But this is not all. Every sentence must fit, it must make sense, in the place where it is located. Listen carefully to what I'm telling you now: The poacher was arrested this morning."

"What poacher?" Daniel asked. "I don't understand..."

"You see? My statement about the poacher is perfectly correct from a grammatical point of view, yet still it makes no sense in the context of our discussion. In the same way, even if a gene were to be transformed into another perfectly functional gene, the new gene wouldn't fit anymore into the system that it is a part of."

"Yes, I understand now. It is a big problem, indeed. A change in a gene has to be accompanied by dozens or hundreds of precise changes in other genes."

"Exactly, those changes would have to be perfectly synchronized, otherwise the system stops working. But here we encounter another problem: Gene copying errors are rather rare. Due to the fact that mutations are usually harmful, if the proteins of an organism underwent dozens of such modifications in each generation, that species would go extinct pretty fast, because its individuals would not make it till the age of reproduction."

"Yes, this is also a problem," Daniel admitted.

"Then, each intermediate stage has to be not only fully functional, but also somewhat better than the previous stage, otherwise it would not have better chances to survive and reproduce. Here's an example: Some time ago, the cars were equipped with a cassette player. Today they are equipped with a CD player. Imagine how you would transform a cassette player into a CD player step by step. You would need a few thousand intermediate stages. Each stage has to be only a very little bit different than the previous one, but at the same time somewhat better and, obviously, perfectly functional. Ah, let's not forget, all this transformation has to be *totally* random."

"I give up," Daniel said after a few seconds, "I can't even imagine how I could transform a cassette into a CD in a few thousand steps…"

"And this is not all; the process should be going something like this: The cassette player is manufactured by workers following some blueprints in which each individual component is described in detail. Let's suppose those workers are like the ribosomes that manufacture cellular components following the instructions in the DNA, they don't have their own intelligence, and if a small error sneaks into the blueprints, they don't realize this and produce the component with the wrong shape or size. Now, at every stage, the blueprint of the cassette player is copied, also through a process devoid of intelligence, which introduces, pretty rarely, an error here and there. What do you say: is it possible for the cassette player's blueprint to be eventually transformed into the blueprint of a perfectly functional CD player? Oh, and all the intermediate stages must also describe perfectly functional devices. Imagine that every time the size of a component changes even by a single millimeter, something also needs to be changed in all the other components that this one is connected to, otherwise the mechanism stops working."

"I give up one more time," Daniel said, this time without thinking.

"Of course, the evolutionists can't answer these questions, either. Some of them claim that these complex components have somehow evolved behind the curtain, without being used, which allowed them to have non-functional intermediate stages, and at some point, a simple mutation activated them. You said it yourself recently that if a gene gets duplicated, the original can keep on doing its job, and the copy can be gradually transformed into something else. But not too many people take this explanation seriously, because it is illogical. Why would a species evolve a protein or an organ that it doesn't use for anything for millions of years? That partial organ would offer no advantage over its rivals, but even more, it would be a disadvantage, because it would unnecessarily consume its resources. Besides, evolution is supposed to be blind, unguided, without an explicit purpose, at random. How then could there be so many thousands and millions of intermediate stages for the development of an organ or a system, in the 'hope' that it will be used later? Blind matter does not hope, blind matter does not make plans for the future, blind matter does not reason. But there is an extremely strong *something* inside the evolutionists that makes them believe in these step by step transitions, although they have never seen them and they are also so improbable."

"Yes, probably," Daniel admitted. "Everything comes down to one's predisposition to believe one version or another."

"Or, better said, to one's desire to believe one version or another," Michael said.

5.3.6. Bacteria and the Citrates

After a short interruption, Michael went on:
"There was a recent case in which it was believed initially that a species has added a new functionality. Researcher Richard Lenski and his colleagues noticed in 2008 that some *Escherichia coli* bacteria had started to feed on citrates[22] in an aerobic environment, that is, in the presence of oxygen. The discovery made headlines around the world, being considered one of the best proof for evolution ever found. It took the researchers a few years to find out exactly what had happened. *E. coli* bacteria already had the ability to eat citrates, but only in an anaerobic environment, that is, in the absence of oxygen. So the complex mechanism required to transport the citrates through the membrane and to digest them was already present in the genome of the bacteria, but it was not always active. What had actually happened? In simple words, the mechanism providing the transportation of the citrates from outside the cell to inside was now also being activated in the presence of the oxygen, because a gene had been copied to a different location."

"So no truly new functionality?"

"No, of course not. The evolutionists were so enthusiastic because they simply didn't have anything better to boast about. But this kind of change will never transform a bacterium into a mammal."

5.3.7. Changes Observed in Today's Life Forms

"However," Daniel said, "there are examples of changes made in living organisms, in order to adapt to the environment they're living in."

"Yes, there are minor changes caused either by the genetic recombination, or by the moving of some genes in other places,

---

[22] Citrate: a salt or ester of citric acid. (Merriam-Webster)

or by the activation or deactivation of some previously existing genes. The organisms have 'by design' the possibility of performing these minor changes. For example, such variations, which for the time being seem to us to be random, can produce birds with shorter beaks and birds with longer beaks. Depending on the environment conditions, the ones with the shorter beaks may be better adapted for survival, and thus they multiply more than those with longer beaks. If the environment conditions change, it is possible that those with longer beaks will multiply more, and the others will almost die off. But this is all there is."

"But can't the genetic mutations be the cause of such changes?"

"If you have a text with a few hundred letters, is it possible to change one or two letters and get a better text? Yes, sometimes it is possible, but these cases are rare and the changes are very limited, you cannot change this way the entire text into another, totally different one. So it is possible to find mutations that add a little improvement to a creature, for example, mutations that make it a little bit faster, or a little bit more silent, or mutations that change its color a little, but these are very rare and very limited."[23]

"Yes, I understand," Daniel said, "we just talked about the problem of the intermediate steps. Tell me one more thing, what do you think about the genetic algorithms?"

"Genetic algorithms are sometimes used by computer programmers in order to find solutions to problems that cannot be solved in other ways. Usually, the algorithm starts with a functional system and changes a few of its parameters to get a better system. For example, it starts with a regular car and it changes little by little the shape of the body till it makes it more aerodynamic. The engineers cannot mathematically calculate the best shape, so they have a computer test millions of possibilities. Genetic algorithms don't produce new and different systems, they

---

[23] The reader can see the last book by Dr. Michael J. Behe, *The Edge of Evolution: The Search for the Limits of Darwinism*, Free Press, 2008, where he will find an analysis of these limits.

don't produce new 'genes' and they don't prove in any way that the theory of evolution is functional."[24]

"I see."

"Now I think we can move on to the last part of our discussion about the theory of evolution and talk about fossils."

5.4. Controlled Evolution?

"One more thing," Daniel said. "What if there was actually a controlled evolution that took place? What if an intelligent being took care to cause the right mutations at the right moments? Maybe the six days mentioned in the Bible were actually six million or billion years?"

"I understand what you mean; this theory is also known as intelligent design. It is accepted by some believers who want to believe both in God and in evolution, but it is a wrong theory."

"Why?"

"Because it is completely different from the biblical account, with which it cannot be reconciled in any way. We read in the Bible that God created an almost perfect world, in which there was no death and no suffering. Neither humans, nor even animals used to kill and eat other animals:"

«Then God said, "Behold, I have given you every seed-bearing herb that sows seed on the face of all the earth, and every tree whose fruit yields seed; to you it shall be for food. I also give every green plant as food for all the wild animals of the earth, for all the birds of heaven, and for everything that creeps on the earth in which is the breath of life." It was

---

[24] http://creation.com/genetic-algorithms-do-they-show-that-evolution-works

http://creation.com/genetic-algorithms-are-irrelevant-to-evolution

so. Then God saw everything He had made, and indeed, it was very good. So evening and morning were the sixth day.»[25]

Michael went on:

"God wouldn't have called *«very good»* the result of billions of years of evolution during which billions of billions of animals would have had to kill other billions of billions of animals in order to survive. This is one of the main problems of this theory. Besides this, the Bible says that the earth, the sun and the stars were created in a different order than modern science claims, I mean the earth was created first."

"Without the sun? What was it revolving around?"

"I don't know; maybe in that primordial world it was the sun and the rest of the universe that were revolving around the earth."

"What happened to that world? Why do you say that it was 'almost perfect' and not perfect?"

"It was 'almost' perfect because there still existed the possibility for it to change, for better or for worse. There is a very good book on this topic, written by an American hieromonk[26], Father Seraphim Rose, and it is titled *Genesis, Creation and Early Man. The Orthodox Christian Vision.*"

"I memorized the title," Daniel said.

"This almost perfect world was turned upside down by the sin of Adam and Eve. God had told them they could eat from any tree, with only one exception. But the devil deceived them and they sinned. And then, rather than admitting their mistake and repent, Adam blamed Eve and Eve blamed the serpent. This fall of our ancestors has turned upside down the entire material world that God had created. *«[C]ursed is the ground for your sake,»*[27]

---

[25] Genesis 1:29-31.

[26] Hieromonk: a monk of the Eastern Church who is also a priest. (Merriam-Webster)

[27] Genesis 3:17.

This quotation is taken from the NKJV, because in the OSB *«for your sake»* has been replaced by *«in your labors.»* The NKJV text (although translated from the Masoretic Text) is in this case closer to the Romanian Orthodox Bible (translated from the Septuagint).

God said to Adam. Since then, death has entered into the world; since then the bodies of Adam and Eve and of their descendants have become mortal."

"Isn't this too severe of a punishment for such a small mistake?" Daniel asked.

"This was not a small mistake at all; Adam and Eve were far superior to us, they were much more intelligent and they had no other concern than to avoid that tree. That was their only restriction."

"And why has the entire creation been turned upside down?"

"The cursing of the earth and the life full of suffering that ensued for our ancestors till today were necessary for the healing of the souls of Adam and Eve and of all their descendants."

"By the way, why do they say that we inherit the original sin, the sin of Adam and Eve?"

"We don't inherit their guilt, only the consequences of their sin. From that moment on, the entire human existence has changed. Man was banished from heaven and could not go there for several thousand years. Righteous and virtuous men mentioned in the Old Testament could not enter heaven after their death; they had to wait for the Resurrection of Jesus Christ, which reopened the door of paradise for humankind. You see, this is actually the foundation of the Christian faith: God created a good primordial world, in which there existed no death, but in which there existed man's free will. Then Adam and Eve fell into sin and, as a consequence, human nature together with the entire creation was corrupted and ended up in the state that we see it in today. And then Christ was incarnated and died on the cross in order to restore the human nature, which was corrupted by the sin of our two ancestors. If we replace this basis with a guided evolution, then Christ's incarnation and sacrifice seem to make no sense at all. If there was no corruption of human nature, then what did Christ restore through His sacrifice? For all these reasons, the idea of an evolution guided by God does not square with the Christian faith. And there is one last reason, which we'll talk about soon."

"Yes," Daniel said, "indeed, the two accounts can't really be reconciled with each other. We have to choose either one or the other. What is that last reason?"

"There are no fossils that would show that there ever was an evolution, guided or not. There are no transitional fossils, not even by far."

6. Lack of Fossils

6.1. The Fossil Record

"There are no fossils to support the theory of evolution?" Daniel wondered. "It seems weird for you to say that; museums are full of fossils."

"In the 19th century, some people believed that God put the fossils in the ground in order to test their faith.[1] And maybe others believed that it was the devil who put them there, in order to deceive them."

"This resembles the Last Thursdayism theory a little," Daniel noticed.

"Yes. In a way, such a conclusion seems admirable to me, it seems those people were determined to believe in God and in the divine six-day creation no matter what arguments were presented to them. But in the end, such a conclusion is not necessary at all. The fossils are indeed showcased in museums and are being advertised as the most visible proof that the theory of evolution is

---

[1] An example can be found in the book *Omphalos: An Attempt to Untie the Geological Knot*, written by Philip Gosse in the year 1857. "Omphalos" (ὀμφαλός) is a word of Greek origin that means "navel." The Omphalos hypothesis suggests that the original world was made to look old on purpose; for example, the hypothesis says that Adam and Eve probably had navels, although they had not been born by other human beings and they had no need of umbilical cords.

true. But few people know that the fossil record[2] shows no transformation of any kind of creature into another."

"No?" Daniel asked surprised.

"Is this a surprise to you? No, the fossils show no such transition. The only thing the fossils are showing is that in the past there also used to exist creatures that today are extinct. But in no case do they show that they were transformed into something else. Let's start with the beginning. Everywhere in the world we find animals and plants buried in the sedimentary strata. The theory of evolution claims that they were buried during billions of years. The creationists believe that these billions of years never existed, but there was a flood of global proportions that covered the entire planet with water and also buried all those animals and plants in the sediments at the bottom."

"Wait a minute," Daniel said, "I thought the fossils are found in a certain order, the primitive ones at the bottom, the mammals above them, because they emerged later, and so on."

"As far as I know, there is no place in the world that contains fossils of all species, from marine snails to mammals and birds, buried in perfectly ordered layers. So this perfect order only exists in the imagination of the evolutionists. In places where fossils are found, there are usually no more than a few dozen species buried together. But, indeed, sometimes a certain order can be seen, that is, they seem to be arranged in layers, but this order can also have other explanations."

"What explanations?"

"Creatures of different species have different buoyancies, that is, they behave differently when they are dead in the water. Some sink faster, others sink slower. If the fossils were buried as a result of the flood described in the first book of the Bible, then we expect that the water sorted them by buoyancy and buried them in the sediments on the bottom in a certain order. In an experiment conducted at Loma Linda University, in Loma Linda, California, the dead bodies of a few creatures of several different

---

[2] The fossil record is the totality of fossils, both discovered and undiscovered.

species were placed in the water. The result was exactly as expected: Eventually the bodies sank and were deposited on the bottom in a certain order, the mammals after the reptiles, and the birds after the mammals. The order was similar to the one presumed by evolution, but this was so only because the evolutionists first observed the order in which the animal corpses were buried during the biblical flood and they presumed that they actually have evolved in that order."

"I suppose that *something* inside me will have to choose either the flood account or the billions of years account."

"Obviously," Michael replied, "none of us were there to see exactly what happened. But there are a few more things to be added here. This sorting of fossils in layers is not perfect, not even by far, and raises many questions. First, many fossils were found in layers where they didn't belong. The evolutionists' explanation is, usually, that these fossils were unburied and reburied again millions of years later, by various cataclysms or geological events. Then there are the so-called 'polystrate trees.' These are trees that are buried vertically, spanning the height of several geological layers, layers that are presumed to have taken tens or hundreds of millions of years to be deposited. Then there are also areas where the fossil layers are found exactly in the reverse order. The biblical flood probably buried them in the right order, the buoyancy order, and the subsequent geological movements turned them upside down."

"So it's not all clear and simple," Daniel said, more to himself than to Michael.

"No, obviously not. The next problem is that a lot of the fossils are incomplete, or they are made up of only a few bone fragments. The evolutionists are using their imaginations to complete them. Have you ever heard of the Nebraska Man[3], or the Piltdown Man[4]?"

"I don't remember," Daniel admitted.

---

[3] https://en.wikipedia.org/wiki/Nebraska_Man
[4] https://en.wikipedia.org/wiki/Piltdown_Man

"The Nebraska Man was found in 1917. He was not an entire man, only a small part of one. Actually, it was just a tooth. That was it, a single tooth. It was believed that it was the tooth of an intermediate species between man and monkey. Many scientific papers were written about it, drawings were published in which he was depicted as a wild man, with monkey-like characteristics, drawings that still can be found by anybody on the Internet. And all this started from a single tooth. *Something* inside some people wanted very much to find a link between monkeys and people. But between 1925 and 1926, the rest of the skeleton was also found. It was neither man, nor monkey; it was a wild pig. In 1927, the scientists publicly admitted their mistake."

"And the Piltdown Man?"

"The Piltdown Man was 'found' in 1912. He was not an entire man, but only a lower jawbone and a few skull pieces. As with the Nebraska Man, many scientific papers were written about it, doctoral theses, drawings were published in magazines, and so on. And all this for 41 years, till 1953, when the truth was discovered: The lower jawbone had belonged to an orangutan, the teeth had been filed, and the other bone fragments were from a human skull."

"Embarrassing," Daniel said.

"The same thing happens today, hundreds of theories about the past are formulated, about the extinction of the dinosaurs, about all kind of hypothetical events that only exist in the minds of those who believe in them. Is it possible that all these scientists are wrong? Certainly it is possible. As some time ago many doctoral theses were written about beings that had never existed, represented only by some incomplete fossils, faked or wrongly identified, so today hundreds of doctoral theses are written about events that never happened, about an evolution that never took place."

"OK, but those mistakes are pretty old."

"100 years ago they 'identified' a pig's tooth as being half human and half monkey. Although many branches of science have advanced a lot during the past 100 years, the technique for identifying the species starting from the shape of some bones has not changed that much. Yes, now we can easily analyze a bone and see whether it was filed or impregnated with various substances to make it look old. But the identification of the species starting from only a few bone fragments is a procedure as subjective and speculative as it was back then. Especially when that species only exists in the imagination of the evolutionists. Please remember what we discussed about the investigation of the past, you cannot go back in time and see with your own eyes whether the conclusions drawn about each individual bone fragment are correct or not. Therefore, everybody is free to produce whatever theory they want. The two examples mentioned before are exceptions, usually the conclusions about the past cannot be scientifically proven to be wrong or correct."

"Yes," Daniel said, "I saw how difficult it is to investigate the past."

"If you want to read more details, the topic of fossils is pretty well addressed in the books *Evolution? The Fossils Say No!*[5] and *Evolution: The Fossils Still Say No!*[6], written by the American biochemist Duane T. Gish."

6.2. What Do the Evolutionists Say about the Fossils?

Michael went on:

"As I was telling you, the most serious problem for the evolutionists is that fossils don't show even a single transformation of any kind of animal into something different. To understand this problem, I think I'd better tell you what they themselves are saying. For example, here's a quote from Dr. David Raup, curator of geology at the Field Museum of Natural History in Chicago,

---

[5] Published by Master Books, 1979.

[6] Published by the Institute for Creation Research, 1985.

one of the largest such museums in the world. Dr. Raup was once considered the greatest paleontologist alive."

Well, we are now about 120 years after Darwin and the knowledge of the fossil record has been greatly expanded. We now have a quarter of a million fossil species but the situation hasn't changed much. The record of evolution is still surprisingly jerky and, ironically, we have even fewer examples of evolutionary transitions than we had in Darwin's time. By this I mean that some of the classic cases of Darwinian change in the fossil record, such as the evolution of the horse in North America, have had to be discarded or modified as a result of more detailed information – what appeared to be a nice simple progression when relatively few data were available [,] now appears to be much more complex and much less gradualistic. So Darwin's problem has not been alleviated in the last 120 years and we still have a record which does show change but one that can hardly be looked upon as the most reasonable consequence of natural selection.[7]

One of the ironies of the evolution-creation debate is that the creationists have accepted the mistaken notion that the fossil record shows a detailed and orderly progression and they have gone to great lengths to accommodate this "fact" in their flood geology.[8]

"What?" Daniel said. "So there is no kind of order to the fossils?"

"As I have told you, sometimes some kind of order can be seen, but only in places where multiple species are found buried together, and only a limited order, caused by different buoyancies. Dr. Raup is an evolutionist," Michael went on, "he probably couldn't have become curator at one of the largest museums in the world if he believed in divine creation. Next we'll talk about

---

[7] *Conflicts between Darwin and Paleontology*, Field Museum of Natural History Bulletin, Jan. 1979, Vol. 50, No. 1, pp. 22-29.

[8] David Raup, *Evolution and the Fossil Record*, Science, July 17, 1981, p. 289.

Dr. Colin Patterson, senior paleontologist at the British Museum of Natural History. Dr. Patterson wrote a book titled *Evolution*, and a reader asked him why he didn't include in that book a single photo of a transitional fossil. On April 10th 1979 the author replied to the reader:"

> ... I fully agree with your comments on the lack of direct illustration of evolutionary transitions in my book. If I knew of any, fossil or living, I would certainly have included them. You suggest that an artist should be used to visualise such transformations, but where would he get the information from? I could not, honestly, provide it, and if I were to leave it to artistic licence[9], would that not mislead the reader?

> I wrote the text of my book four years ago. If I were to write it now, I think the book would be rather different. Gradualism[10] is a concept I believe in, not just because of Darwin's authority, but because my understanding of genetics seems to demand it. Yet Gould[11] and the American Museum people are hard to contradict when they say there are no transitional fossils. As a paleontologist myself, I am much occupied with the philosophical problems of identifying ancestral forms in the fossil record. You say that I should at least "show a photo of the fossil from which each type of organism was derived." I will lay it on the line – there is not one such fossil for which one could make a watertight argument. The reason is that statements about ancestry and descent are not applicable in the fossil record. Is Archaeopteryx the ancestor of all birds? Perhaps yes, perhaps no: there is no way of answering the question. It is easy enough to make up stories of how one form gave rise to another, and to find reasons why the stages should be favoured by natural selection. But such stories are

---

[9] Artistic licence: the freedom of an artist, writer, etc., to change the way something is described or shown in order to produce a work of art. (Merriam-Webster)

[10] Gradualism: the evolution of new species by gradual accumulation of small genetic changes over long periods of time; *also*: a theory or model of evolution emphasizing this. (Merriam-Webster)

[11] Stephen Jay Gould, mentioned in following paragraphs.

not part of science, for there is no way of putting them to the test.

So, much as I should like to oblige you by jumping to the defence of gradualism, and fleshing out the transitions between the major types of animals and plants, I find myself a bit short of the intellectual justification necessary for the job ....[12]

Michael went on:

"Now here's another famous evolutionist, Stephen Jay Gould. He used to be a professor at Harvard and New York University, and he also used to work for the American Museum of Natural History, one of the largest museums in the world. Here's what he has to say in one of his books:"

The history of most fossil species includes two features particularly inconsistent with gradualism:

1. Stasis. Most species exhibit no directional change during their tenure on earth. They appear in the fossil record looking much the same as when they disappear; morphological change is usually limited and directionless.

2. Sudden appearance. In any local area, a species does not arise gradually by the steady transformation of its ancestors; it appears all at once and "fully formed."[13]

"One more," Michael went on. "In 1996, Dr. Eugenie Scott, executive director of the National Center for Science Education, a non-profit American organization that fights for the teaching of evolution in schools, was writing to her fellow evolutionists:"

---

[12] Luther Sunderland, *Darwin's Enigma*, Master Books, El Cajon, CA, 1988, pp. 88-90.

It seems the reader who addressed the question to Dr. Patterson is none other than Luther Sunderland, the author of the quoted book.

[13] Stephen J. Gould, *The Panda's Thumb*, W. W. Norton & Company, 1980, pp. 181-182.

Avoid debates. If your local campus Christian fellowship asks you to "defend evolution," please decline ... you will probably get beaten.[14]

"I'm extremely surprised," Daniel said, "why do these people continue to believe in evolution?"

"You're underestimating the power of that inner *something*, which can make one believe even the absurd. Look at Stephen Gould for example; although he clearly admitted that there are no transitional fossils, nonetheless, he came to an aberrant conclusion, namely that evolution happens only at some moments, and so quickly, that it leaves no traces in the fossil record[15]. Any proof? The very fact that there are no transitional fossils is, for him, a clear proof that evolution happens at great speed and that it leaves no traces. Here's another similar example, this time from the famous British astronomer Fred Hoyle. He is the author of a well-known statement about the so-called unguided evolution of life:"

> The chance that higher life forms might have emerged in this way is comparable to the chance that a tornado sweeping through a junkyard might assemble a Boeing 747 from the materials therein.[16]

"What do you think," Michael went on, "was Fred Hoyle an adept of divine creation? No, he had declared himself an atheist, and he used to believe that life came from somewhere in outer space."

"Again, everything comes down to that inner predisposition to believe either one account, or the other," Daniel noticed.

"Have you ever heard of the Cambrian Explosion? This is the name evolutionists have given to an event that is inexplicable

---

[14] Eugenie C. Scott, *Monkey Business*, The Sciences, Jan.-Feb., 1996, p. 21.

[15] This theory, developed by paleontologists Niles Eldredge and Stephen Jay Gould, is called "punctuated equilibrium."

[16] Fred Hoyle, *The Intelligent Universe (A new view of creation and evolution)*, Holt, Rinehart and Winston, 1983.

from a scientific perspective. In the sedimentary layers that they associate with an epoch named Cambrian, most animal and plant species appear suddenly, with no kind of visible intermediate stages. I think we can make an analogy here. They wrongly call 'dark energy' the cause for the 'stretching out' of the universe, but this fact, if it really took place, was an act of God. And in the same wrong way, they use to call 'Cambrian Explosion' the biblical flood, which buried all those fossils."

"So this is about two completely different ways of interpreting the same observations…"

6.3. Twenty Fossils

"I have talked many times with various evolutionists," Michael said, "and I have presented a problem to many of them, which so far no one was able to solve."

"What problem?"

"The problem is to find 20 fossils, which, placed one next to one another, would show a step by step transition from a reptile to a bird, as they say it happened. Or from a reptile's leg to a bird's wing. So far, no one has found something like this. Be careful, if you start looking, they have to be 20 photos of real, complete fossils, not drawings of how some artist imagines an animal or the skeleton of an animal used to look. You see, most of the images of prehistoric animals you can find in books are not photographs of those animals, not even photographs of their skeletons, but only drawings. Many times all the evolutionists have at their disposal is a single bone, or just a bone fragment, and from it they come up with the drawing of an entire animal. Obviously, the artist's imagination, the artistic license, plays an important role in that drawing."

"I think you're phrasing the problem in kind of a wrong way," Daniel said. "The theory of evolution does not say that the reptiles have evolved into birds, but only that they had a common ancestor. That ancestor, indeed, probably resembled a reptile more than a bird, but it was not a reptile like present day ones."

"OK," Michael said, "let me rephrase it. Find eight fossils that connect the reptiles to that common ancestor, and another 12 that connect the common ancestor to the birds. Be careful, they have to be real, complete fossils, not drawings."

Daniel thought about this for a few seconds.

"Did anybody try to find them?" he eventually asked.

"This seems to be a rhetorical question," Michael said, "if those 20 fossils existed they would be displayed in all biology text-books. Such fossils have not been found, nor will they ever be, for the simple reason that this alleged evolution never took place. Instead, you may find many fossils that show transitions between related creatures, for example between the elephant and the mammoth, and maybe even between the modern tiger and the smilodon[17]."

"How is this possible?"

"The Bible does not talk about species; the categorization of living beings into species is just a modern convention, nothing more. God did not create the animals divided into species, but He created them divided into *kinds*."

«Thus God made great sea creatures and every living thing that moves with which the waters abounded, according to their kind, and every winged bird according to its kind. God saw that it was good.»[18]

Michael went on:

"And those original *kinds* had a very large potential for ge-netic diversity, which today can still be seen especially in dogs. You certainly know how many dog breeds, of various sizes and colors, have been bred only during the past few hundred years, and all this due to the potential for genetic diversity still present in the canine genome. Well then, what today can be seen in dogs, probably during the first thousands of years after the creation, could also have been seen in many other creatures. Therefore, the

---

[17] Also known as the "saber-toothed tiger."
[18] Genesis 1:21.

African elephant, the Indian elephant and the wooly mammoth probably all belong to the same biblical *kind*. If I were to express this in modern language, I would say that both the elephants and the mammoths are breeds of the same species. The brown bear, the black bear and the polar bear also probably belong to the same biblical *kind*. And maybe even the modern tiger and the smilodon. Some would go even further and say that all large and small cats probably descend from the same biblical *kind*, because lions and tigers can still mate, though their offspring are sterile. But this is a speculative statement; maybe it is so, maybe it isn't, there is no way to know for sure."

"And this explains the transitional fossils between related animals?"

"Yes. As in present times you can mate two dogs of different breeds and get something in between, so this was probably happening in the past with many other creatures. This is a big problem for the theory of evolution. How is it that we can find transitional fossils that connect very similar animals, which, evolutionists say, have evolved during a few thousand years from an alleged common ancestor, but we cannot find transitional fossils that connect very different animals, which, they say, have evolved during tens or hundreds of millions of years from another alleged common ancestor? How is it possible that an evolution that lasted for a few thousand years did leave traces in the fossil record, but an evolution that lasted for tens of millions of years left no traces? It is obvious that something is wrong here."

"You said that it is possible that the European bear and the polar one have 'evolved' from a common ancestor. Why isn't it possible that all creatures have evolved this way from a single common ancestor?"

"I didn't say that bears have evolved. There was no evolution, but rather an involution, an entirely different process. If they did indeed have a common ancestor, that ancestor had a very great potential for genetic diversity, which was lost over time. Remember the analogy with the cookie ingredients. The more ingredients you have, the more kinds of cookies you can make. But if you lose some of them, you can't make that many kinds anymore. In the end, if you're only left with flour, yeast and water, you'll only be able to make bread and nothing else. This probably also happened to bears, and to many other animals: they lost a part of their genetic potential, a part of their genes, and thus present-day species show almost no variation at all. But dogs still offer a good example. From a few dozen stray dogs, it is possible to get, in a few dozen generations, new, pure breeds."

"Why stray dogs?"

"Because dogs of pure breeds have already lost a big part of the potential for genetic variation. In the process of selection, either natural or artificial, diversity is usually lost. This is a process of involution. The loss of genes and of the variation potential will never turn a bacterium into a mammal. This would have been possible only if that common ancestor had an enormous potential for variation, probably a DNA much larger and complex than the DNA of all present-day creatures. God could have created such an ancestor, if He wanted to, but the Holy Scripture says that He created multiple *kinds*, and not just one."

"I see. However, I read some time ago that fossils of feathered dinosaurs were found, which proves the evolution of birds from dinosaurs."

"To me it seems like a joke. There were, indeed, a few alleged discoveries of this kind, but so far it couldn't be clearly proven that they were feathered dinosaurs. Some of those finds are just reptilian scales that left traces similar to feathers in the petrified sediments. Others are some bird remains that were buried together with real dinosaurs. And others could be large flightless birds, similar to penguins or ostriches. This is still a very unclear topic and there are many alternative explanations. And even if they were indeed feathered dinosaurs, what would that prove? It would only prove that God also created feathered dinosaurs, nothing more."

"And what about the human fossils, the Neanderthal Man, for example?"

"First, these fossils are extremely few and incomplete; most of them are made up of just a few bones and skull fragments.

Then, all of them can be clearly divided into two main categories: apes and people."

"And the Neanderthal Man?"

"They were humans, just like me and you, despite the fact that they are depicted in books as savages, half man, half ape. They even had religious practices: they used to bury their dead according to various rituals. They looked a little bit different from us because they were a different race. For the same reason Asian people look a little bit different from Europeans. But they were humans, real humans. And something else: Some evolutionists, due to the lack of proof about the evolution of man they were expecting to find, came up with the hypothesis that actually the evolution took place the other way around, that is, that apes have evolved from humans:"

> In the popular mind, man is descended from the chimpanzee. This is not true. Both are descended from some common ancestor, and when pressed the popular mind would admit that what it really thinks is that man and the chimp are descended from something very ape-like, very like a chimp. To translate our suggestion into that form of speech, we think that the chimp is descended from man, that the common ancestor of the two was much more man-like than ape-like.[19]

"Weird," Daniel said, "I have never heard this before. Did anyone take them seriously?"

"I don't think so, but the fact that some people could come up with such a hypothesis demonstrates how few and unclear are the 'proofs' for the evolution of man. A book that addresses the topic of human fossils very well is *Bones of Contention: A Creationist Assessment of Human Fossils*[20], written by Marvin L. Lubenow."

There followed a short silence, after which Daniel said:

"I have to admit that I'm very disappointed by these fossils. I was almost sure that by looking at them one could clearly see

---

[19] John Gribbin and Jeremy Cherfas, *Descent of Man — or Ascent of Ape?* New Scientist, vol. 91, Sept. 3, 1981, p. 594.

[20] Published by Baker Books, 2004.

that the theory of evolution is true. At least this is what we see in almost any textbook or TV program that addresses this topic."

7. Other Arguments

7.1. Vestigial Organs

"Wait a minute," Daniel said, "I remember there also were other arguments for the theory of evolution. For example, the vestigial organs, left behind by the evolutionary process, I mean organs we still have but don't use them for anything, like the appendix."

"First, just about all human organs once considered to be vestigial were proven over time to have a certain role. The last to be removed from that list is the appendix, about which it was recently discovered that it is a warehouse for bacteria that helps rebuild gut flora following a disease."[1]

"But we can live without it," Daniel said.

"We can also live without an arm or without a kidney, but I don't think you'll ever say that the arm or the kidney are vestigial organs. Second, there are, indeed, in other creatures organs that seem to be vestigial, for example the eyes of the mole. But this can only be a proof of involution, not of evolution."

"Tell me one more time, what is the difference between evolution and involution?"

"Evolution is the hypothetical process by which the DNA of a species is enriched with new, functional genes, which add new functionality to the creature. A theoretical example would be the addition to mouse DNA of the genetic information that

---

[1] https://en.wikipedia.org/wiki/Appendix_(anatomy)#Function

'builds' an echolocation device, a change that, together with many other changes, would transform the mouse into a bat. This kind of process has never been observed. Involution is the process by which portions of a species' DNA deteriorate, genes are being lost, and the organism loses some of its existent functionality. This process has been observed many times; a likely example would be the eyes of the mole. Yes, it is true that even this involution can, in some conditions, provide an animal with better chances of survival, and I gave you a few examples before, but these are just exceptions. A bacterium will never become a mammal by losing functional genes and never adding anything instead. A car will never become a helicopter if you keep removing pieces from it and throw them away. It is possible that at some point it will consume less fuel, because it becomes lighter. And if you disable the ABS[2] system, it is possible that the car will brake better, with the great disadvantage that the driver loses control of the direction. Yes, all these could be considered 'beneficial mutations' in certain situations, but the car will never become a helicopter through these kind of changes."

"Yes, I understand," Daniel said.

"A book that addresses the topic of involution pretty well is *Genetic Entropy & The Mystery of the Genome*[3], written by the American scientist Dr. John C. Sanford. Dr. Sanford explains to us that instead of evolving, the human, and not only the human, genetic material is actually degenerating from one generation to the next, because of the harmful genetic mutations that accumulate over time. This also explains very well the existence of the vestigial organs. I mean the organs that are truly vestigial."

---

[2] ABS: Anti-lock Braking System, a system found on almost all modern cars, which allows the driver to maintain control of direction while braking. The ABS prevents the blocking of the wheels, or it blocks and unblocks them a few times per second. Thus, the braking distance can sometimes be longer, or even significantly longer in certain conditions, but the driver maintains control of the direction. The ABS system is especially useful on ice or snow, but also in any situation in which the car starts skidding when brakes are applied.

[3] Published by Feed My Sheep Foundation, 2008.

"But if our DNA is degenerating, why do we now live longer than we did 200 years ago?"

"Most likely due to the progress of medicine. Doctors, hospitals and the pharmaceutical industry act like a system of artificial life support. I think that if we were to go back to the knowledge and to the living conditions of 200 years ago, half of us would die in a maximum of two or three years."

"Some time ago, the vestigial organs were presented in school as a clear proof of evolution," Daniel said.

"The fact that the evolutionists resort to such weak arguments proves how 'solid' their theory is. It is hard to understand how they don't see the logical error in this argument. Even though those organs were indeed completely useless, that only means that at this moment they serve no purpose, or, the worst scenario, that they were created with no specific purpose; but in no way is this a proof that they created themselves, out of the blue. If you were to find in your car a component that serves no purpose, would you say that your car has built itself and that the stories about car engineers and designers are just lies?"

"No, that would be a logical mistake, obviously," Daniel admitted.

"And since we talked about bats, I have to tell you that, indeed, fossilized bats were found whose echolocation device seems to be incomplete and underdeveloped. But those could be genetic defects, the same way sometimes an animal is born without a leg, or with a malformed leg. There is also the possibility that those bats had a different lifestyle and their sonar had become vestigial. But none of us has ever seen such a bat alive, and we also haven't monitored its species for thousands of generations, so in the end *something* inside us will make a choice. It will either believe that the fossilized bats with incomplete sonars were just some malformed animals, or animals with vestigial organs, but descended from normal ancestors; or it will believe that they were an intermediate stage in the process of evolution."

7.2. Ontogeny Recapitulates Phylogeny?

"Yes," Daniel admitted, "I see that even now, everything comes down to that inner *something*'s predisposition to believe—or not—one account or another. I remembered one more argument; they say that the mammal embryo goes through the stages of fish and reptile before it becomes a mammal. Ontogeny recapitulates phylogeny[4], that's what they were calling it in school some time ago."

"This is simply not true. It was believed some time ago that it was so, because the shape of the embryo seemed to look a little bit like a fish, but even evolutionists have abandoned this argument for a long time. It was seen that it was a lie even from the beginning of the 20th century, so about a hundred years ago. I'm surprised that it is still being used."

7.3. Is Evolution a Scientific Theory?

"There's another problem," Daniel said, "many scientists claim that it is not 'scientific' to believe that the universe and life were created by God. In other words, religion is not scientific, and creationism is a fake science."

"Why would anyone care whether religion is scientific or not? The only thing that matters is whether it is true or not."

"I don't understand…"

"The term 'scientific' is just a man-made definition, a standard. It is something comparable to a country's constitution, which is a law that can be changed every time the population decides so. In some countries it may be unconstitutional for a man to change

---

[4] Ontogeny: the development or course of development especially of an individual organism. (Merriam-Webster)

Phylogeny: the [alleged] evolutionary history of a kind of organism. (Merriam-Webster)

his religion. The same goes for the categorization of theories into scientific and unscientific; it is just a human way of seeing things, a way that can change from one year to the next."

"If I understand correctly, it is something similar to the definition of a planet."

"Yes. Recently that definition has changed and Pluto is no longer a planet. However, the object named Pluto has not changed its size at all, or its weight, or its orbit. It is just us who have changed our opinion about it, that's all."

"Yes, that's true," Daniel said.

"At this moment, the definition of science excludes supernatural explanations. If God exists, science will never find Him, because any proof of His existence is considered unscientific by definition. Have you ever heard the expression 'the elephant in the room'? This expression refers to truths so obvious they cannot be ignored or denied by anybody, the same way as the presence of an elephant in a room cannot be ignored or denied by anyone present in that room. Here's an analogy belonging to biochemist Michael Behe, about whom I have spoken before:"

> Imagine a room in which a body lies crushed, flat as a pancake. A dozen detectives crawl around, examining the floor with magnifying glasses for any clue to the identity of the perpetrator. In the middle of the room next to the body stands a large, gray elephant. The detectives carefully avoid bumping into the pachyderm's legs as they crawl, and never even glance at it. Over time the detectives get frustrated with their lack of progress but resolutely press on, looking even more closely at the floor. You see, textbooks say detectives must 'get their man,' so they never consider elephants.[5]

Michael went on:

"See the madness of modern science, which to me seems comparable to the madness of the detectives in Behe's metaphor. The same way as those hypothetical detectives were not consid-

---

[5] Michael Behe, *Darwin's Black Box*, p. 192 (in the 1996 edition).

ering the elephant, so modern science does not consider the possibility that life was created, that life did not evolve from zero out of inanimate matter."

"You mean that the theory of evolution is scientific just because the definition of scientific research has been changed so that evolution is considered to be scientific, and the belief in creation isn't?"

"The theories of evolution and the Big Bang are not even by far scientific, regardless of how much the definitions are changed. Science can only study repeatable phenomena that take place in the present and that can be closely observed. Anything else is pure speculation and a falsehood. Neither the Big Bang, nor the dilation of space, nor the emergence of life, nor macro-evolution can be reproduced in the laboratory, so every theory about them is just speculation and a falsehood, and not at all science."

"Then how is it possible for some false theories to hold on for so many decades?"

"The theories are addressing topics that are impossible to be analyzed scientifically, therefore, regardless of how aberrant they are, nobody can confirm or refute them by laboratory tests. Can anybody dilate space in order to see what effects it has on light? Can anybody observe a galaxy for five billion years to see whether it retains its shape? No, these theories cannot be tested, and for this reason, the madness of modern science cannot be restrained."

"Aren't there any exceptions? Really, isn't it possible to test any of the theories of modern science?"

"Yes, there are some exceptions, but only a few. Sometimes it does happen that such an imaginary theory is proven to be partially or even totally wrong. Here's an example. During the past years, astronomers have formulated dozens of theories about galaxies and black holes, theories considered to be correct by most scientists. But here's a recent discovery that overturned some of these theories. What did they discover? A black hole, they say, 30 times larger than the theories on galaxy formation say there could be.[6] Not 30% larger, not two or three times larger, but 30 times larger, which is 3,000% larger than the maximum size. I don't know whether this find is indeed a black hole or not, but the news is very important to help us understand how weak the theories of modern astronomers are about the cosmic space and how difficult it is to investigate such things."

"I see what you mean. But still, why do so many scientists believe in the Big Bang and evolution?"

"This is like asking why all Muslims believe that Muhammad was a prophet. If they didn't, they wouldn't be called Muslims anymore. When a Muslim stops believing that Muhammad was a prophet, he is not a Muslim anymore. Therefore, all remaining Muslims believe that Muhammad was a prophet. There are plenty of scientists who believe in God and that the world was created in six days, a few thousand years ago. But when a scientist starts to believe something like this, he is no longer considered to be a true scientist, and this is why almost all 'true' scientists believe in the Big Bang and evolution."

"Yes, now I get it," Daniel said smiling, "this is about the definition of the 'true' scientist."

"So there are plenty of scientists who believe in the divine creation and that our planet and the universe are no more than a few thousand years old. But there are also plenty of scientists who, although they believe that God created life, also believe that the earth is billions of years old. Anyway, this is not a very important issue, in my opinion. Even if all scientists in the world believed in evolution, that wouldn't make it a true theory. That would only mean that all scientists in the world are wrong, that's all. Scientists are not super-humans, they can be wrong, too."

"Actually I wanted to ask you, what do you think about the Christians who believe that evolution and the Big Bang are true?"

---

[6] http://edition.cnn.com/2015/09/26/world/black-hole-is-30-times-expected-size/index.html

http://www.ras.org.uk/news-and-press/2718-too-big-for-its-boots-black-hole-is-30-times-expected-size

"A lot of people don't know how weak and devoid of proof these theories are, and try to reconcile them somehow with the belief in God. But such a reconciliation is impossible. Then there are others, who know how groundless the theory of evolution is and they accept divine creation, but maybe it seems too exaggerated for them to also believe that the earth and the universe are no more than seven or eight thousand years old, so they also accept the billions of years age, which they try to reconcile somehow with divine creation. We cannot know and obviously, we also cannot judge each one's reasons."

"Aha, so there are several categories of creationists," Daniel noticed.

"Yes. Consider, for example, the biochemist Michael Behe, about whom I told you before. His book *Darwin's Black Box* was very appreciated by most creationists, because it proves the extreme improbability of evolution at the molecular level. However, although Michael Behe believes that life was created, for reasons that we cannot judge he also believes that the earth is billions of years old. Usually, those who believe that the universe is a maximum of several thousand years old are called 'creationists,'[7] and the theory according to which God created life during billions of years through guided evolution is called 'intelligent design.'"[8]

7.4. Ethical Arguments

"These were just about all the arguments for evolution that I knew of," Daniel said.

"One more thing. Now that we're done with the scientific arguments, let's also see what ethical or moral arguments there

---

[7] Sometimes the belief is referred to as YEC (Young Earth Creationism).

[8] Sometimes the belief is referred to as OEC (Old Earth Creationism).

are against the theory of evolution. Of course, such arguments can in no way be supported or disputed scientifically. But *something* inside us is very sensitive to them, as you will see."

"You've made me curious; I'm listening."

"The theory of evolution claims that we, the people, are just evolved animals, just collections of billions of billions of atoms and molecules, without a soul. But why, if we're just animals, do we have moral standards? Why do we believe that there is good and evil? Why do we believe that it is very wrong to take another man's life? Is it a crime if a wolf kills a deer? Is it a crime if a male leopard kills the cubs of a female, in order to mate with her? Should we start killing all wolves, leopards and other carnivorous animals because of this? Or maybe we shouldn't interfere, but would it be good if other leopards killed their kinfolk that committed such acts? The things that I'm saying don't really make sense, do they? Then why is everything different for humans, if man is also just an animal? Isn't it that *something* inside us feels that man is a special being? Isn't it that *something* inside us has some innate basic knowledge about what is good and what is wrong?"

"You mean that we're born with such knowledge?"

"Yes, we have it from God. Every man hears the voice of his conscience, which tells him that it is wrong to steal, to kill, and so on. This voice can sometimes be silenced, but only if the man strongly desires to do so. We'll talk about conscience later, if you still want to listen to me."

7.5. Joshua's Long Day

"Religious texts mention many miracles and supernatural events," Daniel said. "Many of them look downright impossible to me."

"They are impossible for us, and it is also impossible for them to happen naturally. But for God, Who is almighty, they are not impossible at all."

"Somewhere in the Bible there is an account of a day that lasted way longer than it should have."

"Yes," Michael confirmed, "Joshua's long day:"

«Then Joshua spoke to the Lord on the day God delivered the Amorites into the hands of Israel, when he crushed them in Gibeon. They were crushed before the face of the sons of Israel, for Joshua said:

"Let the sun stand still over Gibeon,
And the moon over the valley of Ajalon."
So the sun and moon stood still
Until God brought vengeance against their enemies.
The sun stood still in the midst of heaven
And did not set in the west until the end of one day.

There was no day like that day either before or after, that God should hear a man, because the Lord joined in war with Israel.»[9]

"Do you realize what this means? The rotation of the planet had to be slowed down or even stopped. Inertia would have thrown enormous amounts of water from the oceans onto the dry land; it would have been a global cataclysm. And somewhere else in the Bible there is an account of the sun going back a few steps on a sundial."

"Yes," Michael confirmed again, "the sign of Hezekiah:"

«[" ' "] Now this shall be the sign to you from the Lord, that God will do this thing: I will turn back the shadow on the ten steps of your father's house—the steps on which the sun goes down." ' " So the sun's shadow that went down on the ten steps turned back.»[10]

«And Isaiah said, "This is the sign from the Lord that the Lord shall do what He said. Either the shadow of the sundial will move forward ten degrees, or should it go backward ten degrees?" Hezekiah answered, "It is easy for the shadow on the dial to move forward ten degrees. There-fore, let the shadow return and go backward ten degrees." So Isaiah the

---

[9] Joshua 10:12-14.
[10] Isaiah 38:7-8.

prophet cried out to the Lord, and the shadow on the dial went backward ten degrees.»[11]

"This involves not only stopping the rotation of the planet," Daniel said, "but even rotating it backward for a short period of time."

"God is almighty; He can stop the planet's rotation in less than a second, and this without anyone feeling anything. You know, God can also cancel out the inertia, if He wants to. And because you mentioned these miracles, let me tell you a few words about them. Such events would have certainly been observed everywhere around the world, right? It would have been something totally out of the ordinary. A day lasting more than usual or, on the other side of the globe, a long night, would have certainly remained in the memory of all people as *totally* extraordinary events."

"Obviously," Daniel agreed.

"Well then, some researchers, like Immanuel Velikovsky[12], Charles Totten[13] and many others, have noticed that all around the world there are old testimonies, written or oral legends, that tell either about a very long day or a very long night, or about a sunrise or a sunset that lasted for many hours. Researcher Fernand Crombette has translated from the Egyptian hieroglyphs a story about a very long day.[14] Also, the Greek historian Herodotus mentions that Egyptian priests had shown him writings about the sun's abnormal behavior. Legends about a very long day are also found in China, Greece, India and Africa. In the folklore of the Indians of North, Central and South America, there were legends found about a night that lasted a very long time, for example,

---

[11] 4 Kingdoms 20:9-11 (NKJV: 2 Kings 20:9-11).

[12] Immanuel Velikovsky, *Worlds in Collision*, Macmillan Publishers, 1950.

[13] Charles A. L. Totten, *Joshua's Long Day and the Dial of Ahaz, A Scientific Vindication and a Midnight Cry*, 1891.

[14] *Cercle historique et scientifique*; quotation probably taken from Fernand Crombette, *Véridique histoire de l'Égypte antique*.

in the annals of Cuauhtitlan, Mexico, in the Aztec[15] and Mayan[16] oral traditions, and also in many other sources.[17] In Peru it was told that the sun remained hidden for about 20 hours during the time of a king who, some researchers calculated, reigned at the same time as the Hebrew ruler Joshua.[18] Bernardino de Sahagún, a Spanish savant who traveled to America a few decades after Columbus and gathered legends from the aborigines, mentions such a legend, too. His legend says that once the sun rose a little above the horizon and remained there."[19]

"A very long sunrise on the American continent… But how does this fit with the legends about a very long night in that part of the world?"

"There is no contradiction," Michael said, "we just have to look at a globe. If the rotation of the earth stopped when the sun in Israel was only a few hours away from setting, then on the east coast of the North American continent, it was just rising, and in the rest of the continent it was night."

"What about China?" Daniel asked.

"In some parts of China the sun was even closer to setting than in Israel, but it was still visible. And these researchers have also found possible references to the backward movement of the sun. I mean they found legends that talk about a day with two sunrises, or with two sunsets, when the sun set, it rose back a little, and only then did it set for good."

---

[15] Alfonso Caso, *The Religion of the Aztecs*, Popular Library of Mexican Culture, Central News Co., Mexico City, 1937, pp. 15-16.

[16] Adrián Recinos, Delia Goetz and Sylvanus G. Morley (translators), *Popol Vuh: The Sacred Book of the Ancient Quiche Maya*, University of Oklahoma Press, 1972, part III, chapters 4-7, pp. 172-190.

[17] William Tyler Olcott, *Sun Lore of All Ages: A Collection of Myths and Legends Concerning the Sun and Its Worship*, G. P. Putnam's Sons, New York, 1914.

[18] Fernando de Montesinos, *Memorias antiguas, historiales y políticas del Perú*, 1882. The work was written sometime between the years 1628 and 1652.

[19] Bernardino de Sahagún, *Historia general de las cosas de la Nueva España*. The work was written sometime between the years 1540 and 1585.

"This is amazing," Daniel said, "I have never heard these things before. How credible are these legends? Do they all perfectly match the time zones of those peoples?"

"This is not a simple question. First, we're talking about two long days, the first one during the time of Joshua, about 3,400 years ago, and the second one during the time of King Hezekiah and prophet Isaiah, about 2,700 years ago. We don't know exactly how long the first day was extended, maybe by 12 hours, maybe by 24 hours, it is impossible to find out. Also, we don't know what period of time the ten steps mentioned by the prophet Isaiah mean.[20] If ten steps means, let's say, five hours, and the shadow went backward at the same speed it was going forward, then the day was extended by ten hours. But this is just a supposition; we don't know how long the ten steps lasted. Then, we don't know exactly the time of day at which the two miracles took place. We might be tempted to say in the afternoon, but we can't know for sure."

"So it's possible that the two events took place at different times of day," Daniel said.

"Yes. Next, most ancient peoples did not record these events in writing exactly when they took place, they orally transmitted them from generation to generation, and of course they have somehow been altered during so many hundreds or thousands of years till they were written down. Each civilization has usually attributed these phenomena to local deities, for example, the Greeks to Phaeton, the son of the god Apollo, and the aborigines of the Pacific islands to Māui, a local semi-god, whose name was also given to one of the islands of the Hawaiian archipelago. Besides this, some tribes have migrated and have ended up inhabiting totally different areas than those they inhabited several thousand years ago. For these reasons, we don't always have a perfect match between the legends and the biblical description. For example, the Chinese account says that the long day lasted

---

[20] Some linguists say that the Hebrew text and the Greek translation known as Septuagint do not necessarily talk about a sundial, but about the shadow of an object on some steps.

for ten days, while the Mexican Indians say that the long night lasted for four regular nights. At that time there were no clocks with which to exactly measure the passing of time. We find, instead, a good match between the legends and the time zones of those peoples, but there are also a few exceptions here and there. But because such legends are found in a lot of ancient civilizations, it is almost impossible for all of them to be just mere coincidences."

"So most of them seem to match the time zones of those peoples?"

"Yes, the great majority do match, some very well, others only approximately, and two of them not really well. Actually, as far as I know, the only one that doesn't match at all is a Lithuanian legend about a long night, but it is possible that that legend has other origins, for example, it may refer to the polar night."

"Maybe it's not the only one with a different origin," Daniel said.

"Obviously, it is possible that there are other legends that do not refer to the two miracles and for this reason, they do not match very well the biblical accounts, but these are exceptions. The great majority match them rather well. Here's an interesting detail: The Egyptian account translated by Fernand Crombette says that the sun stopped, but the moon only slowed down very much, like it kept on rotating around the earth."

"Doesn't the Bible say that the moon stopped, too?"

"The Bible uses different words for the sun and for the moon, and some linguists claim that the verb used for the stopping of the moon is not as strict as the one used for the stopping of the sun, and that it is possible that the moon kept on moving, just a lot slower. I don't know whether it is so or not, but anyway, it is an interesting clue. The only discrepancy is that this Egyptian account seems to place the event in the morning, which seems rather unlikely. I think there is probably an error in the Egyptian writing or there's a translation error. Obviously, I could be wrong; there is no way for me to know for sure. One of the two legends that don't fit very well is a West African legend about a long night, and if that legend was inspired by a real event, then at least one of the two miracles took place when it was morning in Israel."

"Stopping the rotation of the earth would have affected the entire population of the planet in a certain way. Wasn't it possible for God to only work a local miracle?"

"God is all-powerful and He can do anything. Yes, God could have blocked the light coming from the sun in a limited geographical area, and He could have created some other light source instead, which would have rotated together with the earth, and which would have given the impression that the sun was standing still. But I don't think God did it this way, because it seems these two events were observed everywhere in the world. I don't really think that all those legends were inspired by other events and that it is by chance alone that most of them match the time zones of the areas they were found in."

"What about all those people who were negatively affected by the long day or by the long night?" Daniel asked.

"There is no such thing as a totally random event; everything happens with the knowledge and permission of God. If someone was negatively affected by those events, then he was affected for some very specific reasons, known to God alone. We'll talk later about such things."

"Can these legends be dated, so we can see whether they were inspired by events from the time of Joshua or Hezekiah?"

"The great majority cannot be dated. One exception would be the Peruvian legend that I told you about just before. Some time ago, some researchers tried to link the Chinese legend to the Emperor Yao[21], but now it is supposed that Yao lived about 800 years before Joshua, so that association was probably wrong. I say 'probably' because Yao's reigning period is also uncertain; some researchers claim that he lived at the same time as Joshua, and in this case, the association could be correct."

"One last question: Those who studied these legends were all Christian?"

---

[21] Also known as Yeo or Yahou.

"Some were, others weren't. One of the most known researchers of these events, Immanuel Velikovsky, was not a Christian. He was Jewish and he believed that these events did take place, but he believed that they were caused by some rather unusual cosmic phenomena, which disturbed the rotation of the planet. Obviously, almost nobody took his theory seriously, because it is absurd and totally impossible for something like this to happen by natural causes. But God is not restricted by these limits. However, it is sad that a man who investigated so much and who found so many proofs did not believe that these were actually divine actions, which took place in the history of his own people. Even if we suppose, against all reason, that these were naturally caused phenomena, what would the likelihood be for such a phenomenon to take place exactly when Joshua was praying to God to extend the day so he could finalize the battle?"

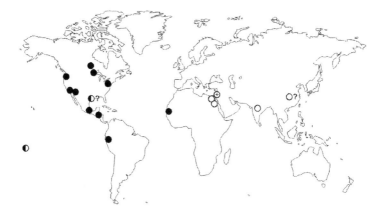

Approximate locations for some of the legends about very
long days and nights.

○: very long day;
●: very long night;
◐: long sunrise or sunset;

We have to keep in mind that there were two different miracles, possibly at different times of day, and some peoples have changed their location during the two to three thousand years till these legends were recorded in writing.

The location of the sunrise mentioned by Bernardino de Sahagún (◐? on the map) is uncertain; the event was probably observed more to the East.

The location of the event in China (○? on the map) is possible to have been more to the West.

If the West African legend about a long night was inspired by a real event, then the miracle took place when it was morning in Israel.

7.6. Noah's Flood

"What about the biblical flood?" Daniel asked. "Where did that much water come from? How did so many millions of animals fit inside Noah's Ark?"

"The first verses of the Bible speak about the *«water above,»*[22] and it's possible that this means that the planet was initially surrounded by a very large amount of water, liquid or gaseous, and maybe that water fell on the ground during the flood. But even if this interpretation is not correct, God, Who created the entire universe in six days, can also create the water needed for the flood, and then He can make it disappear. As for the animals on Noah's Ark, don't think that there really were that many millions of them. First, it is not written in the Bible that Noah took two of each species, but two of each *kind*. The species are just modern conventions of dividing creatures into different categories. The biblical *kind* was probably some significantly larger category. For example, I don't think he took two dogs of each breed, but two dogs in total. As for dinosaurs and other large animals, on the Ark there were probably only cubs, not adults. An American creationist wrote a book that attempts to give detailed answers to all these questions."[23]

"How is it possible for just two dogs to give birth to all dog breeds that we can see today?"

"We have talked recently about the genetic recombination. If the pair of dogs on the Ark had enough potential for genetic variation, it could have easily given birth to all canine breeds of today."

"You have told me about legends," Daniel said. "I've heard that the story of the flood is also found in the Babylonian culture, more exactly in the legend of Gilgamesh, which is said to be older

---

[22] Genesis 1:6-8.

[23] John Woodmorappe, *Noah's Ark – A Feasibility Study*, Institute for Creation Research, 1996.

than the Bible. Some researchers say that the author of the book of *Genesis* was inspired by that older story."

"Moses, who wrote the first five books of the Bible, was inspired neither by the Babylonian story, nor by other stories. The flood was a global event and, although only eight people survived, its account was transmitted from generation to generation till present times. Not only the Babylonians, but also a lot of other ancient civilizations from all around the world have or have had similar accounts in their oral or written traditions: the Greeks, the Indians, the American Indians, the natives of the Pacific Islands, and many others.[24] European missionaries were astonished when they were encountering such legends in the cultures of the peoples they were trying to Christianize. Obviously, some of these accounts differ somewhat from the biblical version of events, but this is so because they have been orally transmitted for thousands of years. Thus, some details were lost, and other details were transformed into something else. But I believe that the biblical version is the most accurate, because Moses did not write down stories orally transmitted from generation to generation, he wrote from divine inspiration."

---

[24] Byron C. Nelson, *The Deluge Story in Stone*, Bethany Fellowship, Minneapolis, Minnesota, 1968, pp. 169-190.

http://www.nwcreation.net/noahlegends.html

https://en.wikipedia.org/wiki/List_of_flood_myths

Flood legends from around the world[25],[26] (1) ■ full representation of biblical facts ▲ partial representation of biblical facts	Assyria-Babylonia 1	Assyria-Babylonia 2	Persia	Syria	Asia Minor	Greece	Egypt	Italy	Lithuania	Russia
Man in transgression (Genesis 6:5-6, 11-12)	■			■		■	■	■		
Divine destruction (Genesis 6:7, 13, 17; 7:4, 23)	■	■				■	■	■	■	■
Favored family (Genesis 6:8, 18)	■	■	■		■	■		■		
Ark provided (Genesis 6:14-16; 7:1, 7-9)	■	■	▲	■	■	▲		■	▲	▲
Destruction by water (Genesis 6:17; 7:4, 10-24)	■	■	■	■	■	■	▲	■	■	■
Humans saved (Genesis 6:18; 7:1-7, 13-16, 23)	■	■	■	■		▲	■	▲	■	■
Animals saved (Genesis 6:19-20, 7:2-3)	■	■	■	■						▲
Universal destruction (Genesis 7:21-23)	■	■	■	■	■	■	■	■	■	■
Landing on mountain (Genesis 8:4)	■	■	▲	▲	▲	■	▲	■	▲	▲
Birds sent out (Genesis 8:7-12)	■	■	▲		■					
Survivors worship (Genesis 8:20)	■	■				■	■	■		
Divine favor on saved (Genesis 9:1-17)	■	■					■			

---

[25] There are hundreds of such legends; tables 1 and 2 only mention a few of them.

[26] Adapted from Byron C. Nelson, *The Deluge Story in Stone.*

Flood legends from around the world[27] (2) ■ full representation of biblical facts ▲ partial representation of biblical facts	China	India	Cree (Canada)	Cherokee (US)	Tohono O'odham[28] (Mexico)	Aztecs (Mexico)	Peru	Leeward Islands	Fiji Islands	Hawaii
Man in transgression (Genesis 6:5-6, 11-12)								■	■	■
Divine destruction (Genesis 6:7, 13, 17; 7:4, 23)		■						■		
Favored family (Genesis 6:8, 18)		■	■	■	■	■	■	■		
Ark provided (Genesis 6:14-16; 7:1, 7-9)	■	■	■	■	■		▲	▲	■	■
Destruction by water (Genesis 6:17; 7:4, 10-24)	■	■	■	■	■	■	■	■	■	■
Humans saved (Genesis 6:18; 7:1-7, 13-16, 23)	■	■	■	■	■	■	■	■	■	■
Animals saved (Genesis 6:19-20, 7:2-3)			■							
Universal destruction (Genesis 7:21-23)	■	■	■	■		■	■	■	▲	■
Landing on mountain (Genesis 8:4)	■	■								
Birds sent out (Genesis 8:7-12)	■	■		▲						
Survivors worship (Genesis 8:20)	■									■
Divine favor on saved (Genesis 9:1-17)	■									■

[27] Ibid.

[28] North American people, previously known as the Papago.

7.7. Dinosaurs

"Were there dinosaurs on Noah's Ark, too?"

"There were probably dinosaur cubs, not mature animals. And there was no need to take two of each species, as modern science defines species nowadays, but only two of each *kind.*"

"And what happened to them after the flood?"

"They died off, otherwise we could still see them today. But I don't think they died immediately; the world is full of legends about 'great serpents' and 'dragons,' so it is possible that they survived for several hundreds or even thousands of years after the flood. It's possible that we also have the description of a dinosaur in the Bible:"

«But look now at the wild animals with you. They eat grass like oxen. Behold now, his strength is in his loins, and his power is in the center of his stomach. He sets up his tail like a cypress; his nerves are tightly knit. His ribs are like ribs of bronze, and his backbone like bars of iron. This is the ruler of the Lord's creation, made to be mocked at by His angels.[29] When he goes up to a rough mountain, he causes joy to the four-footed animals in Tartarus.[30] He lies under trees of every kind, alongside the papyrus, and reed, and bulrush. The great trees shade him with their branches; so do the branches of the willow. If there should be a flood, he will not notice it; he is confident, though the Jordan beats against his mouth, though he takes it in his eyes, or one pierces his nose with a snare.»[31]

---

[29] Alternative translations for Job 40:19:

«He is the chief of the creatures of God, and made to be the greatest among (or the ruler over) the other beasts.» (Romanian Orthodox Bible (Septuagint))

«He is the first of the ways of God; only He Who made him can bring near His sword.» (NKJV (Masoretic Text))

[30] Alternative translations for Job 40:20:

«The mountains give him food, and all the wild beasts are terrified when they see him.» (Romanian Orthodox Bible (Septuagint))

«Surely the mountains yield food for him, and all the beasts of the field play there.» (NKJV (Masoretic Text))

[31] Job 40:15-24.

"You think that in this quotation God is talking about a dinosaur?" Daniel asked.

"In some editions the word is translated as *hippopotamus*, but I think this is an error. In the ancient Greek translation, known as the Septuagint, the word for that animal is *thēria (θηρία)*, the plural for *thērion (θηρίον)*, which means beast, and this is exactly how it was translated in the Romanian Bible from 1914, *beast*."

"Why isn't it called a dinosaur?"

"The word 'dinosaur' was coined in the 19th century, when researchers wanted to give a name to the fossils they had just discovered. When the Old Testament was translated into Greek and English, this word didn't exist. The Hebrew version uses a word (בְּהֵמוֹת) whose meaning was not clearly known when the Bible was translated into English, so the translators employed a transliteration, that is, they coined a new word, which was being pronounced approximately as they thought the original Hebrew word was being pronounced. And this is how the word *behemoth* was introduced into the English language, a word that today has other meanings, too."

"And you think that that animal is in fact a dinosaur?" Daniel asked.

"In my opinion, it's very likely that it is a dinosaur. I think that the hippopotamus is not *«the ruler of the Lord's creation,»* nor is it *«the greatest among the other beasts.»* Then, the statement *«all the wild beasts are terrified when they see him»* does not seem to suit a hippopotamus. Also, the tail of a hippopotamus doesn't really resemble an imposing tree."

"Indeed," Daniel said, "the description better suits a dinosaur than a hippopotamus."

"And right in the next chapter of the book of Job, another fabulous animal is briefly described, called a *leviathan*. Besides these biblical descriptions and the legends mentioned before, there are also numerous drawings and sculptures that are hundreds and even thousands of years old that seem to represent dinosaurs. One of the most popular is the one in the Ta Prohm temple in Cambodia, built in the 12th and 13th centuries after Christ."

The Cambodian bas-relief
that very well resembles a stegosaurus.
(source: http://www.bible.ca/)

8. The True Religion

Daniel looked at his watch. It was past five, but sunset was still a few hours away. He thought for a few seconds, then said:

"I have listened to you for about five hours, and I've found out many new and interesting things, which I didn't know till now. But the greatest revelation I had was to become aware of the existence of that inner *something*, which is present in all aspects of our lives. Although now it seems obvious to me, I have never before seen things from this point of view."

"I'm glad that you have come to the obvious conclusion, namely that the inner *something* is real, that it exists," Michael said.

"But at the same time, I'm also indignant," Daniel went on. "When I came here I was hoping to find out for sure, with certainty, whether there is a God or not. And all I've found out so far is that it is impossible to scientifically investigate this topic, that although there are arguments on both sides, science is entirely powerless. God could exist and science would never find out about this. To some believers, the existence of God seems way too obvious, and they consider any discussion to be useless and a waste of time. Also, to some nonbelievers, the veracity of the theories of the Big Bang and evolution seems way too obvious, and they consider any discussion useless and a waste of time. But I don't belong to either of these two categories, though maybe I wanted to. In conclusion, I'm indignant because everything comes down to that inner predisposition to believe or not to believe something. I'm indignant because things are not clear enough. If there is a God, why isn't He more visible, why aren't there miracles happening more often, so everybody will see and believe?"

"I think you realize that modern science cannot answer this question."

"Of course it can't," Daniel admitted.

"So the answers I'm offering you are addressed exclusively to your inner *something*. You're wondering why God isn't working many great miracles, so that everybody will believe. But I'm asking you, what makes you think that seeing many great miracles would make people believe in God? What makes you think that *something* inside them wouldn't find other explanations for them?"

"What explanations can you find for a clear, obvious miracle?"

"You still don't grasp the power of that inner *something*... Let's suppose that a great miracle happens, something unheard of; let's say that in the timeframe of a few seconds, the moon breaks apart into millions of small fragments and those fragments are arranged in the sky forming a clear text, that any earthling can read: 'THERE IS A GOD!' Then that writing stays visible in the sky for a couple of months. Do you understand?"

"This would indeed be a clear proof," Daniel said. "Who could still dispute it?"

"Who? But what if some famous astronomer, an expert in astrophysics and quantum mechanics, tells us not to rush to conclusions, maybe an alien civilization, much more advanced than ours, is subjecting us to a psychological experiment, to see how we react? Won't there be many who believe him? What if most of the atheist scientists say the same? Eventually, it's still that *something* inside us that will have to choose whom to believe, this time without having any scientific argument, for or against."

Daniel remained speechless for several good seconds.

"Somehow," he eventually said, "this resembles the Last Thursdayism theory; I mean, it is impossible to argue scientifically, one way or another."

"But why should we think of alien civilizations?" Michael asked. "Maybe another astronomer will say that a very smart, but a little insane, scientist has probably invented a completely new and unknown to us technology by which he can remotely manipulate matter in any way he wishes to, and that it was that scientist who has fragmented the moon and wrote that there is a God with the resulting pieces, in order to make fun of us. Can any scientific argument for or against this new explanation be produced? Won't there be enough people to believe it?"

"Indeed," Daniel admitted, "it is impossible to argue scientifically, one way or another."

"Let us think about another 'miracle.' What if one day some shiny disks come down from the sky, and out of them emerge some humanoid beings, who say that they are aliens and that it was them who created us? In other words, they will say that they are 'God.' Will you believe them? If the representatives of some religions accept this explanation, will you also accept it? But what if the representatives of other religions don't believe them, but say instead that these are demonic 'miracles' and that the humanoids are in fact fallen angels, that is, demons? Whom are you going to believe? How will you argue scientifically?"

"I don't think you can argue scientifically..."

"What if one of those humanoids will also work 'miracles'? What if *«[h]e performs great signs, so that he even makes fire come down from heaven on the earth in the sight of men. And he deceives those who dwell on the earth by those signs which he was granted to do»*[1]? Thus is described in the book of Revelation, the last book of the Bible, the final deception that the apostate humankind will fall into. Think about the spiritual state of present-day people, how many of them will believe that those 'aliens' are their creators?"

"I understand what you mean and I totally agree with you, it is absolutely impossible to scientifically investigate something like this. *Only* that *something* inside us can make a decision; only it can incline to one side or another. Now I also remember this problem from philosophy: It is said that there is no absolute objectivity; everything, or almost everything, is subjective, more or less. But I don't understand *why* is it so? Why can't we also know things

---

[1] Revelation 13:13-14.

some other way, a way that would give us certainty? Why does everything have to pass through that inner *something*?"

"Because, I believe, this is what God is looking for in us. God is not looking for our intelligence; He is not looking for our ability to analyze the cosmic space and the molecules in order to find answers about the origin of the universe and of life. God is looking for that inner *something* of ours; God is looking for our predisposition to believe that He exists. God is looking for our 'bias,' our 'prejudice,' in the good way, for our subjectivity, and even for our desire to believe. And the fewer arguments we need in order to believe, the better for us."

"What exactly made you come to this conclusion?"

"The words that Jesus Christ told Thomas when they met after His Resurrection. Jesus had first appeared to the other disciples, when Thomas was not there, but Thomas did not believe when he was told. He only believed later, when Jesus appeared to him, too. And then Jesus told him:"

> *«Thomas, because you have seen Me, you have believed. Blessed are those who have not seen and yet have believed.»*[2]

"What about those who won't believe regardless of how much proof they see?" Daniel asked.

"We have this kind of example, too. In the Bible, we read that Jesus worked countless miracles: He healed sick people, He cast out demons from possessed people, He also raised some dead people, but a large part of the Jews[3] still didn't believe in Him. They could not deny the miracles that were happening in front of them, but *something* inside them was telling them that they were works of witchcraft, that they were not miracles worked with the power of God. And this is a very serious sin; it is also called the sin against the obvious. After Jesus healed a possessed man, some people were saying: *«This fellow does not cast out demons*

---

[2] John 20:29.

[3] The words 'Jew' and 'Hebrew' are not fully synonyms, though many times they are used as such. The Jews are the only known descendants of the ancient Hebrew people.

except by Beelzebub, the ruler of the demons.»[4] It was then, in those circumstances, that Jesus said that there are sins that will never be
forgiven. We find somewhat similar accounts if we read the Lives
of Saints. In the first centuries after Christ, Christianity was out-
lawed by the Roman emperors, and countless Christians were tortured and killed for their faith. During these persecutions, miracles happened very often, but the persecutors were interpreting
them as being works of witchcraft. We have so many accounts of
Christians who were put into fire but were not burned at all, or
Christians whose eyes were removed or destroyed, but by the
next day God had healed them, restoring their sight. But not all
the Roman soldiers who were committing, or only witnessing,
these atrocities were interpreting the miracles as witchcraft.
Sometimes, *something* inside them was being convinced and they
were becoming Christians, too, being then also killed in their turn.
We have such an example in the life of holy martyrs Rufinus and
Aquilina, commemorated on April 7th. They were martyred
around the year 310 together with the 200 soldiers who believed
in Christ after seeing the miracles worked through them."

"Now you're talking about your religion," Daniel noticed.
"But there are multiple religions. It seems that inner *something*
does not work the same way for all believers, otherwise there
would only be a single religion. So there are many religions, and
each one of them claims to be true and based on the divine revelation. How can I know which one is the true one? Obviously,
they can't all be true. Christians and Buddhists, for example, believe totally opposite things. So it seems obvious that at least one
of them is based only on hallucinations or on a demonic 'revelation.' How does your inner *something* help you make the difference?"

"*Something* inside you will be attracted to one of them. This
is true for everybody. The atheist, too, is being attracted toward
something, namely toward the idea that there is no God. The
atheist cannot prove such a thing, but *something* inside him is predisposed to believe even the most absurd arguments of the theory

---

[4] Mathew 12:22-32.

of evolution. And if sometimes he can't find the arguments he's looking for, he fabricates them himself, and then he believes them."

"And an even more important question: How do you know that your inner *something* is not wrong? In the case of many people, obviously, it is wrong, otherwise there would be a single religion in the entire world. So how do you know that in your case it is not wrong? As you say, modern science cannot help you in this regard."

"He who loves the truth will find it. The opposite seems to be true as well: He who loves the lie will find it. Here's an observation made by Blaise Pascal:"

> Truth is so obscure in these times, and falsehood so established, that, unless we love the truth, we cannot know it.[5]

8.1. Some Basic Beliefs

8.1.1. Creation

"Let's start from the beginning," Michael said. "The first thing I believe is that the universe, the planet we're living on and the creatures that populate it have been created, that they have not emerged following an explosion and a random evolution. For this there are enough arguments that *something* inside me considers to be more than obvious."

"Let's say that so far I agree with you. But how do you know that the universe was not created by an alien civilization, or that it isn't just a giant simulation that only exists in a super-computer belonging to a super-alien? How do you know that we're not liv-

---

[5] Blaise Pascal; quoted in Archim. Seraphim Alexiev, Archim. Sergius Yazadzhiev, *Orthodoxy and Ecumenism* (in Romanian), Babel Press, 2012, p. 10.

ing in something similar to the fake world in the movie *The Matrix*? How do you know that all world religions are not just experiments performed by those aliens on us? Or how do you know that God is indeed good? How do you know that all world religions are not just some experiments conducted in order to see how we react? Or how do you know that there are not multiple gods, each one with his own universe, and who are competing against each other to see whose universe is doing better?"

"It is impossible to *know* such things. You can only *believe* or *not believe*. And those who propose these absurd theories can't know, either; they only want to believe in something else than the Christian God. *Something* inside a Christian is attracted to a certain direction, it desires something, namely to believe that Jesus Christ is God. God fulfills his desire and bestows him this belief, which is so strong, that the Christian is absolutely sure that God exists and that He is good. He who has this belief is ready at any time to lay down his life for his religious conviction."

"So the belief is given by God? Isn't it a product of that inner *something*?"

"Yes, the belief is from God, but it is only given to the one who asks for it, I mean to the one whose inner *something* desires it and is looking for it. You remember how unlikely the theory of evolution is? Well then, even if it were likely, the Christian would still believe in God. Even if it were possible for him to travel or to see back in time, in the past, and if he saw the Big Bang or evolution with his own eyes, the Christian would still believe in God. He would believe that that 'travel' or that 'seeing' in the past is just a demonic illusion, and there would be no way for anyone to scientifically demonstrate to him that it is not so. This is how powerful the belief is. But it is a gift from God, given to the one who desires it and asks for it; it is not a product of that inner *something*."

"What about those who strongly believe that there is no God? Or those who believe that we were created by some aliens, either from this universe, or from another one?"

"That belief cannot be from God, maybe it is from the devil, but again, I think the devil can only give it to the one who desires it and is looking for it. Nobody is forced in any way."

"I see," Daniel said. "Go on, please, I want to see how you get to the conclusion that your religion is the right one. And how do you know that the inner *something* is not wrong in your case?"

"How do I *know* that I'm not wrong...? Obviously, from the point of view of modern science, I don't know. I only know that the inner *something* can be subject to change; I mean one can change his predisposition to believe or not to believe during his life. I know this because I have seen nonbelievers who have become believers, and the other way around. This is about all that I *know*. For the rest I can only *believe*. And this is true for everybody, everybody *believes* one thing or another, though many like to lie to themselves by telling themselves that they *know*."

"But what if that inner *something* is not your soul, but just your psyche? What if the belief in God is just a product of your psyche? Your opinion is that the belief is from God, but what if this opinion, too, is just a product of your psyche? In the end, you don't know these things, you only believe them, and what you believe could be just a product of your psyche."

"You also don't know these things, you only believe them. You cannot escape circular reasoning, it's absolutely impossible. Think about the statement that the inner *something* is just the psyche. If the statement were true, then it (the statement) would be a product of the psyche, too. Further on, the statement that religious belief is a product of the psyche, wouldn't it (the statement) be a product of the psyche, too? If the products of my psyche are not absolute truths, then neither are the products of your psyche absolute truths."

Daniel pondered for a few seconds.

"Indeed, you cannot avoid circular reasoning," he eventually admitted. "If I believe that religious convictions are a product of the psyche and cannot be relied upon, then that belief of mine would also be a product of the psyche and could not be relied upon. And if you believe that religious convictions are a gift from God, then that belief of yours is probably also from God."

"I was only speaking about the religious convictions that are true, only those I believe to be from God."

"Yes, I understand. What do you think about those who say that there is no truth?"

"A self-defeating statement. How could it be true, if there is no truth?"

"Maybe the truth is relative…"

"Then that statement would also be relative."

Daniel waited for a few seconds, then said:

"Let's go on. So you only *believe* that you're not wrong."

"Yes. And I also *believe* that if you really want to find the Truth, you need three things."

"What things?"

"First, you need humility. Yes, before anything else you need to admit that there is no way for you to find the true religion by your own means, or with the help of science. Even if all scientists and all institutions of scientific research in this world joined their forces with this purpose, they still couldn't find the true religion. It is simply *totally* beyond their means. Father Sophrony Sakharov, a disciple of Saint Silouan the Athonite, expresses this very beautifully:"

> With iron drills men drill the earth's crust for oil, and are successful. With their intellectual powers they drill heaven for the fire of Divinity but are rejected of God because of their pride.[6]

Michael went on:

"So first you have to admit that you can't find the true religion by yourself. You need God to reveal it to you; that is, you need God to offer you the right arguments. God can give you these arguments either through some books, or through a mere man, who in turn has found them from other sources. It doesn't matter which way the arguments are offered to you, the important thing is that you accept them. Besides these arguments, I strongly

[6] Archim. Sophrony Sakharov, *St. Silouan the Athonite*, St. Vladimir's Seminary Press, Crestwood, New York, 1991, p. 169.

believe that there's also the witness of the Holy Spirit in your soul, as the Scripture says[7], but you have to accept that witness. This is the first thing I think you need."

"And the second one?"

"Second, if one pays attention to himself, to the arguments that go through his inner *something*, he will begin to realize that his will plays a very important role in accepting and rejecting them. In other words, the second thing I think you need is to want to believe, to desire to believe in the existence of God. Everything begins with our free will, both in the case of the believers, and in the case of the nonbelievers. If one doesn't want to believe, he won't believe, no matter how many arguments he is given. We read in the New Testament that Jesus Christ Himself, God incarnate, preached to many people, and many of them still didn't believe in Him, although He worked so many miracles right in front of them. Our will is so strong that it can reject even the strongest and most tangible arguments. The opposite is also true: our will can accept even the weakest arguments, or even more: it can fabricate, or make up its own arguments, which it desires to believe. And our will is free—neither God, nor the devil force it in any way."

"Here I agree," Daniel said, "the will plays a very important role. And the third thing you think I need?"

"The third thing, I think, is to begin to purify your inner *something*, that is, to begin the healing of the soul. I say 'to begin,' because this healing is a process that goes on for your entire life, and it is completed only in the afterlife. I told you just before that I believe that God wants to see that man is attracted by the Truth, that he accepts the Truth with the fewest arguments and tangible proofs. Well, I think God expects this from people because this should be man's normal, natural tendency. Man should be naturally attracted toward his Creator and toward the revelation offered by Him. But this doesn't happen to all people because our souls are sick. But once the process of healing the soul begins, man starts again, little by little, to feel the attraction toward his

---

[7] Romans 8:16.

Creator, and he begins to wish to believe in God. Someone once said:"

> Sin is that which prevents us from believing. Not logic. For this reason, if you tell an unbeliever to live for six months according to the ethics of the Gospel, and he does it, he will become a believer without even realizing it.[8]

"And how is this healing being accomplished?" Daniel asked.

"You can begin to try to heal your soul, to be a good man, to forgive from all your heart all those who upset you, and so on. But you will soon realize that your progress is very limited and short lived. And this is because it is not in your power to really change your soul for the better. Only God can accomplish this healing, all you can do is to want and to ask this thing from Him. No matter how much you try to change, you won't be able to without His help. Obviously, you too have to struggle to become better, but you have to be aware that your will and your struggle do nothing more than to show God how much you desire this thing; the actual healing of souls is done by Him. Therefore, you need humility again. You need to admit that you cannot change by yourself, and to ask God to help you in this regard."

"And this humility, which you said is the first thing needed, how does one get it?" Daniel asked.

"I forgot to mention it: It is again God Who gives it to you, when you realize that you need it and you desire it and you ask it from Him and at the same time you fight against your pride."

"If what you say is true, almost everything has to come from God; we're doing almost nothing ourselves."

"The main thing we do is to will. This is the only thing that is truly ours: our will. Then we also have to fight with ourselves and with our spiritual diseases, which are also called passions. But despite all our efforts, which sometimes last for decades and seem to us to be superhuman, victory in this fight comes from God,

---

[8] From the Life and Teachings of Father Epiphanios Theodoropoulos.

and not from us. Let me give you an example. Let's say we have to travel to a remote city, 15,000 kilometers[9] away. The airport is two or three kilometers[10] away from us and the airline is giving us the ticket for free. All that is needed now is for us to do our part. First, we have to *want* to go to that city. The pilot and the flight attendants will not come to forcibly grab us from our homes if we don't want to go. Then, we have to wake up in the morning, go to the airport, board the plane, and not leave the aircraft for the entire duration of the trip. This is our part, small and insignificant; God is doing the rest. But God will not do His part if we don't do ours, from all our hearts."

"Let's say that it is as you say it is. However, it seems to me that our part is also pretty significant. For example, I walk on the sidewalk and a poor man asks me for some food and I give it to him. Or a friend in need asks me to lend him a significant amount of money, and I give it to him, although I don't know for sure whether he'll ever be able to give it back to me. Aren't these all examples of things that belong to my part?"

"Yes, in a way. But after a careful analysis you will notice that the money you say is yours is actually from God, too. Your healthy body and your intelligence needed to earn money are from Him, too. The earth that we live on and that feeds us every day is from Him, too. The same for the water that we drink and the air that we breathe. And so on. Saint John Chrysostom, Patriarch of Constantinople at the end of the 4th century and the beginning of the 5th century, used to warn the rich people in his sermons that their riches actually belonged to God, and were only entrusted to them in order to feed the poor at the right time. Here's a biblical quote:"

> «*Who then is a faithful and wise servant, whom his master made ruler over his household, to give them food in due season? Blessed is that servant whom his master, when he comes, will find so doing. Assuredly, I say to you that he will make him ruler over all his goods. But if that evil servant says in his heart, 'My master is delaying his coming,' and*

---

[9] 15,000 km = (about) 9,334 miles.
[10] 2-3 km = (about) 1.25-1.87 miles.

begins to beat his fellow servants, and to eat and drink with the drunk-
ards, the master of that servant will come on a day when he is not looking
for him and at an hour that he is not aware of, and will cut him in two
and appoint him his portion with the hypocrites. There shall be weeping
and gnashing of teeth.»[11]

"And Saint John's commentary:"

For to this servant are they like, who have money, and give
not to the needy. For thou too art steward of thine own pos-
sessions, not less than he who dispenses the alms of the
church. As then he has not a right to squander at random
and at hazard the things given by you for the poor, since they
were given for the maintenance of the poor; even so neither
mayest thou squander thine own. For even though thou hast
received an inheritance from thy father, and hast in this way
all thou possessest: even thus all are God's. And then thou
for thy part desirest that what thou hast given should be thus
carefully dispensed, and thinkest thou not that God will require His own of us with greater strictness, or that He suffers
them to be wasted at random? These things are not, they are
not so. Because for this end, He left these things in thine
hand, in order 'to give them [the poor] their meat in
due season.'

[...]

What! are they thine own things which thou hast? With the
goods of the poor hast thou been entrusted, though thou be
possessed of them by honest labor, or though it be by inheritance from thy father. What, could not God have taken away
these things from thee? But He doth not this, to give thee
power to be liberal[12] to the poor.[13]

"You see," Michael said, "for these reasons, I believe that
only the exercising of our free will is something that is truly ours."
"Hasn't the will been given to us by God, too?"

---

[11] Matthew 24:45-51.
[12] To be generous to the poor.
[13] St. John Chrysostom, *Homilies on the Gospel of Matthew*, Oxford,
1843, Homily LXXVII.

"Yes, but it is free. We use it as we want to; it is us who decide which way we go. That's why I say the decisions that we make are ours, otherwise we would be just some robots remotely commanded from above. Without free will, we would be predestined to do one thing or another."

"OK, I understand. Let's now get back to what makes you think that your religion is the right one."

8.1.2. Revelation

"So first I believe that there is a God, that He is good, and that He is the One Who created everything. Then I notice that several religions claim to be based on the divine revelation. *Something* inside me tells me that one of these religions, one and only one, has to be true."

"Why one and only one?" Daniel asked. "Why couldn't all be false, and be the work of the devil or of someone else?"

"I strongly believe that God would not allow the devil or someone else to lie to us this way, without Him offering us the truth, too, so we can choose. Even more, due to our inability to discern which revelation is the true one, I believe the genuine divine revelation would be accompanied by the greatest miracles. God would not allow the devil to work miracles greater than His miracles, and to deceive us this way. This is a belief, obviously; there is no way for me to argue for it scientifically, but I am as sure about it as I am sure that the universe was not created this morning. And I also find a confirmation for this belief in the second book of the Bible, *Exodus*, when Moses goes before Pharaoh and works various miracles in order to convince him to release the Hebrews from slavery. Then the Egyptian sorcerers also work several miracles, with the help of the devil probably, but the miracles worked by God through Moses are significantly superior. In the Old Testament we often find cases in which those whom a prophet of God is speaking to also ask for a sign, to be sure that the prophet is indeed speaking the words of God."

8.1.3. About Islam

"OK," Daniel said, "but all religions of the world claim that their founders are working or have worked miracles."

"This isn't quite true. The Quran, for example, does not mention any miracles worked by Muhammad. Although it was asked of him many times, Muhammad said that he could not work miracles. Although he admitted that to other prophets before him was given the power to work miracles, he said that his only 'miracle' was the Quran.[14] Muhammad believed that this Quran was dictated to him by an angel, more exactly, by Gabriel."

"So Muhammad received a supernatural revelation, too?"

"I don't know, I wasn't there to see, but *something* inside me tells me that if indeed the Quran was dictated to him, then it certainly wasn't dictated by an angel sent by God, let alone by the archangel Gabriel. If someone did dictate to him, then I believe that that someone was a demon. This also explains why Muhammad couldn't work any miracles at all."

"And why do Muslims believe in him, if he worked no miracles?"

"Certain texts of secondary importance from the Muslim tradition[15] do mention several miracles worked by Muhammad. But all of them are mentioned in writings that are newer than the Quran, and many times they seem to be copied from the Christian miracles. But the main book of the Muslims, the Quran, contradicts these texts pretty clearly. Why does the Quran say so often that Muhammad's opponents were reproaching him for not working miracles, and he never denies this?"

"Are you trying to say that it's possible that all those accounts are lies?" Daniel asked.

---

[14] Quran 3:183; 13:7; 29:50-51; 17:90-93. The word "Quran" means "recitation" in Arabic.

[15] Also known as "hadith."

"Yes, this is one possibility. Another possibility is that some of them were demonic miracles, like the miracles worked by Pharaoh's[16] sorcerers. It's also possible that they were fake miracles, illusions to be more exact, which can also be reproduced nowadays by some fakirs and shamans, with the help of the devil. An example of such a diabolical illusion seems to be the account about how Muhammad split the moon in two. I mean there was no breaking of the moon in two, but it only seemed to be so to those present there, through the work of the devil. This, of course, if the account is not a fabrication."

"So ancient people were expecting a prophet of God to work miracles in order to prove his authority," Daniel noticed.

"Exactly! We also find a lot of examples in the Old Testament. And Jesus Christ worked the greatest miracles, and the greatest of them is His very Resurrection. We were not there to see these miracles with our own eyes, but others did see them and recorded them in writing. And now we can believe those accounts, if we want to. Remember, *«Blessed are those who have not seen and yet have believed.»* But unlike us, who can only believe without seeing, the apostles of the Lord were in a different situation. They *knew*, they had seen with their own eyes how Christ had worked so many miracles, they had seen Him resurrected and ascending to heaven. And the apostles preached these things to the end of their lives. Most of them were arrested, beaten, and eventually killed for the faith they were preaching. Think about this carefully: nobody suffers and sacrifices his life for something he *knows* it is not true. If the Christian religion was not true, if it were a fabrication, a fantasy, the apostles would have *known* this and certainly they wouldn't have sacrificed their lives for a lie."

"Michael," Daniel said, "it seems to me that you're very biased. You reject way too easily the Muslim miracles, even though they are not mentioned in the Quran, but instead in later writings of secondary importance. At the same time, you accept way too easily the Christian miracles, mentioned in the Bible."

---

[16] Exodus (second book of the Bible), chapters 5-15.

"Of course I am biased, *something* inside me is strongly attracted by the Christian side. The Muslim is also biased, *something* inside him is strongly attracted by Muhammad's side. The atheist is also biased, *something* inside him is strongly attracted by the idea that there is no God. Those events took place in the past and they cannot be observed or scientifically studied by us. So it is impossible to be impartial or unbiased; neither of us is unbiased, nor can anybody be. And the most deceived of all is the one who comes to believe that he is unbiased, the one who comes to believe that he can find out the truth by his own means, more exactly through scientific research. I think a savage pagan who worships the sun and the moon is less deceived than a scientist who puts his trust is the ability of science to offer him the Truth."

"So everything comes down to that inner *something*..."

"Yes, even though this is very hard for the modern man to admit it, because he is usually sick with pride. This is what I think God wants from us, our inner *something*, our bias, oriented in the right direction. And I also believe that our spiritual diseases, our passions, are the reason for why sometimes we are attracted to the wrong direction. This is, in my opinion, the cause that sometimes makes us like the lie and dislike the truth."

Daniel waited for a few moments, then asked:

"Wouldn't it be possible, though, that both Christianity and Islam are divinely inspired religions? For example, Christians consider Judaism to be divinely inspired, so why couldn't Islam be divinely inspired, too?"

"Judaism was revealed by God to the Hebrews in ancient times, but its role ended with the coming of Christ. So yes, Judaism was of divine origin, but it was replaced by a new, superior revelation, namely Christianity. For this reason, now it cannot be reconciled with Christianity, because adepts of Judaism reject the new revelation of God; in other words, they fight against God."

"What about Islam?"

"Christianity does not claim things contrary to the Judaism of two thousand years ago. Christ did not come to tell the Jews that their religion was a lie; He did not come to destroy the Old Law, but to fulfill it. He said:"

«Do not think that I came to destroy the Law or the Prophets. I did not come to destroy but to fulfill.»[17]

Michael went on:

"But Christianity and Islam imply *totally* contradictory beliefs. Christians believe that Jesus is God, the second Person of the Holy Trinity. Muslims believe that Jesus was just a man. Christians believe that Christ was crucified, that He died and was raised back to life on the third day, but the Quran says that it isn't so. Jesus Christ says that in the afterlife people don't get married anymore, that is, there is no more sexual activity, but the Quran says that the sex life of the inhabitants of heaven is blooming. If the two religions are both from God, then God is lying, God forbid. No, it is impossible for them to be reconciled. *Something* inside us has to choose one of them, but certainly not both of them."

"Many consider Islam to be a barbaric religion," Daniel said. "And this is probably so because of the fact that most suicide terrorists are Muslim."

"Not only because of this, but also because it was spread in the world by force, through wars. The Quran says that the holy war, the *jihad*, is a duty for every Muslim. I think you can also judge a religion by the extremes that it produces, that is by its most devout believers, who take that religion seriously and strictly follow all its teachings. I'm not going to give you examples of Muslim extremists; you can identify them yourself. But I will give you examples of Christian 'extremists.' Most of them you can find by reading the *Lives of Saints*. And others, pretty few, lived during our own times, like Saint Paisios of Mount Athos, who lived between the years 1924 and 1994."

---

[17] Matthew 5:17.

8.2. What Are Heaven and Hell?

"OK," Daniel said, "let me tell you now what my main problem is, why I find it very hard to believe in the Christian God. I'm having a hard time understanding how it is possible that a good and loving God can send some people to suffer for eternity in hell. I understand that evil deeds must be punished, but for eternity? For an endless number of years? No judicial system in the word is that harsh. And in Christianity, even having sexual relations with your wife before marriage is a sin. How is it possible to eternally torment a man for something like this?"

"I understand your problem, and you're not the only one who has asked himself such questions. The first thing I want to say here is that people should not think they are smarter than God; I mean they should not think they know better who deserves to end up in hell and for how long, and who doesn't deserve to be there. The second thing is that people should not think that God has left us useless rules in His Church. If God has said that certain deeds are a sin and that they can seriously affect our soul in the afterlife, then we should believe Him and we should obey the rules left for us in the Church, without doubting. *«Blessed are those who have not seen and yet have believed.»* I think this verse can also mean *Blessed are those who have obeyed God's commandments without looking for the purpose of each one of them.*"

"Is that what you did?"

"No, I wasn't one of those blessed ones. My faith was weak and it needed answers. I have looked for those answers and I have found them. But if you want to be one of those blessed ones, tell me to stop now and quit talking."

"Keep going," Daniel said, without thinking too much. "What answers did you find?"

"At first sight, the problem seems to be a rather complicated one. How can a man be sentenced to suffer for eternity, no matter what he did? Even for a serial murderer, maybe after a few thousand years of burning in hell, we could consider that he is done serving his sentence, right? But what if he asks forgiveness? Even we would eventually forgive him. Wouldn't God forgive him, too? Let us also consider the reverse problem: what if one of those in heaven, after a few million years spent there, starts to commit evil deeds, will God send him to hell?"

"Interesting questions…"

"Maybe, but I think we have to elucidate something else first, namely what are heaven and hell."

"OK, let's start with this."

"First of all, the afterlife is a mystery that far surpasses our comprehension. In the Bible, too, it is mainly described to us in the form of metaphors, because the reality beyond death simply cannot be described in human language. However, although we don't know all the details, everybody seems to know that those who die in sins go to hell forever, and the virtuous ones go to heaven forever. So the second aspect is that wherever we end up after the Last Judgment, we remain there for eternity. Those in hell can no longer become good in order to enter heaven, and those in heaven can also no longer become evil and be sent to hell. The third aspect is that the eternal life is eternal, everlasting, it never ends. Some people try to imagine eternity as an enormous period of time, like billions of billions of years, followed by other billions of billions of years, and so on. But I think this is only a metaphor; time as we perceive it ends when this life ends. I don't know what the 'time' on the other side looks like, but I'm inclined to believe that it is not made up of hours, days and years like this time is."

"And what is heaven?" Daniel asked.

"Good question, what is that heaven? Many people believe that heaven is a beautiful place, where everything is clean and green; where there is plenty of food, free for all; a place where all people are always perfectly healthy and where you don't have to work hard to pay your debts to the banks. This may be considered a good description, but God has offered us in the Bible a higher understanding of heaven. When Jesus Christ was asked:"

«[W]hen the Kingdom of God would come, He answered them and said, "The Kingdom of God does not come with observation; nor will they say,

'See here!' or 'See there!' For indeed, the Kingdom of God is within you.»[18]

"Then Saint Paul the Apostle writes to the Romans:"

«[F]or the Kingdom of God is not eating and drinking, but righteousness and peace and joy in the Holy Spirit.»[19]

"I don't really understand," Daniel said. "So it is not something visible, and it's also not food and drink. But what is it?"

"From these quotes I understand that heaven is, first of all, a state of the soul—an eternal and unchangeable state of the soul. This is the reason for the eternal happiness of those there, the inner state of their souls. Yes, there is probably also a visible side of heaven, I mean trees with fruit and other things like this, but these are of secondary importance. The eternal happiness is not due to the external elements, but instead due to the inner spiritual state of those in there."

"And what about hell?"

"Why wouldn't hell be a similar thing, too? An eternal suffering caused only by the spiritual state of those in there. An eternal and unchangeable state of the soul. As the body suffers when it is sick, why wouldn't the soul suffer, too, when it is sick? And even more because it knows that its disease can never be healed."

"I have never heard this explanation in my entire life," Daniel said. "Please give me more details, because I don't really understand it."

"Let's take it gradually. First, let's see what sin is and what repentance is. Most of us understand that sin is a deed, an action of ours that goes against the rules that God has established for us. God told us that we are not allowed to steal, to lie, to kill another human being, and so on. But there is also a more profound meaning of sin. The outwardly visible deed we call sin is actually a manifestation of some inner spiritual problems, problems that are called spiritual diseases or passions. These passions

---

[18] Luke 17:20-21.
[19] Romans 14:17.

sometimes make us manifest them externally by committing visible sins. But not always, sometimes the passion can also exist without being outwardly visible. Christ has said in one of His sermons:"

> «*You have heard that it was said to those of old, 'You shall not commit adultery.' But I say to you that whoever looks at a woman to lust for her has already committed adultery with her in his heart.*»[20]

Michael went on:

"This is an example of passion that does not manifest itself outwardly. But the spiritual disease exists, without being seen by others."

"So it's a sin to look, too," Daniel said, a little discouraged, "and it's probably also a sin to think about women. But why? I'm not doing any harm to anyone."

"You're doing harm to yourself," Michael replied. "Let us now see what repentance is. This is a word used very often in the Bible, both in the Old and New Testament. Both the Savior Christ and Saint John the Baptist started their missions with this urging: «*Repent, for the Kingdom of heaven is at hand.*»[21] Nowadays, many people have come to believe that repentance is a mere formality, they go to the priest and tell him what sins they have committed, the priest reads a prayer over them and that's it, they are forgiven and they can go on with their lives. But repentance has a much more profound meaning. The original Greek word is *metanoia*[22] and it means something more, namely a change of the mind, a change of man's inner nature, a healing of the soul. This change first means that man realizes that he is a sinner, he becomes aware of his inner spiritual diseases, even though many times they do not manifest outwardly. Then he has to feel sorry for being like that, to feel sorry that he is spiritually sick and to

---

[20] Mathew 5:27-28.

[21] Matthew 4:17; 3:2.

[22] In Romanian, the Greek word "metanoia" (μετανοια) also gave birth to the word "metanie," which means a kneeling and a prostration to the ground.

desire and to fight with all his strength to change, to stop committing both visible and invisible sins, to stop sinning in thought, too. This is what repentance is and, if taken seriously, it involves a fight that lasts for a lifetime and leads in the end, and with the help of God, to the soul being healed of passions and to the Kingdom of heaven."

"I still don't understand why it is a sin to look at or to think about women," Daniel said.

"It is a sin to look lustfully, this is what Christ is saying. We'll get to this soon. Now let's see what is going on in the afterlife. It is true that sinners go to hell forever, but this is not because God does not want to forgive them anymore, but because they can no longer repent. This change of mind and change of nature that I was telling you about, this *metanoia*, is possible *only* during the earthly life. God is very good and He would always be ready to forgive them and welcome them into heaven, even after their deaths, but they cannot repent anymore, they can no longer change their minds and their inner nature. Here's what Saint Theophan the Recluse, a Russian bishop who lived in the 19th century, says about this:"

> The Lord is so merciful, that He would also forgive us after death, if we repented. But our tragedy is that, after death, there is no hope for us to repent.[23]

"What about the suffering in hell, what causes it?" Daniel asked.

"The man who dies without having repented, the man who dies without having first healed his soul, that man passes into the afterlife with a sick soul, subdued by those passions. And the healing of the soul is no longer possible after the death of the body. As our body suffers when it is sick, so the soul will suffer eternally because of its diseases of which it will never be able to get rid of. You asked me a couple of times why it is wrong to look lustfully at a woman. First, Christ would not have mentioned this

---

[23] *Words from Saint Theophan the Recluse (Letters)*, (in Romanian) Egumeniţa Press, 2005, pp. 95-104.

sin if it were not a serious one. And this is why it is wrong: this lustful look feeds the sexual desire you already have. And if you don't kill this desire during your earthly life, you will take it with you to the other side, and there the desire will never die. There is no sexual life after death, the Savior has said pretty clearly that in the afterlife people *«neither marry nor are given in marriage, but are like angels of God in heaven.»*[24] Do you understand the problem now? He who does not get rid of this desire during this life, in the eternal life he will forever want something that he will never be able to have. This is the reason why God has left us so many rules about the sexual life, but too bad, modern society now considers them to be outdated. This is one of the things that torment the sinner in hell, the burning desires that never die and that can also never be satisfied."

"I have never imagined hell this way," Daniel said. "I have never imagined that, if there were a heaven and a hell, the suffering of those in hell would be caused by the impossibility of fulfilling some desires."

8.3. Hell in the Vision of the Orthodox Church

8.3.1. Saint John of Damascus

"Here's what Saint John of Damascus, who lived between the years 675[25] and 749, tells us about hell:"

> We say that the torment is nothing other than the fire of unsatisfied passion. For those who obtained changelessness in passion do not desire God but sin. But there in that place the commission of evil has no place. For we neither eat nor

---

[24] Matthew 22:30.

[25] The year of his birth is not known with certainty, but it is estimated to be 675 or 676.

drink, nor get dressed, nor marry, nor gather wealth, nor does envy or another evil satisfy us. Therefore, by desiring and not partaking of the things desired, they are burned by passions as if by fire. But those who desire the good–namely God alone, Who is and exists eternally–and who partake of Him rejoice according to the intensity of their desire according to which they also partake of the Desired One.[26]

Michael went on:

"Do you get the idea? Saint John of Damascus says it pretty clearly: after the death of the body, the man loses the ability to change, he becomes unchangeable, and he keeps on wanting forever things that he can never have."

"Yes, the quote is pretty clear," Daniel said.

8.3.2. Saint Theophan the Recluse

"This is just one aspect of hell; there are many others, but I can only show them to you through metaphors. Each spiritual disease that man is not healed of during this life will torment him in a special way in the afterlife. Malice, envy, anger—all these and many others are serious spiritual diseases or mortal sins, as they are also called. All these will cause eternal suffering to the soul if the man has not set himself free of them during his life. And if a sinner from hell were to be taken from there and moved into heaven, that wouldn't help him at all; even more, his suffering could be greater in heaven. Here's what Saint Theophan the Recluse also says:"

Imagine a sinner in Paradise! What a nonsense! What is he going to do there? For him, heaven is hell, because he does not have the senses necessary to enjoy its sweetness. Everything he will see there will upset and disturb him. He won't

---

[26] St. John of Damascus, *Dialogus contra Manichaeos*, *Patrologia Graeca* (P.G.), vol. 94, col. 1573; quoted in [F r .] Dumitru Staniloae, *The Experience of God*, vol. 6 (The Fulfillment of Creation), Holy Cross Orthodox Press, 2013, pp. 43-47.

find peace of soul anywhere, because all will be contrary to his inner disposition.

Call an illiterate man into a group of learned men. Among such persons he will feel very bad. The same will happen to a sinner who entered heaven together with all his uncleanness.

In that moment, maybe you will say: let someone cleanse him; isn't such a thing possible for God?

I will answer to you: if it were possible, then here, on earth, there would have been no sinners. God would say that all to become saints, and His commandment would immediately be fulfilled. But this is the problem: cleansing can only be done if we also want to. And if here, on earth, we do not want to, the less we'll want in the other life; the beginning of the cleansing is repentance. But there is no repentance in the afterlife.[27]

"This is the first time that I've heard such a thing," Daniel said. "How is it possible for the suffering of the sinner to be greater in heaven?"

"Because of his spiritual diseases, for him 'heaven is hell,' as Saint Theophan also says."

8.3.3. Saint Paisios of Mount Athos

"Let's see now what another saint says, this one contemporary to us, Saint Paisios of Mount Athos. He spent most of his life as a monk on that mountain and, although he was living in utmost poverty, he was well known in all of Greece and even beyond its borders. Thousands of people were coming to him every year to ask for his advice. A lot of visitors confess that many times Saint Paisios knew their problems and was giving them an answer for them before they got a chance to say a word. And this is what he tells us about hell:"

---

[27] *Words from Saint Theophan the Recluse (Letters)*, pp. 95-104.

Even hell was allowed by God out of love, for the sinner and those like him to go there and be 'comforted.' Because these people, even though God were to put them in heaven, would still suffer.

Imagine what someone who doesn't love Christ would feel if he were to participate in an endless Holy Liturgy. It would be hard for him, he would be bored and would hardly bear it.[28]

Since God has said: *«You shall not covet [...] anything belonging to your neighbor,»*[29] how could we desire something that belongs to someone else? After that our life becomes a living hell. *«But each one is tempted when he is drawn away by his own desires and enticed,»*[30] says Saint James, the relative of the Lord. These desires will also torment the soul in hell. And if God takes us in heaven, without us being delivered from envy, then even there we won't find peace, because we'll have the same irrational desires.[31]

The conscience… a frightening thing! There is no greater fire, no greater hell than the burning of the conscience. There is no more frightening and tormenting worm than the worm of conscience. Those sentenced will suffer eternally, because they will be tormented by the thought that they have lost the good things in heaven for the few years of earthly life, although these were filled with sadness and unrest. Then the acquired passions won't satisfy them anymore, and this will be another torment.[32]

---

[28] Athanasios Rakovalis, *Talks with Father Paisios*, Orthodox Kypseli Publications, 2000. (translated from the Romanian edition).

[29] See Exodus 20:17; Deuteronomy 5:21.

[30] James 1:14.

[31] Elder Paisios of Mount Athos, *Spiritual Counsels*, vol. 5 (*Passions and Virtues*).

It seems an English translation is not yet available. The translation above was done from the Romanian edition.

[32] Elder Paisios of Mount Athos, *Spiritual Counsels*, vol. 3, p. 147. (translated from the Romanian edition).

Let me tell you a story that I've heard:

Once there was a simple man who kept asking God to show him what paradise and hell are like…

So, one night, in his sleep, he heard a voice saying: 'Come, let me show you what hell looks like.'

He suddenly found himself in a room, where many people were seated around a table. In the middle of that table was a pot filled with food. But all those people were hungry, because they were unable to eat. They each held a very long spoon in their hand. They were able to take food out of the pot, but couldn't bring the spoon to their mouth.[33] Because of this, some were complaining, others were shouting, others were weeping…

Then he heard the same voice saying to him: 'Come now, and let me show you what Paradise also looks like.'

He again found himself suddenly in another room, where many people were seated around a table, just like the one before, and in the middle of that table was–again–a pot full of food. Those people also held the same kind of long spoon in their hand. But every one of these people was full and happy, because each would dip his spoon in the pot and feed the person near him.[34]

"I don't understand the parable of the spoons," Daniel said.

"It's pretty easy," Michael replied. "Both those in heaven and those in hell were in the same situation. But those in hell were unhappy because of their egotism, because they were only thinking of themselves and they were only trying to feed themselves.

---

[33] The end of the spoon was tied to their hand, and the spoon was longer than the hand. For this reason they were unable to bring it to their mouth.

[34] Elder Paisios of Mount Athos, *Spiritual Counsels*, vol. 5.

It seems an English translation is not yet available. The translation above was reproduced from:

http://oodegr.co/english/esxata/Hell1.htm

This is a metaphor; don't imagine that in the afterlife we'll have spoons attached to our hands."

"Yes, I thought it was a metaphor, too."

8.3.4. Saint Silouan the Athonite

"Now here's a short quote from Saint Silouan the Athonite,[35] a Russian ascetic who lived between the years 1866 and 1938:"

> But he who loves not his enemies will never find peace, even though he were to be set down in paradise.[36]

"The same idea," Michael said. "If we take with us a spiritual disease, it will eternally cause problems for us in the afterlife. Even though we were in heaven, we'd suffer there, too."

8.3.5. Saint John Maximovitch

"Here's what Saint John Maximovitch, a Russian bishop who lived between the years 1896 and 1966, says. He belonged to the Russian Orthodox Church Outside of Russia[37] and he used to be Archbishop of Shanghai and San Francisco. About him, too, we have many wonderful testimonies: he 'was seen in glowing light, levitated during prayer, was clairvoyant, worked miracles of healing.'[38] This is what he tells us about hell:"

---

[35] He spent most of his life on Mount Athos, hence the title of 'the Athonite.'

[36] Archim. Sophrony Sakharov, *St. Silouan the Athonite*, p. 422.

[37] Also known as ROCOR or ROCA (Russian Orthodox Church Abroad), it was first a jurisdiction of the Russian Orthodox Church, from which it separated in 1927, when the latter began to compromise with the communist leadership. The two Churches were reunited in 2007.

[38] Fr. Seraphim Rose, *God's Revelation to the Human Heart*, St. Herman of Alaska Brotherhood, Platina, California, 1997, pp. 17-18.

This is an extraordinary book, very short, which the author of this book warmly recommends to all readers.

And the Lord will appear in glory on the clouds. Trumpets
will sound, and loud, with power! They will sound in the soul
and conscience! All will become clear to the human conscience. The Prophet Daniel, speaking of the Last Judgement, relates how the Ancient of days, the Judge, sits on His
throne, and before Him is a fiery stream.[39] Fire is a purifying
element; it burns sin. Woe to a man if sin has become a part
of his nature: then the fire will burn the man himself.

This fire will be kindled within a man: seeing the Cross, some
will rejoice, but others will fall into confusion, terror, and
despair. Thus will men be divided instantly. The very state of
a man's soul casts him to one side or the other, to right or to
left. The more consciously and persistently a man strives toward God in his life, the greater will be his joy when he hears:
«Come unto Me, ye blessed.»[40] And conversely: the same words
will call the fire of horror and torture on those who did not
desire Him, who fled and fought or blasphemed Him during
their lifetime!

The Last Judgement knows of no witnesses or written pro-
tocols! Everything is inscribed in the souls of men and these
records, these *«books»*[41], are opened at the Judgement. Everything becomes clear to all and to oneself [, and man's
spiritual state will make him go to the
right or to the left].

And some will go to joy, while others — to horror.

When *«the books are opened,»* it will become clear that the roots
of all vices lie in the human soul. Here is a drunkard or a
lecher: when the body has died, some may think that sin is
dead too. No! There was an inclination to sin in the soul, and
that sin was sweet to the soul, and if the soul has not repented
of the sin and has not freed itself from it, it will come to the
Last Judgement also with the same desire for sin. It will never
satisfy that desire and in that soul there will be the suffering

---

[39] Daniel 7:9-10.
[40] Matthew 25:34.
[41] Daniel 7:10; Revelation 20:12.

of hatred. It will accuse everyone and everything in its tortured condition, it will hate everyone and everything. *«There will be gnashing of teeth»*[42] of powerless malice and the unquenchable fire of hatred.

A 'fiery Gehenna' — such is the inner fire. *«Here there will be wailing and gnashing of teeth.»* Such is the state of hell.[43]

He who rejoices in the glory of God and in everything that reminds one of it in this life will also rejoice in the age to come. He who in this life strove toward God will rush to Him joyfully when at the Dread Judgment he hears the words, *«Come unto Me, ye blessed....»* All those that do not know how to rejoice in the glory of God, in whom the divine realm and its laws call forth a state of unhappiness, who love gloom or semi-gloom, who do not love the light, will not answer to the call of *«Come unto Me....»* They will shrink back in indignation, unhappiness, in jealousy and anger, from the humble and the meek who will go toward the light, from God Himself, Whom they will begin to blame for their being in such a state. They will even shrink from themselves, thought they will not want to admit their guilt. Such a state is true suffering. Hades is not a place, no, but a state of soul. It begins already here on earth. Just so, paradise too begins in the soul of man already in the earthly life.[44]

8.3.6. Saint Nephon

"Here's an older source, an excerpt from a vision of the Last Judgment by Saint Nephon, bishop of Constantia. Constantia was an ancient city on the island of Cyprus, and Saint Nephon

---

[42] Matthew 25:30 (and also in many other places).

[43] *Sermons and Writings of Saint John Archbishop of Shanghai and San Francisco*, Book 2, Holy Dormition Sisterhood, St Marys, NSW, Australia, 2004, pp. 17-18.

The sentence in [brackets] is taken from the Romanian translation.

[44] *Sermons and Writings of Saint John Archbishop of Shanghai and San Francisco*, Book 1, pp. 18-19.

was a bishop there sometime in the 4th century. And this is what he saw in his vision about the Last Judgment:"

> As soon as the Judge voiced that decision,[45] at once an enormous fiery river spilled over from the East and went rolling violently toward the West. It was broad like a big sea. When the sinners on the left saw it they were very stunned and began to tremble frightfully in their despair. But the impartial Judge ordered everyone—just and unjust—to pass through the flaming river, so that the fire could try them.
>
> The ones at His right hand started first. They crossed and came out gleaming like solid gold. Their deeds did not burn, but instead proved to be brighter and clearer with the test. That's why they were filled with joy.
>
> After these, the ones at His left hand came to pass through the fire, so that their deeds might be tried. But, because they were sinners, the flame began to consume them and kept them in the middle of the river. Their deeds were burned up like straw while their bodies remained unharmed to burn for years and endless ages along with the devil and the demons.
>
> No one was able to come out of that fiery river! The fire imprisoned all of them, because they deserved condemnation and punishment.[46]

Michael went on:

"It resembles a little the vision with those sitting at the table with the long spoons. They were all in the same reality, but each one of them perceived it in a different way, according to his spiritual state. Almost the same thing seems to be true about the river of fire: to some it did good, but others were burned by it."

---

[45] *«Come, you blessed of My Father, ...» «Depart from Me, you cursed, ...»* (Matthew 25:34-45).

[46] *Stories, Sermons, and Prayers of St. Nephon: An Ascetic Bishop,* Light & Life Pub. Co., 1989, pp. 64-65.

8.3.7. Saint Paul the Apostle

"Related to fire," Michael went on, "here's what Saint Paul the Apostle tells us:"

«one's work will become clear; for the Day [of the Lord] will declare it, because it will be revealed by fire; and the fire will test each one's work, of what sort it is. If anyone's work which he has built on it endures, he will receive a reward. If anyone's work is burned, he will suffer loss;»[47]

"And in the Old Testament we are told:"

«For the Lord your God is a consuming fire.»[48]

8.3.8. Saint Isaac the Syrian

"Do you begin to get the idea? After death we are all confronted with the same reality, but each one of us perceives it differently, according to his spiritual state. If you want an example from this world, think of two men exposed to sunlight. The first one has a healthy skin, but the other one has a sick skin[49] and he can't stand the sun at all. For the first one, the sunlight is good, but the second one is tormented by it. And this is not so because there is anything wrong with the sun, but because he is sick. This is a somewhat inexact analogy, because those who are affected by these diseases are very few, but we are all affected by spiritual diseases, more or less. Besides, spiritual diseases are always curable, with the help of God, if we really try to repent. About this 'reality,' which is perceived differently by each one of us, some say that it is the very presence of God or the love of God. For some, this presence is an unimaginable happiness, for others it is an unimaginable suffering. Here's a few words from Saint Isaac

---

[47] 1 Corinthians 3:13-15.

[48] Deuteronomy 4:24.

[49] For example, *xeroderma pigmentosum* is a disease where, in some cases, any kind of exposure of the skin to sunlight is completely forbidden.

the Syrian, who lived in the 7th century after Christ and for a while was a bishop in the city of Nineveh, the former capital of the Assyrian Empire:"

> I also maintain that those who are punished in Gehenna are scourged by the scourge of love. For what is so bitter and vehement as the torment of love? I mean that those who have become conscious that they have sinned against love suffer greater torment from this than from any fear of punishment. For the sorrow caused in the heart by sin against love is more poignant than any torment. It would be improper for a man to think that sinners in Gehenna are deprived of the love of God. Love is the offspring of knowledge of the truth which, as is commonly confessed, is given to all. The power of love works in two ways. It torments sinners, even as happens here when a friend suffers from a friend. But it becomes a source of joy for those who have observed its duties. Thus I say that this is the torment of Gehenna: bitter regret. But love inebriates the souls of the sons of heaven by its delectability.[50]

8.3.9. Saint Nicholas Cabasilas

"Next, here's a quote on the afterlife from Saint Nicholas Cabasilas, who was born sometime between the years 1319 and 1323, and lived till the year 1391:"

> The Life in Christ originates in this life and arises from it. It is perfected, however, in the life to come, when we shall have reached that last day. It cannot attain perfection in men's souls in this life, nor even in that which is to come, without already having begun here. [...] But if the life to come were to admit those who lack the faculties and senses necessary for it, it would avail nothing for their happiness, but they

---

[50] *Ascetical Homilies of St. Isaac the Syrian*, Holy Transfiguration Monastery, 2011, Homily 72: *On the Vision of the Nature of Incorporeal Beings*. In other books this homily is titled "Homily 27" or "Homily 28" and in the Romanian edition it is "Word 84."

would be dead and miserable living in that blessed and immortal world. The reason is, that the light would appear and the sun shine with its pure rays with no eye having been formed to see it. The Spirit's fragrance would be abundantly diffused and pervading all, but one would not know it without already having the sense of smell.[51]

Michael went on:

"To me it seems to be pretty clear what Saint Nicholas Cabasilas means: the afterlife is only happy for those who have the 'senses' formed to perceive it; for the others it is a torment, they can't 'see' or 'smell' anything. And these 'senses' are being formed in this life. Obviously, this is about spiritual 'senses,' not about eyes or noses as we have in our bodies now."

"Yes, I understand," Daniel said.

8.3.10. Saint Maximus the Confessor

"Also, here's a quote from Saint Maximus the Confessor, who lived between the years 580 and 662:"

God is the sun of justice, as it is written, Who shines rays of goodness on simply everyone. The soul develops according to its free will into either wax, because of its love for God, or into mud, because of its love of matter. Thus just as by nature the mud is dried out by the sun and wax is automatically softened, so also every soul which loves matter and the world and has fixed its mind far from God[52] is hardened as mud according to its free will and by itself advances to its perdition, as did Pharaoh.[53] However, every soul which loves God is softened as wax, and receiving divine impressions and

---

[51] Nicholas Cabasilas, *The Life in Christ*, Saint Vladimir's Seminary Press, Crestwood, New York, 1974, p. 43.

[52] In other translations: "receives teaching from God and opposes it."

[53] Exodus, chapters 5-15.

characters it becomes *«the dwelling place of God in the Spirit.»*[54, 55]

8.3.11. Saint Gregory the Great

"Let's now see what Saint Gregory the Great, who used to be Pope of Rome between the years 590 and 604, says in one of his dialogues:"

PETER: I beseech you: Is there one fire in hell, or, according to the diversity of sinners, be there so many sorts of fire prepared in that place?

GREGORY: The fire of hell is but one: yet doth it not in one manner torment all sinners. For every one there, according to the quantity of his sin, hath the measure of his pain. For as, in this world, many live under one and the same sun, and yet do not alike feel the heat thereof: for some be burnt more, and some less: so in that one fire, divers manners of burning be found, for that which in this world diversity of bodies doth, that in the next doth diversity of sins: so that although the fire be there all alike, yet doth it not in one manner and alike burn and torment them that be damned.

[...]

PETER: Willing I am to know how that sin can justly be punished without end, which had an end when it was committed.

GREGORY: This which you say might have some reason, if the just judge did only consider the sins committed, and not the minds[56] with which they were committed: for the reason

[54] Ephesians 2:22.

[55] Maximus Confessor, *Selected Writings*, Paulist Press, Mahwah, NJ, 1985, p.130 (*Chapters on Knowledge*, 1:12).

[56] In other translations: "the hearts." In the Latin text we find the word "corda," which is usually translated as "hearts."

why wicked men made an end of sinning was, because they also made an end of their life: for willingly they would, had it been in their power, have lived without end, that they might in like manner have sinned without end. For they do plainly declare that they desired always to live in sin, who never, so long as they were in this world, gave over their wicked life.[57]

Michael explained:

"We have two important clues in the words of Saint Gregory. First, the 'fire' is the same, but each one perceives it differently, according to the spiritual state he was brought to by his sins. And the second clue, the suffering is eternal because it is caused by the evil in their hearts, not necessarily by their deeds. Actually, the deeds, the visible sins, are just an outwardly manifestation of the evil within. If the evil within would go away, the suffering would go away, too. But in the afterlife there is no more change, there is no more repentance."

"I don't think there is anything more terrifying than eternity," Daniel thought aloud. "The human mind can't really comprehend such a time interval. Actually it's not a time interval, it's an infinity…"

Hoc recte diceretur, si districtus judex non *corda* hominum, sed facta pensaret.

The idea is that their suffering never ends because their hearts and their minds never change.

[57] Gregory the Great, *Dialogues*, translated into English by P.W., published in 1608, re-edited by Edmund G. Gardner in 1911, chapters 42-44.

For his dialogues, St. Gregory is also known as St. Gregory the Dialogist.

8.3.12. Egyptian Paterikon

"Here's another clue, taken from a collection of sayings of certain monks from the first centuries of Christianity, of whom many are recognized as saints:"

> Said some elder: There is no worse and bitter thing than the bad habit and custom. Because a long time and much diligence and labor are needed by such a man in order to get rid of and uproot his bad habit and custom. Now many did have the labor, but they did not have the time, because the sickle of death hastened and reaped them together with their habit and custom, and only God Himself knows what He's going to do with those in the Day of Judgment.[58]

"What does 'the bad habit and custom' mean?" Daniel asked.

"It could mean any habit of sinning: speaking evil of others, anger, envy, pride, vainglory, malice and, obviously, the sins of sexual nature, including sins committed in thought alone. Although the quote is not attributed to a certain saint, I think it helps us see that even from the first centuries, Christians knew that we take our spiritual diseases with us in the afterlife, where they cause us problems."

"And what's the meaning of the fact that 'only God Himself knows what He's going to do with those in the Day of Judgment'?"

"I think it means that it is impossible for us, men, to judge what eternity is going to look like for those I just mentioned. Besides, I think that today each of us has at least one such bad habit, and it is important that we struggle to get rid of them."

"The elder quoted by you says: 'many did have the labor, but they did not have the time.' Why didn't God allow them to live longer, if they were struggling to get rid of those bad habits?"

"This is a question that only God can answer, but I believe that if they were indeed going to get rid of those habits, without

---

[58] *Egyptian Paterikon* (in Romanian), second part (unnamed elders), the chapter on humility.

acquiring new ones, and without harming their souls in other ways, then they would have lived longer. Here's what Saint John Chrysostom says about the death of a sinful man:"

> And if indeed he departed a sinner, his wickedness is stayed; for certainly, had God known that he was being converted, He would not have snatched him away before his repentance [.] [59]

"The will of God is to save everybody," Michael concluded.

"Yes, I understand. Do you know any other clues about the nature of hell?"

8.3.13. The Encyclopedia

"Here's also an 'official' explanation for hell, from an Internet encyclopedia:"

> The Eastern Orthodox Church teaches that heaven and hell are relations to or experiences of God's just and loving presence. [...] One expression of the Eastern teaching is that hell and heaven are dimensions of God's intensifying presence, as this presence is experienced either as torment or as paradise depending on the spiritual state of a person dwelling with God. For one who hates God and by extension hates himself as God's image-bearer, to be encompassed by the divine presence could only result in unspeakable anguish.[60]

8.3.14. Dostoyevsky

Daniel resumed the conversation:

"You're presenting to me a vision of hell totally different than everything I have heard of before. I didn't really believe

---

[59] St. John Chrysostom, *Homilies on the Gospel of Matthew*, Homily XXXI.

[60] https://en.wikipedia.org/wiki/Christian_views_on_hell#Orthodox_conceptions_of_hell

there was a hell, however, I used to imagine it with lots of caul-drons filled with boiling pitch, in which the sinners are boiling in horrifying torments that never end."

"The horrifying torments that never end are real, but I don't think there's any cauldrons of pitch. We have in the Bible a few references to the «fire» and the «worm,»[61] but they're probably met-aphors. I mean, the fire is inside the souls of those in there, and the worm is the conscience, as some saints say. You have heard of Dostoyevsky[62], the Russian writer, haven't you? Although Dostoyevsky is neither a saint, nor was he a priest or a monk, here's how his characters see hell:"

> Fathers and teachers, I ponder, "What is hell?" I maintain that it is the suffering of being unable to love.
>
> [...]
>
> They talk of hell fire in the material sense. I don't go into that mystery and I shun it. But I think if there were fire in material sense, they would be glad of it, for I imagine that in material agony, their still greater spiritual agony would be forgotten for a moment. Moreover, that spiritual agony cannot be taken from them, for that suffering is not external but within them. And if it could be taken from them, I think it would be bitterer still for the unhappy creatures. For even if the righteous in Paradise forgave them, beholding their tor-ments, and called them up to heaven in their infinite love, they would only multiply their torments, for they would arouse in them still more keenly a flaming thirst for respon-sive, active and grateful love which is now impossible.[63]

---

[61] «where 'Their worm does not die and the fire is not quenched.'» (Mark 9:44).

[62] Fyodor Mikhailovich Dostoyevsky, (1821 - 1881) was one of the most important Russian writers.

[63] F. M. Dostoyevsky, *The Brothers Karamazov*, part II, book VI *(The Russian Monk)*, chapter III *(Conversations and Exhortations of Father Zossima)*, subchapter i *(Of Hell and Hell Fire, a Mystic Reflection)*.

8.3.15. About Metaphors

"Yet still, what are the sources of the stories about the caul-drons full of pitch from hell?" Daniel asked.

"Various visions of hell have been preserved for us in the tradition of the Church, and some of them indeed talk about flames and other instruments for physical torture. But the Church has understood even from the beginning that these were meta-phors, meant to help us stay away from sins. Here's what Saint Gregory the Great, Pope of Rome, says about the vision of a cer-tain Reparatus, who saw in hell a woodpile being prepared for the burning of a sinner:"

> And the reason why Reparatus saw that great wood-pile burning, was not that we should think that the fire of hell is nourished with any wood: but because he was to make rela-tion of these things to them that remained still in this world, he saw that fire prepared for the wicked, to be made of the same matter of which our fire is, to the end that, by those things which we know and be acquainted with, we should learn to be afraid of those, which yet we have not seen nor have any experience.[64]

Michael went on:

"People can be on several spiritual levels. Some do good and avoid sins because they are afraid of hell, others because they ex-pect a reward from God, and still others because they love God and their neighbor. And many times people are on two or even on all three levels at the same time. God would want all of us to belong to the third category, that is, to do good only because of our love for Him and for our neighbor, but He also accepts those who belong to the first two categories. But the metaphors about heaven and hell are not all suited for all intellectual and spiritual levels, and they should not be taken literally, as Saint Gregory the Great also explains. Here's what he says about a vision in which someone saw in heaven a house being built with bricks of gold."

---

[64] Gregory the Great, *Dialogues*, chapter 31 (of the death of Repa-ratus).

PETER. What, I beseech you, was meant by the building of that house in those places of delight, with bricks of gold? For it seemeth very ridiculous, that in the next life we should have need of any such kind of metal.

GREGORY. What man of sense can think so? but by that which was shewn there, whosoever he was, for whom that house was built, we learn plainly what virtuous works he did in this world: for he that by plenty of alms doth merit the reward of eternal light, certain it is, that he doth build his house with gold.[65]

Michael went on:

"Saint Nephon, whom I mentioned just before, in his vision about the Last Judgment saw that Christ and all the saints went where there were the things that *«Eye has not seen, nor ear heard, nor have entered into the heart of man»*[66]:"

But the servant of God Nephon wasn't able to describe them to me. Even though many times I pressured him, he didn't tell me the slightest thing. "My son," he would say with a sigh, "I can't portray those there with my words, nor compare them with any earthly thing. They were beyond every thought and imagination, beyond everything visible and invisible."[67]

"Here's also what Saint Isaac the Syrian tells us about metaphoric speech:"

Doest thou see, how the Fathers change their designations of spiritual things? This is because accurate designations can only be established concerning earthly things. The things of the world-to-be do not possess a true name, but only simple cognition, which is exalted above all names and signs and forms and colours and habits and composite denominations. When, therefore, the knowledge of the soul exalts itself above this circle of visible things, the Fathers use concerning

---

[65] Ibid., chapter 36.
[66] 1 Corinthians 2:9.
[67] *Stories, Sermons, and Prayers of St. Nephon: An Ascetic Bishop*, p. 68.

this knowledge any designations they like, though no one does know the real names in order that the psychic deliberations may be based on them. We use denominations and riddles, according to the word of the holy Dionysius[68] who says: We use signs and syllables, conventional names and words in behalf of the senses. But when by spiritual working our soul is moved unto divine things, then the senses and their workings are superfluous to us, as also the spiritual forces of the soul are superfluous as soon as our soul becomes the image of the godhead through unification with the incomprehensible and radiant in the rays of the sublime, by those impulses which are not for the eyes.[69]

8.3.16. Conclusion about Hell

"So it is pretty clear," Michael said, "that the visions about the afterlife are, most of the time, metaphoric, because otherwise we wouldn't be able to understand them. However, I think you can still form an idea, although a very vague one, about what heaven and hell are. Imagine neither enormous amounts of food and drink in heaven, nor cauldrons of pitch in hell. However, be careful not to be deceived by this image of hell. Although the cauldrons of pitch don't exist, the sufferings of those in there are unimaginable and without end. And although God does everything possible to save everybody, it seems most people will end up in hell."

"How's that?" Daniel asked, a little scared.

"Christ Himself is warning us:"

«Enter by the narrow gate; for wide is the gate and broad is the way that leads to destruction, and there are many who go in by it. Because narrow is the gate and difficult is the way which leads to life, and there are few who find it.»[70]

---

[68] Probably St. Dionysius the Areopagite.

[69] *Mystic Treatises by Isaac of Nineveh*, A. J. Wensinck edition, Amsterdam, 1923, pp. 114-115.

[70] Mathew 7:13-14.

"And Saint John Chrysostom reminds us of the words of the Lord:"

> Christ Himself says that the larger part of humankind will perish and only a small part will be saved.[71]

"This is truly depressing," Daniel objected.

"It's very sad, indeed, but this is the result of each person's free will. God is ready to save everybody, but He can only do it if we also want to be saved:"

> *«Say to them, 'As I live, thus says the Lord: "I do not will the death of the ungodly man. So the ungodly man should turn from his way and live. Turn heartily from your way, for why should you die, O house of Israel?' "»[72]*

Michael went on:

"In conclusion, the torment of those in hell is not caused by God's 'anger' or 'revenge,' as some have come to believe, but only by their spiritual diseases."

"I have one more question: Why doesn't God kill those in hell? I think that it would be better for them to simply disappear than to be tormented eternally."

"I cannot answer this question, but what exactly makes you think that they would really want this? Are you sure that they will want to die and God will refuse them?"

"No, obviously, there is no way for me to know such a thing…"

8.3.17. Sartre's Hell

Michael kept quiet for a few moments, while Daniel was thinking.

---

[71] St. John Chrysostom, *Against Those Who Oppose the Monastic Life.*
[72] Ezekiel 33:11.

"Have you ever heard of Jean-Paul Sartre[73]?" Michael asked eventually.

"Yes," Daniel said, "he was a French writer."

"An atheist writer. Would you like to see how an atheist sees hell?"

"I find it surprising that you propose to me the vision of an atheist. What did a believer like you find in a nonbeliever like Sartre?"

"His vision of hell presented in the play *No Exit*[74], although wrong, is much closer to reality than the image of the cauldrons of pitch that is so widespread in the West. The three main characters end up in hell, all three of them in one room. There they expect to find a torturer, who would torment them for their sins, but there is no such thing. Instead, the characters begin to verbally and mentally torture one another, such that, near the end, one of them exclaims: 'There's no need for red-hot pokers. Hell is other people!'"

"And what exactly is wrong in this vision of Sartre?"

"It can be seen even from his text, at a careful analysis. The cause of each one's suffering is their very passions, the spiritual diseases of which they were not healed during their lifetime, not the other people in there. Joseph Garcin, for example, is obsessed by the idea of convincing others that he is not a coward, probably because he was sentenced to death and executed for desertion during a war. The other characters also suffer from, among other things, a sexual desire that can never be satisfied anymore."

"And how is it possible for an atheist to have such a vision of hell? I understand that his version is imperfect, but indeed, it is significantly better than the version with the cauldrons of pitch."

"Remember the quotes from just before, in which it was being said that heaven and hell are, in a way, eternal continuations

---

[73] Jean-Paul Charles Aymard Sartre (1905-1980), French writer and philosopher, an adept of existentialism. He was awarded the Nobel Prize in 1964, but he refused it.

[74] *Huis-clos*, a French play that was first performed in the year 1944.

of the spiritual state acquired in this life. I think that Sartre, as an atheist, was beginning to feel the hell that he was heading to, and he presented his vision by means of these characters. I don't mean that he had a real vision of hell, only that he was beginning to feel it."

"An interesting idea," Daniel said.

8.3.18. A Sinner in Heaven

"Now here's how a sinner sees heaven," Michael said. "This is about an ordinary man from Russia, who died of pneumonia in a hospital at the end of the 19th century or at the beginning of the 20th century. As he himself says, he was not a nonbeliever, he believed in God, but he did not believe in the afterlife. He was going to Church only once a year. And though he was not a true believer, after death, the angels were taking his soul to heaven. But when he got there, he noticed that for him heaven was not that unlimited peace and happiness of which the saints talk about. For him heaven was a blinding light, in which he could not see anything, and an unexplainable fear:"

> Having passed through some of its distance, I saw a bright light above me, it resembled, as it seemed to me, our sunlight, but was much more intense. There, evidently, is some kind of kingdom of light.

> 'Yes, namely a kingdom, full of the power of light,' guessing by means of a special kind of feeling yet not understood by me, I thought. Because there was no shade with this light. 'But how can there be light without shade?' Immediately my perplexed conceptions made their appearance.

> And suddenly we were quickly carried into the field of this light, and it literally blinded me. I shut my eyes, brought the hands up to my face, but this did not help since my hands did not give shade. And what did the like protection mean here anyway?

> 'My God, what is this, what kind of light is this? Why for me it is like regular darkness! I cannot look, and as in darkness,

can see nothing,' I implored, comparing my earthly vision to that of my present state, and forgetting, or perhaps even not realizing that now such a comparison was of no use here, that now I could see even in the dark.

This incapacity to see, to look, increased in me the fear before the unknown, natural in this state of being found in a world unknown to me, and with alarm I thought: 'What will come next? Shall we soon pass this sphere of light, and is there a limit to it, an end?'

But something different happened. Majestically, without wrath, but authoritatively and firmly, the words resounded from above: 'Not ready!'

And after that thereafter an immediate stop came to our rapid flight upward–we quickly began to descend.

But before we left this realm, I was endowed with the capacity to learn of one most wonderful phenomenon.

Hardly had the said words resounded from above when everything in that world it seems, each particle of dust, each slightest atom, responded to these words with their accord, as though a multimillion echo repeated them in a tongue unable to be perceived by hearing, but perceived and understood by the heart and mind, expressing its unison with the decision so decreed. And in this unity of will there was such wonderful harmony, and in this harmony so much inexpressible, exalted happiness, before which all our earthly charms and raptures appeared like a gloomy day without sunlight. This multimillion echo resounded in the form of an inimitable musical chord, and one's whole soul extended out toward it, wholly responding to it in a state devoid of any cares and in an ardent transport of zeal to be at one with this omnipresent, most wonderful harmony.[75]

---

[75] *Unbelievable For Many, But Actually a True Occurrence*; from *Orthodox Life*, Vol. 26, No. 4 (July-August, 1976), pp. 1-36.
Reproduced from:
http://orthodoxinfo.com/death/unbelievable.aspx

"Why were the angels taking his soul to heaven if he was not a true believer?" Daniel asked. "Do angels also make mistakes?"

"I believe that the angels of God only make 'mistakes' on purpose. Besides, the angels don't take the souls of the dead where they decide to, but where God tells them to, and certainly God never makes mistakes. So the angels were probably taking his soul to heaven so that all those who would hear about or read this account to understand that heaven is a pleasant place only for those who live an authentic Christian life."

"Why did he hear millions of voices agreeing to God's decision?"

"Probably so that we understand that in heaven there's no one who still has his own will, but all are following the will of God. Jesus Christ has also told us many times something like this, namely that we have to abandon our will and do the will of God:"

> *«Therefore the disciples said to one another, "Has anyone brought Him anything to eat?" Jesus said to them, "My food is to do the will of Him who sent Me, and to finish His work. ["] »*[76]

> *«I can of Myself do nothing. As I hear, I judge; and My judgment is righteous, because I do not seek My own will but the will of the Father who sent Me.»*[77]

> *«For I have come down from heaven, not to do My own will, but the will of Him who sent Me. This is the will of the Father who sent Me, that of all He has given Me I should lose nothing, but should raise it up at the last day. And this is the will of Him who sent Me, that everyone who sees the Son and believes in Him may have everlasting life; and I will raise him up at the last day.»*[78]

> *«So He said to them, "When you pray, say:*
> *Our Father in heaven,*
> *Hallowed be Your name.*
> *Your Kingdom come.*

---

[76] John 4:33-34.
[77] John 5:30.
[78] John 6:38-40.

Your will be done
On earth as it is in heaven. [...″] »[79]

«*And He was withdrawn from them about a stone's throw, and He knelt down and prayed, saying, "Father, if it is Your will, take this cup away from Me; nevertheless not My will, but Yours, be done."*»[80]

«*For whoever does the will of God is My brother and My sister and mother.*»[81]

«*Not everyone who says to Me, 'Lord, Lord,' shall enter the Kingdom of heaven, but he who does the will of My Father in heaven.*»[82]

Michael went on:

"And here's also another clue, from Saint Arsenios the Great, an ascetic of Roman origin who lived in Egypt during the 4th and 5th centuries:"

The thousands and ten thousands of the heavenly hosts have but one will, while men have many.[83]

Daniel thought for a few moments, then asked:

"How is it possible for all of them to have a single will?"

"In order to enter heaven, every one must abandon his own will and do the will of God, as it is also so clearly written in the Bible. Even though in this life the will of God is not always known to us, we must have the inner predisposition to always prefer it at the expense of our own will, when it is known to us."

"And how can this perfect harmony be preserved for an eternity? Is it really impossible for two saints in heaven to have an argument?"

"In the afterlife, both in heaven and in hell, people are no longer subject to change. The same way as a sinner in hell can no longer become good and get into heaven, so a saint in heaven can

---

[79] Luke 11:2.

[80] Luke 22:41-42.

[81] Mark 3:35.

[82] Mathew 7:21.

[83] *The Sayings of the Desert Fathers*, revised edition, Cistercian Publications, Kalamazoo, Michigan, 1984, p. 11.

no longer become evil and get into hell. For this reason, perfect harmony lasts for all eternity, because no one in heaven undergoes the slightest change toward evil."

8.3.19. Eternity

"Something's still not clear for me," Daniel said. "There are many people who have various desires that they cannot fulfill anymore. Some because they don't have the money, others because of some diseases they suffer from, others for lack of a sexual partner. Yet still, for these people the unfulfilling of their desires does not seem to cause an immense and endless suffering, as you say it will be for those in hell."

"For each man, the unfulfilling of a desire causes a certain suffering, smaller or greater, depending on the intensity of the desire and on the way he approaches the difficulty of fulfilling it, difficulty which can be temporary or permanent. Some people hope that they will be, sometime, able to fulfill their desires, others are resigned and only dream of them, and still others simply try to get them out of their minds. Let's think for a moment about a man who has a very strong desire, not necessarily of a sexual nature. Usually we think of the desires of a sexual nature because they are so widespread in almost everybody, but this can be any kind of desire, of any other nature. Well then, I think that if that man realizes that that desire will never be satisfied, then he will feel for a short while and in a very small measure the fire of hell inside him."

"Why only for a short period of time?" Daniel asked.

"Because in this ephemeral life, we are subject to change, and thus the desire can die, little by little, especially when we also try to get it out of our minds. I think we can say that one in such a situation undergoes a forced repentance, unwillingly. This unless he stubbornly tries to keep the desire alive in his soul."

"And why only in a very small measure? In hell, is he going to feel the impossibility of fulfilling his desire in an amplified manner? What exactly is it that amplifies the suffering in hell?"

"It's possible that there are multiple factors, but right now I'm only thinking about eternity. Eternity alone is enough to amplify the suffering in an unimaginable way. Imagine that you are a little bit upset today. It's not a big problem, this is a fleeting state, and tomorrow you'll feel better, won't you?"

"Yes," Daniel admitted.

"But what if you were aware that this bad disposition will never go away, that you will eternally be upset, for billions of billions of years, for endless eons? Is this still a minor problem?"

"Obviously not," Daniel said. "Just thinking about it seems terrifying to me."

"Well, behold, even a nonbeliever, as you say you are, understands what great amplifying power eternity has. As the well-known hieromonk Cleopa Ilie, who was contemporary to us, said:"

> Of all the torments of hell, eternity is the most terrible one, when those in there remember that there will never be a redemption and a departure from there.[84]

"And here's also an analogy, known by many people from other sources:"

> The word 'eternity' is frightful! To understand in part what eternity means, I shall give you an example. Imagine that the whole earth is one big piece of granite, end every thousand years a bird comes to sharpen its beak on this rock. When the entire rock is worn away by the bird sharpening its beak, then we shall have some faint notion of what eternity means—not that we have actually understood eternity, immortality, or life without end! So this life of ours here on earth determines our eternity, like flipping a coin: paradise or hell! Therefore, how much caution must we have![85]

---

[84] *Words from Father Cleopa* (in Romanian), vol. 18, Sihăstria Monastery Press, 2012, p. 34.

[85] Elder Ephraim of Philotheou, *Counsels from the Holy Mountain*, second edition, St. Anthony's Greek Orthodox Monastery, Florence, Arizona, 1999, p. 150.

"Terrifying," Daniel said. "Do all desires lead us to hell?"

"No, of course, only sinful desires. Good desires, like the desire to be good, the desire to do good, the desire to help a poor man, the desire to forgive someone who has upset us, the desire to know and to do the will of God, all these and many others take us closer to heaven."

8.4. Why Are There So Many Religions?

"There's something I don't understand," Daniel said. "Why are there so many religions? If God is all-powerful, and there is only one true religion, then why does God allow the existence of so many other religions, like Islam or Buddhism? If the other religions are the work of the devil, why doesn't God intervene to eradicate them?"

"Although God is all-knowing and all-powerful, in this ephemeral world there are still many things happening contrary to His will. But there is absolutely nothing that happens by chance alone; everything that happens happens because God allows it to happen, even though many times He does not agree with it. Here's an example: A murderer decides to kill someone. God tells him in various ways not to do this, usually by means of the conscience and the teaching of the Church, or by thoughts that advise him not to do evil deeds. Thus God reminds him that this is a mortal sin, that he can lose his soul and that he can end up in hell for eternity. But if the man refuses all these warnings, usually God does not stand against his free will and allows him to do what he has set his mind on."

"But what about the victim?" Daniel asked. "What if the victim is innocent? Why doesn't God intervene to prevent the murder?"

"There are no truly random events in this world or in this life. God is the One Who gives life and He is also the One Who takes it away, when He knows that it has to be taken. Nobody, young or old, dies by chance alone, but he dies because God has decided that his earthly life has to be ended—except suicides, of course. And God can end one's earthly life in very many ways. He can send a disease, an accident, an earthquake, or He can allow a cold-blooded murderer to kill him. It's not God Who makes the murderer kill, the murderer himself decides this, but he can only kill a person who God has already decided to take away from this world. That's why the murderer is responsible for his deed, despite the fact that God uses him to conclude someone's earthly life."

"It is hard for me to understand these things…"

"For example, we see in the news that an earthquake caused the death of thousands of people in a certain country, many of them being tourists who happened to be there 'by chance.' No, nobody died by chance. All those who died, died because God decided so. None of the earthquake's victims died by chance. Or we see that a group of terrorists killed a few tourists in a certain country. Those tourists did not die by chance. God knew very well what the terrorists were up to and, although He did not approve their deeds, He allowed them to kill those people because He decided that their earthly lives had to end. If those terrorists didn't exist, God would have found other ways for those tourists to die."

"This seems to me to go against many ethic and moral norms," Daniel said. "If it were in my power to prevent a murder, I would prevent it."

"I would do the same, too. It is our duty to save the lives of others, when we can. Only God decides who has to die and when; if we ever get in a situation where we can prevent a murderer to kill, then we should prevent him, we should not say that it is God's job to prevent him. If it were only God's job, we wouldn't have gotten into that situation. See that here, too, there's nothing that happens by chance alone. We can only prevent a murder if God allows us and helps us prevent it, otherwise we won't be able to."

"But many of the victims of accidents, earthquakes and murderers are so young, some are just children… And many of the young people who die like that are nonbelievers. Why isn't God allowing them to live longer, maybe they would become believers and save their souls?"

"God knows perfectly both the past and the future of every human being. And He does not know this by calculating, as we calculate what time the sun will rise tomorrow. No, God knows this because He is outside time, He is looking at our entire lives as we look at a movie on a DVD player, a movie in which we can skip both forward and backward, a movie we can pause and in which we can analyze every frame. The difference is that we cannot make changes to that movie, but God can intervene in various ways in our lives. Thus, God knows the future of each one of us and certainly He would not allow the death of a person who in a few years would repent and would save his soul. For example, now you're saying you're a nonbeliever."

"Something like that," Daniel confirmed.

"However, although you don't know what you'll do in the future, you don't know whether you'll ever become a believer or not, God does know. And if He knows that you are going to become a believer and that you are going to save your soul, then God will not allow you to die before that. Even if all murderers in the world set their eyes on you and decide to kill you, they wouldn't be able to, because God won't allow it."

"And what if there is a great earthquake?" Daniel asked.

"God will somehow take care of you."

"And what if I drive the car way too fast and I have a deadly accident? Or if I practice a very dangerous extreme sport, like rock climbing without a safety rope?"

"There's also an exception to what I told you before. God keeps alive those for whom this is profitable, but not against their will. If you decide to adopt a suicidal lifestyle, God will warn you a couple of times, but in the end He will let you do what you want, and you may lose your life. So be careful, don't push it."

"I wasn't going to," Daniel said. "I was just asking, out of curiosity."

"I will now tell you a story that I heard from an acquaintance of mine. About five or six years ago, this acquaintance had a teacher who was not really convinced about the existence of God. Once she had to prepare an assignment for school and chose to present the proof against the theory of evolution. She thought the teacher might be convinced by some serious arguments, so she included the arguments she considered to be the best and she left for school to present it."

"So? Was the teacher convinced?"

"The teacher died that morning in a car accident on her way to school. She never got to hear the arguments."

"I wonder why it happened this way?"

"We cannot know such a thing. But certainly, if it were profitable for her soul to see the presentation, she would have lived and would have seen it. Although we might be tempted to think that she wouldn't have accepted the arguments and this is why God took her sooner, so she wouldn't cause even more harm to her soul, I think, however, that we should refrain and not form an opinion about this. These are things only God knows."

"And didn't your acquaintance feel guilty?" Daniel asked. "Maybe if she hadn't chosen that topic for her homework, the teacher wouldn't have died."

"Our duty is to help anybody who we see needs help, and in this case, it seemed to her that the teacher needed some information. If it was the will of God for her to live longer without seeing those arguments, then that homework wouldn't have gotten to her or it wouldn't have even been written."

"I was going to ask you whether you were absolutely sure that the account is true, that that acquaintance of yours remembers exactly all the details from five or six years ago. But now I realize that the answer is irrelevant, because there were probably many such events in the past, too. I'm thinking about the preaching of Christianity by the 12 Apostles, and I'm wondering how many thousands or tens of thousands of people died just years, or days, or even hours before the apostles got to preach the Gospel to them?"

"I'm telling you one more time: Death is from God, it doesn't come by chance alone. Except suicides, of course. If it were beneficial for their souls to live a few more hours and to hear the Gospel, then they would have lived and would have heard it. We have to accept that God knows what He's doing and that He desires the good for each one of us. God is not interested that we live a long and happy life, healthy and wealthy. God is interested that we save our souls or, if we go to hell, at least that we sink as little as possible. This life is fleeting, but the other life is eternal, and it is obvious that the duration and the quality of the earthly life must be seen from the point of view of the after-life. Here's a comparison: A child has lived his whole life in illness and poverty, then he died at the age of 10 and he ended up in heaven for eternity. Someone else has lived 100 years rich and healthy, then he died and ended up in hell for eternity. Isn't it obvious that the one who lived for only 10 years in such harsh conditions is infinitely better off than the one who lived for 100 years in luxury?"

"If it is so, then it's better for us to be poor and ill…"

"Only God knows what is better for each one of us, and only He can decide which conditions are better for one to live in. If a poor man asks us for something to eat, we have the obligation to give it to him. We must not say that it is better for his soul that he goes hungry; only God can decide something like this, not us. If it is indeed better for his soul that he goes hungry, then God would have taken care that he met nobody who would feed him. In the same way, we must not get sick on purpose. If it is good for our soul that we get sick, then God will take care of this."

"OK, let's now get back to the problem of other religions," Daniel said. "Why does God allow them to exist?"

"You're not the only one who has asked such questions. For example, here's what questions Saint Anthony the Great was asking, who was one of the first monks and lived between the years 251 (probably) and 356:"

When the same Abba[86] Anthony thought about the depth of the judgements of God, he asked, 'Lord, how is it that some

---

[86] Abba: Greek word (ἀββᾶ in Ancient Greek) taken from Aramaic (אַבָּא) that means parent or father. Sometimes it is translated as 'elder' or 'starets.' The word 'starets' (ста́рец in Russian) is derived from the

die when they are young, while others drag on to extreme old age? Why are there those who are poor and those who are rich? Why do wicked men prosper and why are the just in need?' He heard a voice answering him, 'Anthony, keep your attention on yourself; these things are according to the judgement of God, and it is not to your advantage to know anything about them.'[87]

"What does it mean that it is not to our advantage to know?" Daniel asked.

"It means that we gain no spiritual profit if we get to know these things. Or maybe we can't even understand them. You see, modern man has come to believe that he can understand everything, but I don't think that it is so. I think that there are things that only God can understand, and even if He were to explain them to us, our minds simply couldn't handle them, and couldn't comprehend them. Imagine that you explain the Pythagorean theorem to a two-year-old child. Will he understand it? No. And the distance between God and us is certainly greater than the distance between us and a two-year-old child."

"You mean that we cannot understand why God also allows the existence of other religions, despite the fact that, as you say, they are the work of the devil?"

"Of course we cannot understand all the reasons. But we have some clues. Here's what God is telling us in the Bible, by means of a metaphor:"

«For the Kingdom of heaven is like a man traveling to a far country, who called his own servants and delivered his goods to them. And to one

---

Slavonic word 'starĭtsĭ' (old man), which is derived from 'starŭ.' In the Romanian language, the word 'starets' usually means the leader of a monastery, but in other languages the word also has other meanings. Thus, St. Paisios of Mount Athos is many times referred to as a 'starets,' although he was a hermit, he wasn't living in a monastery.

[87] *The Sayings of the Desert Fathers*, p. 2.

he gave five talents[88], to another two, and to another one, to each accord-ing to his own ability; and immediately he went on a journey. Then he who had received the five talents went and traded with them, and made another five talents. And likewise he who had received two gained two more also. But he who had received one went and dug in the ground, and hid his lord's money. After a long time the lord of those servants came and settled accounts with them. So he who had received five talents came and brought five other talents, saying, 'Lord, you delivered to me five talents; look, I have gained five more talents besides them.' His lord said to him, 'Well done, good and faithful servant; you were faithful over a few things, I will make you ruler over many things. Enter into the joy of your lord.' He also who had received two talents came and said, 'Lord, you delivered to me two talents; look, I have gained two more talents besides them.' His lord said to him, 'Well done, good and faithful serv-ant; you have been faithful over a few things, I will make you ruler over many things. Enter into the joy of your lord.' Then he who had received the one talent came and said, 'Lord, I knew you to be a hard man, reaping where you have not sown, and gathering where you have not scattered seed. And I was afraid, and went and hid your talent in the ground. Look, there you have what is yours.' But his lord answered and said to him, 'You wicked and lazy servant, you knew that I reap where I have not sown, and gather where I have not scattered seed. So you ought to have deposited my money with the bankers, and at my coming I would have received back my own with interest. So take the talent

---

[88] Talent (Latin: Talentum, from Ancient Greek: τάλαντον "scale, balance") was one of several ancient units of mass, a commercial weight, as well as corresponding units of value equivalent to these masses of a precious metal. It was approximately the mass of water required to fill an amphora. A Greek, or Attic talent, was 26 kilograms (57 lb), a Roman talent was 32.3 kilograms (71 lb), an Egyptian talent was 27 kilograms (60 lb), and a Babylonian talent was 30.3 kilograms (67 lb). Ancient Israel, and other Levantine countries, adopted the Bab-ylonian talent, but later revised the mass. The heavy common talent, used in New Testament times, was 58.9 kilograms (130 lb).

(https://en.wikipedia.org/wiki/Talent_(measurement))

However, it seems that besides the 'heavy common talent' men-tioned in the Wikipedia article quoted above, in Israel was also being used the 'light talent,' which weighed around 34 kilograms (about 75 lb).

from him, and give it to him who has ten talents. For to everyone who has, more will be given, and he will have abundance; but from him who does not have, even what he has will be taken away. And cast the unprofitable servant into the outer darkness. There will be weeping and gnashing of teeth.'»[89]

Michael went on:

"First a common sense observation. This is a parable, a metaphor. In no case should we understand that in order to make it into heaven we have to conduct business and multiply this worldly money. The talents mean the gifts that each one of us has received from God: the mind, the intelligence, the physical strength, the talent of writing or singing, the true religion. All these must be used to earn a place in heaven. They must be used for spiritual purposes, of course. If God gifted one with a beautiful voice, but he uses it to sing worldly songs, I don't think it will bring any profit for him. And as it can be seen from the previous parable, from each one God expects something depending on how many talents He has given him."

"And what about the one with only one talent? What was he supposed to do?"

"It can be seen from the very quote above that there was something very simple that was being asked of him for saving his soul, namely to give the money to the bankers. But he didn't do it. You should not understand that the Bible encourages usury, God forbid. It's only a metaphor. And here's another quote from the Bible, and this time it is not a metaphor:"

«Then He [Jesus] began to rebuke the cities in which most of His mighty works had been done, because they did not repent: "Woe to you, Chorazin! Woe to you, Bethsaida! For if the mighty works which were done in you had been done in Tyre and Sidon, they would have repented long ago in sackcloth and ashes. But I say to you, it will be more tolerable for Tyre and Sidon in the Day of Judgment than for you. And you, Capernaum, who are exalted to heaven, will be brought down to Hades; for if the mighty works which were done in you had been done in Sodom, it would have remained until this day. But I say to you that it shall be

---

[89] Matthew 25:14-30.

more tolerable for the land of Sodom in the Day of Judgment than for you."[90]

Michael went on:

"This is a quote that should give many people food for thought. Sodom was a city whose sins were so great that God destroyed it[91], but look, the souls of those who saw Christ's miracles and still haven't repented will end up in a worse state than the souls of those in Sodom."

"What does this have to do with those of other religions? Actually, what will happen to them? Will they go to hell? What will happen to a Muslim goat shepherd who has never heard of Christianity in his entire life? What about an African pygmy who lived a few hundred years before the Christian missionaries got there? Are you trying to say that the one with only one talent from the previous parable represents these people?"

"This is a very complicated problem and it is impossible to give a complete and clear answer. But *something* inside us should assure us that God will not be unjust to anybody, in anyway. First, there is nothing that happens by chance alone. One is not born by pure chance in the midst of a Christian or Muslim people, or in the midst of a tribe that worships the stars. All these are happening with the permission of God, for reasons that He alone knows and fully understands. You're saying that to you it seems unfair that some people were born in the midst of an African tribe and died without ever knowing Christianity."

"Yes, so it seems to me," Daniel said.

"But what makes you think that if they had known Christianity they would have accepted it and they would have saved their souls? This way, even if they end up in hell, there they'll be in a less bad state than those who have known Christianity, but have

---

[90] Matthew 11:20-24.

[91] Genesis 13:13, 19:24-25.

From the name of the city of Sodom was derived the name for (almost all) sexual sins against nature, sodomy. In other languages, two distinct sins were named thus, one after Sodom, the other after Gomorrah.

rejected it. If it had been profitable for their souls to find out about Christ, certainly God would have taken care of this. Let's not imagine that we know better than God what is better for some and for others. God loves everybody and He takes care of everybody. Even those who end up in hell, God tries to make them sink as little as possible, so that their suffering will be as reduced as possible. God would save everybody and would make all of them saints, but He cannot do this against their will."

"Is this the official explanation, God allows the existence of the wrong religions so that those people, who wouldn't have accepted Christianity anyway, would suffer less in hell?"

"It is not the official explanation, and it is not even a personal opinion, it is only a possibility that should make us think that, although we don't know all the answers, God, however, has a very good reason for everything He does or allows to happen."

"So all those of other religions are going to hell?" Daniel asked.

"I didn't say that. Here are two visions of heaven preserved in the tradition of the Orthodox Church:"

Once, when I was wandering through the caves of the Holy Mountain, I encountered an ascetic with whom I sat down and talked, and I asked him some things. Among other things, I asked him whether those who are not baptized will be saved. And he replied:

"I will tell you, my son, what once happened in Asia Minor. Some time ago a Turk was living there, who loved Christians a great deal. He helped the Church a great deal. He even helped to build a monastery. Wherever there was a poor man, he would go to help him. And although he was the best man – better even than the Christians –, he had not been baptized; he had not decided to get baptized. He kept postponing it for later.

But after a while he died. And he died before getting baptized. The abbot of the monastery was very sad because this man departed this life before being baptized. But Hasan [this was his name] was such a good man. He prayed for a long while and one day an angel came and said to him:

'Do you want to go and see where Hasan is?'

'Yes,' the abbot replied.

Then the angel took him and they went up, and up, and up... till they got to a very brightly lit church. Everything there was shining! Hymns could be heard from everywhere... The abbot was at a loss for words. When he entered this brightly lit church, he forgot about Hasan... he forgot about everything! He did not want to leave that place!... But after a while, the angel approached him and said:

'Let's go. Let's leave.'

As they were leaving, the angel asked the abbot:

'Did you see Hasan?'

Only then did the abbot remember about Hasan and said to him:

'No, I didn't see him.'

'You didn't see him?'

'No, I didn't see him.'

'Then let's go back, so you can see him.'

As soon as we got back, outside the Church, up on the stairs, opposite the light, there was a blind dog that sat there as though basking in the light. Then the angel told the abbot:

'This is Hasan's soul. He does not realize where he is, he sees nothing and he hears nothing... but he is not in the fire of hell. [']

And concluding, the Elder told me: 'The same also happens to the souls of the heretics. If they are good people, they don't go to the Gehenna of hell, but neither do they go to the delights of heaven.' "[92]

"And here's the second one, from the vision of Saint Nephon, about whom I have told you before:"

After them [those persecuted for Christ] entered [into heaven] a large number of idolaters who did not know the law of Christ, but by nature observed it by obeying their conscience. Many glowed like the sun because of their purity and goodness, and the Lord gave them Paradise and radiant crowns braided with roses and lilies. However, they were blind since they had been denied Holy Baptism. They could not see the glory of God at all, because Holy Baptism is the light and eye of the soul. That's why, he who does not receive it, even if he does an infinite amount of good, he certainly inherits the bliss of paradise and experiences something of its fragrance and sweetness, but he sees nothing.[93]

"Blind in heaven?" Daniel asked, surprised.

"This is probably about a metaphorical blindness," Michael said. "I don't think we have to imagine them walking around blindly in heaven, colliding with and stumbling upon the angels and the saints whom they cannot see."

"What does it mean that they 'did not know the law of Christ, but by nature observed it'?"

"Every man has his conscience, which tells him broadly what is good and what is wrong. Even one who has never heard of God in his entire life feels inside himself that it is wrong to steal,

---

[92] From the bimonthly edition of the Organization "Friends of the Saint Nicodemus Congregation," no. 38, June 2006. Also available online, in Romanian:

http://marturieathonita.ro/se-mantuiesc-oare-cei-care-nu-sunt-botezati/

And in Greek:

http://www.diakonima.gr/2014/10/28/σώζονται-άραγε-αυτοί-που-δεν-είναι-βαπ-2/

[93] *Stories, Sermons, and Prayers of St. Nephon: An Ascetic Bishop*, p. 67.

to kill, to harm other people. And the more one obeys this conscience, the more things it tells him."

"I see that there is a great difference between the state of
Hasan and the state of the idolater pagans."

"Yes, and this is not because Islam is worse than worshipping the sun and the moon. Hasan had known Christianity
firsthand and, although he was a good man, he refused to get
baptized. But the pagans had never heard of Christ. This makes
all the difference, I think. Thinking about the parable of the talents, the pagans seem to me like a man who only received one
hundredth of a talent, but look, they managed to earn another
hundredth during their lives."

"Why didn't Hasan live longer? Maybe he would have eventually accepted the baptism."

"If he had gotten baptized eventually, then he would have
lived longer. Death is from God, it never comes by chance
alone."

"If the suffering in hell is caused by spiritual diseases not
healed during our lives, why do those who find out about Christianity but reject it suffer a lot more?"

"Although it is hard to explain in human words, rejecting the
Truth revealed by God is an extremely serious spiritual disease.
When confronted with the divine revelation, man must choose
whether to accept it or to reject it. He can no longer go back and
forget that he found out about the existence of Christ; his soul is
forced to make a decision, to go toward good or toward evil. It is
possible to change this decision later in life; for example, a nonbeliever might become a believer, and also a believer might become a nonbeliever, but he can never go back before the moment
God offered him His Truth; his soul can never return to the state
of unknowing he was in before he found out about the existence
of Christ. You see, although the soul is subject to change in this
life, although it can change both for the better and for the worse,
there are also certain irreversible 'changes.' Before our discussion
you could have said that you could not believe in God because
the idea of hell seemed absurd to you. But look, God has offered

you, by means of a simple man like me, an answer to this problem. There's nothing else you can do now, you must choose between accepting and rejecting this answer. You will never be able to return to the state you were in this morning, when you weren't aware of this explanation. *Something* inside you is forced to make a decision."

"But why does God, Who you say is all-knowing, offer His revelation to those He knows very well that they will reject it? Look, in our own country, where the majority of people declare themselves to be Orthodox Christians, there are many atheists."

"A few minutes ago you were saying that it seemed unfair to you that some people die without finding out about Christianity. Now it probably seems unfair to you that some do find out, although they reject it."

"Yes, I know that I seem a little bit undecided," Daniel admitted.

"Remember the parable of the talents: *«And to one he gave five talents, to another two, and to another one, to each according to his own ability.»* Do you imagine that you know better than God how many talents each one should have received? Let's make an effort and accept that we are limited beings and that we cannot know better than God how many talents should have been offered to each one of us."

"Do you think God has chosen the best option for everyone? Do you think that those who reject the divine revelation would have been even more unhappy in hell if they hadn't known about it at all?"

"I don't know and I'm not even trying to find answers to these problems, because they are way beyond the human capacity of understanding. But I strongly believe one thing: God knows what He's doing, and He desires the good of every human being. For me this is enough. And in order to conclude this topic, here's what Father Seraphim Rose is saying:"

> In later years, when Fr. Seraphim [Rose] was asked about the Orthodox attitude toward non-Christian religions, he replied that each person is responsible for what he is given: "Once you *accept* the revelation [of the Gospel], then of

course you are much more responsible than anyone else. A person who accepts the revelation of God come in the flesh and then does not live according to it—he is much worse off than any pagan priest or the like."[94]

8.5. Aliens

"I have another question," Daniel said. "What do you think, are there any extraterrestrials? There are thousands of people who claim that they saw UFOs[95] and even some who claim that they met these beings from another world."

"The word 'extraterrestrial' means something or someone from outside our planet, something or someone that is not terrestrial, the same way as 'extraordinary' means, originally, something that is not ordinary. So this word has many meanings. The moon and the sun are two extraterrestrial celestial bodies. A meteorite is an extraterrestrial object, because it doesn't come from this planet, which we also call Terra. Even angels and demons can be called extraterrestrial beings, because they do not live on Terra, they are from outside this planet."

"I understand," Daniel said, "according to the definition, except our planet, the entire universe is extraterrestrial, as well as anything and anyone that might exist outside it. But I only had in mind those hypothetical, material beings, made up of atoms and molecules as we are, who are supposed to live on other planets in this universe."

"I see," Michael said. "Those aliens you're talking about have absolutely no place at all in the world created by God. Man is the

---

[94] Hieromonk Damascene [Christensen], *Father Seraphim Rose, His Life and Works*, 2nd edition, St. Herman of Alaska Brotherhood, Platina, California, 2005, p. 677; the quote is also found in Fr. Seraphim Rose, *God's Revelation to the Human Heart*, p. 42.

[95] UFO: Unidentified Flying Object, also known as "flying saucer."

only being who has a body and an immortal soul. Man is the crown of the material creation, not aliens. The material world got into this state because of the sin of Adam and Eve, not because of the sins of some aliens. The Son of God became incarnate and He was born with a human body, not with an alien body. The Son of God was crucified and resurrected in order to restore the human nature, not the alien nature."

"However, there are so many people who claim that they've seen them…"

"Of course they saw something, but I believe they only saw some demons or demonic visions, not material beings from other planets.[96] There are some very serious questions about these UFOs."

"Such as?"

"First, they never leave behind material remnants, like a small wheel or a piece of metal. The only material things left behind are burned vegetation and soil, but none of their components."

"Interesting, anything else?"

"Then, their movements seem to defy the laws of physics. Sometimes they change direction by 90 degrees in an instant, other times they accelerate from small speeds to enormous speeds in only a few hundredths of a second. Even if there were such powerful engines, classical matter would disintegrate if it were subjected to such accelerations. Movements like these are characteristic to spiritual beings, not to material ones."

"This is also interesting, anything else?"

"The third thing that has to be mentioned is the negative psychological effects they have on people, especially on those who say that they were 'abducted' by these aliens. Seeing such a being is a terrifying experience for any man. Here's how a victim named Whitley Strieber describes such an encounter:"

---

[96] This topic is also addressed by Fr. Seraphim Rose in his book *Orthodoxy and the Religion of the Future*, St. Herman of Alaska Brotherhood, Platina, California, 2004, chapter 6 (*Signs from Heaven*).

> I felt an absolutely indescribable sense of menace. It was hell on earth to be there and yet I couldn't move, couldn't cry out, and couldn't get away. I lay as still as death, suffering inner agonies. Whatever was there seemed so monstrously ugly, so filthy and dark and sinister. [...] I still remember that thing crouching there, so terribly ugly, its arms and legs like limbs of a great insect, its eyes glaring at me.[97]

"It seems horrifying just to hear the account," Daniel said.

"This man also says that these beings have a specific odor, of sulfur or brimstone. The tradition of the Church tells us that it is the demonic visions that bring about this smell. He also writes:"

> Increasingly I felt as if I were entering a struggle that might be a struggle for my soul, my essence, or whatever part of me might have reference to the eternal... It was clear that the soul was very much at issue. People [have] experienced feeling as if their souls were being dragged from their bodies. More than one person had seen the visitors in the context of near-death experience.[98]

Michael went on:

"It is truly shocking that this man, Whitley Strieber, refuses to realize whom he's dealing with. Despite all these terrifying experiences, he calls them 'visitors' and writes in some other places that it is up to us to try to establish contact with them, and that this could lead to our spiritual development. Saint Ignatius Brianchaninov, a Russian bishop who lived between the years 1807 and 1867, warns us:"

> The perception of spirits with the eyes of sense always brings harm, sometimes greater and sometimes less, to men who do not have spiritual perception. Here on earth images of truth are mixed together with images of falsehood (St. Isaac the

---

[97] Whitley Strieber, *Transformation: The Breakthrough*, William Morrow & Co, 1988.

[98] Ibid.

Syrian, Homily 2), as in a land in which good is mixed together with evil, as in the land of banishment of fallen angels and fallen men.

One who perceives spirits sensuously can easily be deceived to his own harm and perdition. If, on perceiving spirits, he shows trust or credulity toward them, he will unfailingly be deceived, he will unfailingly be attracted, he will unfailingly be sealed with the seal of deception, not understandable to the inexperienced, the seal of a frightful injury to his spirit; and further, the possibility of correction and salvation is often lost. This has happened with many, very many. It has happened not only with pagans, whose priests were for the most part in open communion with demons; it has happened not only with many Christians who do not know the mysteries of Christianity and out of some circumstance or other have entered into communion with spirits; it has happened with many strugglers and monks who have perceived spirits sensuously without acquiring spiritual perception of them.[99]

"This is horrifying," Daniel said, "but why does God allow the devil to do something like this?"

"The sins of men give the devil the right to do this. Two American Protestant authors[100] have studied many cases of people who claimed to have been 'abducted' by aliens and they discovered an interesting thing. All those studied had been involved more or less in occult activities, that is, spiritism, witchcraft, talking with the dead, channeling, and others like these. These are extremely serious sins, strictly forbidden by the Church, both in the Old and New Testament. Those who do these things don't realize that they are actually talking with demons, and not with the spirits of the departed or of 'aliens.' The experiences of those 'abducted' by aliens are nothing else than cases of demonic possession, which are brought about by their sins."

---

[99] Bishop Ignatius Brianchaninov, *Collected Works*, vol. 3, Tuzov ed., St. Petersburg, 1883; quoted in Hieromonk Seraphim Rose, *The Soul After Death*, St. Herman of Alaska Brotherhood, 2004, p. 59.

[100] David Lewis, Robert Shreckhise, *UFO: End-Time Delusion*, New Leaf Press, 1991 (reprinted in 2001).

"What about the one you just mentioned, Whitley Strieber?"

"Yes, Whitley Strieber is known as an author of horror stories and he used to collaborate on various occasions with the Gurdjieff Foundation, an organization with occult practices.[101] Such sins give the devil various rights on the one who commits them. Here's an example of a dialogue between victim and 'aliens,' that is, demons:"

'You have no right to do this to me. I am a human being.'

'We do have a right!'[102]

"Or, in another case:"

He tried to resist but was told that the 'alien' had the right to enter without his permission.[103]

Michael went on:

"Of course, the devil lies and he could have said that he had the right without actually having it, but if he hadn't had the right, then obviously he couldn't have done anything to those poor victims. And what makes the situation even sadder is that some of them continue to believe that they had to deal with 'aliens' and not with fallen angels, that is, demons."

"Does the devil show himself to man only as a consequence of the man's sins? There were cases in which the UFOs were seen by thousands of people; have they all been involved in occult activities?"

"Not all those who saw UFOs, only those who ended up being 'abducted,' that is, possessed. There's a difference. Anyone can have demonic visions or dreams, even virtuous people. Many times the devil shows himself as an angel or as a saint, in order to deceive the believer, as the Bible also warns us:"

«And no wonder! For Satan himself transforms himself into an angel of light. Therefore it is no great thing if his ministers also transform

---

[101] https://en.wikipedia.org/wiki/Whitley_Strieber
[102] D. Lewis, R. Shreckhise, *UFO: End-Time Delusion.*
[103] Ibid.

themselves into ministers of righteousness, whose end will be according to their works.»[104]

"And how can you tell the difference?" Daniel asked.

"Usually an ordinary man cannot tell the difference, which is why the Church teaches us to ignore dreams and visions, because we lack the capability to discern which are from God and which are from the devil."

"If we cannot tell them apart, why does God still send them to us?"

"Usually it's not God Who sends them, but the devil. Sometimes the devil appears to a man in his dream and begins to tell him various things, even 'prophecies' that are later fulfilled, in order to gain his trust. Thus he makes the man feel that he is special, that he was chosen by God to have visions. In other words, the devil targets that inner *something* that is sick with self-love, a serious spiritual disease. And if the man starts to believe him, his spiritual destruction follows soon. This is how false prophets are made, false visionaries, and so on. 'You are our chosen one,' the demons said to Whitley Strieber, as he himself confesses. Many times, *something* inside us is attracted by these lies. However, the Church teaches us exactly the opposite, namely that we all should consider ourselves to be sinners, and in no case special or 'chosen.'"

"Can the devil predict the future?"

"The devil cannot see the future the same way God sees it. But he can calculate various things, the same way we calculate the time the sun rises every day, only he can make way better calculations than ours, and thus he sometimes gives the impression that he can predict the future. Besides this, the devil knows, for example, what is now being discussed in a certain closed room in the building in front of us, and he can give this information to a man whose trust he has gained, and thus that man comes to know things impossible to know for an ordinary mortal, and he comes to be known as a visionary and as a man with paranormal powers."

---

[104] 2 Corinthians 11:14-15.

"And who can tell a demonic vision from a divine one?"

"There are certain criteria, but they can only be applied by certain people, namely by those who are close to sainthood. But nowadays it is very difficult, almost impossible to find such people. But here's a quote about dreams and visions from Saints Barsanuphius and John, who lived during the 6th century, in Palestine:"

Question: Tell me, Master, how can the devil dare in a vision or a fantasy during sleep to show the Master Christ or Holy Communion?

[Saint Barsanuphius' answer:]

Answer: He cannot show the Master Christ Himself, nor Holy Communion, but he lies and presents the image of some man and simple bread; but the holy Cross he cannot show, for he does not find means of depicting it in another form. Inasmuch as we know the true sign and image of the Cross, the devil does not dare to use it (for our deception); for on the Cross his power was destroyed, and by the Cross a fatal wound was given him. The Master Christ we cannot recognize by the flesh, which is why the devil tries to convince us by lying that it is He, so that having believed the deception as if it were truth, we might perish. And thus, when you see in a dream the image of the Cross, know that this dream is true and from God; but strive to receive an interpretation of its significance from the Saints, and do not believe your own idea. May the Lord enlighten the thoughts of your mind, O brother, so that you might escape every deception of the enemy.[105]

"Do you get the idea?" Michael asked. "Even if the dream is from God, the way we interpret it could be wrong. This is one more reason to not believe in dreams. The same thing is true for

---

[105] Sts. Barsanuphius and John *Guidance toward Spiritual Life* (Answers to the Questions of Disciples), St. Herman of Alaska Brotherhood, Platina, California, 2002, p. 105.

The note in [brackets] is taken from the Romanian translation.

the Bible; although it is inspired by God, our interpretation is not always correct."

"What are these aliens actually up to?" Daniel asked.

"The devil only has one goal, namely to take as many souls as possible with him to hell. The devil is a good example of an extreme spiritual disease. He is full of hatred and malice and he wants to make us like him, too. But he can't do it, unless we allow him to, unless we let him deceive us. In order to achieve his goal, the devil uses various means, and one of them is to show himself as a UFO or as an alien. He tries, I think, to somehow take the place of God, to give some people the illusion that we were created by aliens, not by God."

"Do you think that, at some point, some UFOs will come down from the sky, and these demons will emerge from them and they'll say that it was them who created us?"

"I can't know for sure, but it is very possible; the devil seems to be preparing this for a long time."

"How's that?"

"Have you ever heard of the 'ancient aliens'? This is a theory that claims that in the past we were visited by beings from other planets, who have influenced us in various ways, and who were called 'gods' by the ancient civilizations."

"Ah, I think I've heard this before," Daniel said.

"This is how they explain some unusual archaeological finds. For example, as some people say, some ancient civilizations from Central and South America built 'airports' and pyramids for the 'gods.' In other places, cave paintings were found that are hundreds or even thousands of years old, and which seem to represent humanoid beings wearing astronaut suits or helmets. In Egypt, a very old wooden sculpture was found, which seems to resemble an airplane, and many other such things. Obviously, those drawings depicting humanoids with helmets are not very clear, and they can also be interpreted as representing auras or halos."

"And you believe that the devil has known for thousands of years that people will some day dream about spaceships and interplanetary voyages, and he thus paved the way for showing himself to them as an alien? Was it for this reason that he also showed himself to those ancient people as an astronaut?"

"The devil, who used to be an angel of God, knows the material world much better than we do. So he has known for a long time about up to which point science and technology can possibly advance, not because he could see into the future, but only because he makes suppositions and various calculations, which sometimes prove to be correct, and other times not."

"It seems to me like a clear case in which our inner *something* will make a decision, will incline to believe one version or another, without having the slightest scientific argument."

"Of course, there is no way to subject the 'aliens' to laboratory tests and see what their nature is. You cannot do this either to those who appear in the present, or to those who appeared in the past."

"You know," Daniel said, "in a way I envy those people who lived in ancient times, or in the Middle Ages. They didn't have these problems, they had never heard of aliens, or of the Big Bang, or of evolution; their inner *something* didn't have to make such difficult choices. Why is it so complicated for us?"

"I don't know, maybe because of our pride, maybe because we see ourselves as being so smart, and so well-informed when compared to our ancestors. Maybe because we put our trust in ourselves, in our intellectual powers, and not in God, as the Church teaches us. Maybe if we humbled ourselves a little, God would help us and it wouldn't seem that hard anymore... Let us remember the words of the Lord:"

> «In that hour Jesus rejoiced in the Spirit and said, "I thank You, Father, Lord of heaven and earth, that You have hidden these things from the wise and prudent and revealed them to babes. Even so, Father, for so it seemed good in Your sight. [..."]»[106]

"You see?" Michael said. "Let us also try to be like babes, and not like the wise ones who Christ is talking about, and maybe God will reveal to us what we need to know."

---

[106] Luke 10:21.

"I still can't help wondering, if there is a God, why isn't He more visible? Why doesn't He help us more with such decisions? Why doesn't He appear and talk to us directly, face to face, saying, for example, 'Do this!' or 'Don't do that!' or 'This is the right religion!'?"

"Do you remember what Christ said, *«Blessed are those who have not seen and yet have believed.»*? Maybe not all of us were that blessed, maybe some of us truly believed in divine creation only after seeing the arguments against the theories of the Big Bang and evolution. Well, I don't have a clear and definitive answer for what you have just asked, but what if this is another chance for us to be blessed, as Jesus said? What if God, in His immeasurable mercy and goodness, is giving us another opportunity to be blessed, if we accept purely by faith alone, without having any kind of tangible proof, that it is better for our souls to make a decision with only these arguments, which may seem to be few and incomplete to you, but which are way more than enough for others?"

"Does this have anything to do with the parable of the talents?"

"I believe it has. In my opinion, God already is very visible, and asking that He is even more visible, that He appears and talks to us face to face, is like we were asking for 100 talents. But if God does this, then I wonder, are we going to produce 100 more talents in return? Therefore I wonder again, is it not better that we're satisfied with the talents that we already have?"

Michael stopped talking for a few seconds, then got back to the initial topic:

"And then there is another pretty serious question that has to be asked about these 'ancient visitors.'"

"What question?" Daniel asked.

"Many of these alleged encounters with aliens took place between the 10th and 15th centuries, before the European colonists came to America. Why did these 'aliens,' so intelligent and advanced, go to such savage peoples, who were often making human sacrifices and were practicing cannibalism?[107] Why haven't they contacted the Europeans, who, despite their shortcomings at that time, probably seemed like little angels compared to the savage populations of South and Central America? Was it that these 'aliens' were the ones who were asking for the human sacrifices? The Bible tells us clearly that these 'gods' are actually demons:"

«For all the gods of the nations are demons»[108]

«Rather, that the things which the Gentiles sacrifice they sacrifice to demons and not to God»[109]

"And there's one more clue to make us think that the devil is somehow preparing to lie to us and tell us that it was the aliens who created us."

"What clue?" Daniel asked.

"Almost all the observed 'aliens' have a humanoid shape. That is, they have two hands, two legs, a head, two eyes, and a mouth. Why do they look so much like us? If they emerged and evolved on another planet, as the advocates of evolution suggest, how is it possible for them to resemble us so much? Why don't they look like an octopus, or like a snail?"

"Yes, this is an interesting observation. For one who believes in aliens, the fact that they look like us will certainly make him think that there is a connection between us and them... And when do you think the devil will do this? When will he attempt this global delusion?"

"He can only do it when God will let him do it, because of the sins of men. It could happen tomorrow, in a thousand years, or never. Only God truly knows the future."

---

[107] The Spanish and Portuguese conquistadors have left us many written accounts about these peoples. One can see, for example, Bernal Díaz del Castillo, *The True History of The Conquest of New Spain*, Hackett Publishing Company, 2012.

[108] Psalms 95:5.

[109] 1 Corinthians 10:20.

8.6. The Eastern Orthodox Church

Michael stopped talking. Daniel waited for a few moments, then said:

"I wanted to ask you a while ago, but I kept postponing it. Who are these 'saints' from whom you keep reading quotes to me? Why can they tell divine dreams and visions from demonic ones, and why can't we? I know that the Orthodox Church and the Roman Catholic one believe in saints, but Protestants say that this is a mistake. Why do you trust their sayings, and why do you think that they cannot be deceived by the devil? Why don't you rely on the Bible alone, which you say is the main book of Christianity? Why do you guys use other books, too?"

"Let's take it step by step. *Something* inside me strongly believes that Christianity is the true religion. My inner *something* was irresistibly attracted by Jesus Christ, and I believed in Him and in His words. Here are some of those words:"

> *«Most assuredly, I say to you, he who believes in Me, the works that I do he will do also; and greater works than these he will do, because I go to My Father.»*[110]

> *« ["] He who believes in Me, as the Scripture has said, out of his heart will flow rivers of living water." But this He spoke concerning the Spirit, whom those believing in Him would receive; for the Holy Spirit was not yet given, because Jesus was not yet glorified.»*[111]

> *«[O]n this rock I will build My church, and the gates of Hades shall not prevail against it.»*[112]

Michael went on:

"In these quotes, Jesus Christ tells us two very important things. First, the Lord says that those who will believe in Him will also work miracles, and even that *«out of his heart will flow rivers of living water.»* The New Testament mentions many prophecies and

---

[110] John 14:12.
[111] John 7:38-39.
[112] Matthew 16:18.

miracles worked by the 12 Apostles, and not only by them, but also by many Christians of those times. So it is not at all unusual that some Christians, who have gotten to high spiritual levels, can work miracles, can heal the sick, can raise the dead, or can see into the future. But they can only do all these things with the help of God, of course; no one can do something like this by his own means. Here are two examples from the Bible, which we say was written through divine inspiration. Two of the four Evangelists were not from among the 12 Apostles, and still, they wrote Gospels inspired by God. So behold, these gifts were given not only to the apostles, but also to other people."

"And the second important thing?"

"The second important thing said by Christ is that He will establish *His Church*, which cannot be defeated by the devil. The Church is not a human organization. The Church is a divine-human organism, and there's only one such organism; there's no such thing as two Churches, let alone ten or a hundred. The head of the Church is Jesus Christ, and all believers are members, or organs, as the New Testament also says. It is true that not all those who declare themselves to be Christians are indeed Christians. Nowadays it is even possible that only a small minority of them are indeed so, and for this reason maybe just a small percentage of the 'official' members of the Church succeed in saving their souls. But it is not our business to judge these things."

"And is the Church being based on the Bible?" Daniel asked.

"No, no way. The Bible is indeed considered to be the most important Christian book and it is also called the Holy Scripture. It is the only book that we believe contains no errors of any kind, with the possible exception of a few translation shortcomings. But in no case do we say that the Bible is the base of the Church. Although you said you were a nonbeliever, you seem to be strongly influenced by Protestant theology."

"So what is the Bible for you?"

"The Savior wrote no books during His earthly life. The Bible only mentions that He once wrote something in the sand.[113]

---

[113] John 8:6.

When the Savior ascended to heaven, He left behind no books with His teachings. But He did leave behind a group of people who, ten days later, at the descent of the Holy Spirit, were to become His Church. That day, ten days after the Ascension, God did not send from heaven a book, nor did He dictate a book to anyone, as the Muslims claim that it was dictated to Muhammad by an angel. That day God sent the Holy Spirit, the third person of the Holy Trinity, Who taught the first believers everything they needed to know, as Christ had said.[114] Under the influence of this Holy Spirit, the New Testament was written. Do you understand the difference? It was the Church who produced the Bible, and not the other way around. The Bible is simply a witness of the work of God in the history of mankind. The Protestants are right to say that the Bible is the most important book, but they use it in a wrong way. For 15 centuries nobody thought about using the Bible the way they use it, that is, to ignore the entire tradition of the Church, to start only from the Bible and to produce a new 'church' based on their interpretation. No wonder this method has produced dozens of Protestant and Neo-Protestant 'churches.' But the Lord has only talked about a single Church."

"And the writings of those saints are also divine revelations, as the Bible is?"

"No other writing has the same importance as the Bible. However, we also read and follow the teachings of the saints, because they were closer to God than we are, and for this reason they saw spiritual matters much better then we see them. And many of them certainly had divine revelations, too, but we still don't ascribe to their writings the same value as we ascribe to the Bible."

"How do you know that all those whom you call saints are indeed saints?"

"Christ has said that His Church, led by the Holy Spirit, will never fall. Therefore, we believe that the Church cannot be wrong in this regard and can only consider someone a saint who really is so. However, nowadays saints are very rare."

---

[114] John 14:26.

"And how do you recognize a saint?" Daniel asked.

"Officially, the Holy Synod of a local Orthodox Church declares one to be a saint, but this act is only a formality, a recognition of the fact that God has counted that person with the saints. The Holy Synod does not produce saints, it only recognizes them. However, many times the multitude of believers becomes convinced of one's sainthood long before it is recognized by the Holy Synod. A recent example is Saint Paisios of Mount Athos. Millions of Orthodox Christians from around the world were considering him to be a saint immediately after his death in 1994, but the official recognition only took place in 2015. And one more thing, one can be officially recognized as a saint only after the end of his earthly life."

8.6.1. About Humility

"Are there also some criteria for recognizing a saint, so the false saints, the ones deceived by the devil, whom you have mentioned before, won't be mistaken for real saints? I think that a saint has to be a good Christian, longsuffering, forgiving, generous to the poor. Is there anything else?"

"Yes, there is something else. The supreme virtue, without which no one can be saved, and which every saint must have more than an ordinary believer, is humility. The more one advances on the spiritual path, the more humble he becomes and sees himself more sinful and insignificant."

"How's that?" Daniel asked.

"Abba Dorotheus, a saint from 6th century Palestine, explains it to us:"

> I remember once we were speaking about humiliation and one of the great lights of Gaza[115], hearing us say, "The nearer a man is to God the more he sees himself to be a sinner," was astonished, and said, "How is this possible?" He did not know, and wanted to know the answer. I said to him "Master

---

[115] In other translations: "a nobleman from Gaza."

of the First Rank, tell me, how do you regard yourself in respect to the other citizens here?" And he said, "I regard myself as great, and first among the citizens." I said then, "If you went away to Caesarea[116], how would you regard yourself then?" "I would value myself somewhat less than the great folk there." So I said, "If you went away to Antioch[117], what then?" And he replied, "I would regard myself as one of the common people." I said, "And if you went from the city of Caesarea into the presence of the Emperor[118], what would you think of yourself then?" He replied, "I should think of myself as just one of the poor." Then I said to him, "There you are! In the same way, the saints, the nearer they approach to God, the more they see themselves as sinners!" Abraham, when he saw God, called himself *«dust and ashes.»*[119] And Isaiah, said, *«Unhappy am I, for my lips are unclean.»*[120] [...] [121]

"Look," Michael said, "we see in the history of the Church that all saints were very humble, and they saw themselves as very sinful. We find in their writings phrases like 'me the great sinner,' 'I did nothing good in my life,' 'I am the most sinful of all people,' and so on. We also have a good example right in the Bible, Saint Paul the Apostle says:"

---

[116] Caesarea: former ancient city, between the current cities of Tel Aviv and Haifa in Israel.

[117] Antioch: one of the great ancient cities. It belonged to the Roman province of Syria, and its ruins are located near the city of Antakya in Turkey.

[118] In other translations: 'if you went away! to the city of Constantine' or 'to Constantinople.' Nowadays the city is called Istanbul and it belongs to Turkey.

[119] Genesis 18:27.

[120] The complete biblical passage is translated into English thus:

«I said, "Woe is me, because I am pierced to the heart, for being a man and having unclean lips, I dwell in the midst of a people with unclean lips; for I saw the King, the Lord of hosts, with my eyes!"» (Isaiah 6:5).

[121] St. Dorotheus (of Gaza), *Discourses and Sayings*, Cistercian Publications, 1977, pp. 98-99.

«This is a faithful saying and worthy of all acceptance, that Christ Jesus came into the world to save sinners, of whom I am chief.»[122]

«For I am the least of the apostles, who am not worthy to be called an apostle [...] .»[123]

Michael went on:

"This is not a false modesty, but it is the result of getting closer to God. This closeness causes the opening, little by little, of the spiritual eyes, through which the believer begins to see himself as he truly is, namely very sinful when compared to the holiness of God. Here's an account about the death of Saint Sisoes, one of the great saints of the Egyptian desert, who lived during the 4th and 5th centuries after Christ:"

> It was said of Abba Sisoes that when he was at the point of death, while the Fathers were sitting beside him, his face shone like the sun. He said to them, "Look, Abba Anthony is coming." A little later he said, "Look, the choir of prophets is coming." Again his countenance shone with brightness and he said, "Look, the choir of apostles is coming." His countenance increased in brightness and lo, he spoke with someone. Then the old men asked him, "With whom are you speaking, Father?" He said, "Look, the angels are coming to fetch me, and I am begging them to let me do a little penance."[124] The old man said to him, "You have no need to do penance, Father."[125] But the old man [Abba Sisoes] said to them, "Truly, I do not think I have even made a beginning yet." Now they all knew that he was perfect. Once more his countenance suddenly became like the sun and they were all filled with fear. He said to them, "Look, the Lord is

---

[122] 1 Timothy 1:15.
[123] 1 Corinthians 15:9.
[124] In other translations: "to let me repent for a little while."
[125] In other translations: "you don't need to repent, Father."

coming and He's saying, 'Bring Me the vessel from the desert.' " Then there was as a flash of lightening and all the house[126] was filled with a sweet odour.[127]

"I understand, but it still seems amazing to me," Daniel said. "It is hard to comprehend how it is possible for some people who had gotten to such a level that God was speaking through them to see themselves as so insignificant."

"If you don't mind, I will dare to make an analogy, too. Think about a pipe through which clean water flows. The pipe has no merit for its existence, because it didn't manufacture itself, it was manufactured by others. The pipe has no merit for the place it is located in, because somebody else installed it there. The pipe has no merit for the water that flows through it, because the water is coming from other sources. And eventually, if the pipe gets rusty and alters the quality of the water, it will be immediately replaced by another pipe. This is kind of how I think a saint sees himself. He has no merit for his own existence, because it was God Who created him. He sees no merit of his own for the place he is in or for the position in the hierarchy of the Church that he occupies, because it was God Who put him there. He sees no merit of his own for his good deeds, because it was God Who gave him the means to accomplish them, and it was his duty to do good deeds, anyway.[128] He sees no merit of his own for the teaching he is offering to the people, because it was God Who gave him the mind, the faith, and the ability to talk or write. And eventually, if he strays from the right path, God can replace him anytime with someone else. It is for these reasons that I think the saints saw themselves as so insignificant, and of course this is how we should see ourselves, too, and the fact that we usually don't see ourselves this way is, I think, proof that shows us how far away we are from sainthood. Man's only merit, I think, is the choice to do the will of God. Even our free will, we have it as a

---

[126] In other manuscripts: "the place." (According to a note in the *Egyptian Paterikon* (in Romanian).)

[127] *The Sayings of the Desert Fathers*, pp. 214-215.

[128] Luke 17:10.

gift from God. Only the way we use it, that is, the choices we make with it, we can say are ours. Even many times it seems to us that we're fighting with all our strength to do the will of God, however, after a careful analysis we notice that even this 'strength,' we have it from God, too."

"So everything that we have is a gift from God?"

"Yes, of course. And if we do good deeds, we should not become proud because of this. First, we do them with the means provided by God. Second, it is our duty to do them, as the Lord Himself told us[129], and as I quoted recently from Saint John Chrysostom. This is why God gave us the talents and the means that He gave us, to do good deeds with them and to save our souls. And with a careful analysis, I think we'll notice that we haven't really met the expectations, therefore there is nothing to be proud of. This is humility, as I understand it. This is approximately what the well-known Father Justin Pârvu was also saying:"

Humility is a correct self-assessment of the dimension of man in this universe.[130]

"What I have told you now is just an analogy, an imperfect one, of course. The pipe has no will of its own, it can neither accept, nor resist if we want to install it somewhere. But we can, either accept, or refuse God."

"I suppose that the opposite of humility is pride," Daniel said.

"Yes, the opposite of humility is pride, the sin of the devil. Pride has many 'branches,' like vanity, vainglory, and many others. I like what Blaise Pascal was saying on this topic:"

Vanity is so deeply rooted in man's heart, that a soldier, a criminal, a cook, or a porter will boast and expect to have admirers. And even philosophers want them; and even those who write against this will themselves want to enjoy the glory of having written well; and those who read this want the

---

[129] Luke 17:10.

[130] Grația Lungu Constantineanu, *Fr. Justin Pârvu* (in Romanian), second edition (revised and appended), Iași, 2007, p. 553.

glory of having read those critics; and perhaps I who write this have the same desire; and perhaps also those who will read it.[131]

"So nice of him," Daniel said, "he admits that he's suffering from the same problem, too."

"We're all suffering from it, more or less, but most of us don't want to admit it."

8.6.2. About Icons

"Tell me please," Daniel said, "why do you, the Orthodox, like the Roman Catholics, use icons? Isn't this idolatry, isn't it written in the Bible that *«You shall not make for yourself a carved image»*[132]?"

"That Old Testament commandment was referring to idols, not to icons, as the Protestants are interpreting it. A few verses further we read:"

> *«Then you shall make two cherubim of gold; of hammered work you shall make them at the two ends of the mercy seat.»*[133]

"Is the cherubim a *«carved image»*?" Michael asked. "And in some other place we find this text:"

> *«In the most holy place he made two wooden cherubim and overlaid them with gold.»*[134]

"There, Solomon placed in the House of the Lord two cherubim. *«Carved image»*? Obviously not. Then we have to see exactly what an icon is. The Greek word *eikōn (εἰκών)* means 'image.' In the Old Testament there were no icons, because God had not shown Himself to the people in the flesh, so there was nothing

[131] Blaise Pascal, *Pensées*; quoted in Archim. Seraphim Alexiev, *The spiritual life of the Orthodox Christian* (in Romanian), Predania Press, Bucharest, 2006, pp. 191-192.

[132] Exodus 20:4 (NKJV).

[133] Exodus 25:18.

[134] 2 Chronicles 3:10.

believers could paint. Besides, Old Testament saints had not entered heaven yet, because they had to wait for Christ's Resurrection. In the New Testament, however, God was incarnate from the Virgin Mary, and thus it became possible for us to paint His human image. The same goes for the Mother of God and for all the saints, we can paint them because they had bodies, and those bodies will rise at the Judgment Day in order to be reunited with the immortal souls."

"What about the icons that depict angels?" Daniel asked. "Do the angels have bodies, too?"

"The angels are spiritual beings, but they have shown themselves to people in visible form, like they had a human body, although they don't, and for this reason they can be painted in icons. In the Old Testament, too, there were representations of some angels in the House of the Lord, that is, in the Temple in Jerusalem."

"But what about the icons of the Holy Trinity, in which both God the Father and God the Holy Spirit are represented?"

"First of all, God the Father and God the Holy Spirit cannot be truly painted, because They have not taken on a human body as did God the Son, Whose human nature the painters are representing in icons. But both the Father and the Holy Spirit have shown Themselves to people in the form of symbols. At the Baptism of the Lord, the Holy Spirit showed Himself as a dove, but this does not mean the Holy Spirit took on the body of a dove, God forbid; it's just a symbol. In the Book of Revelation we see that Jesus Christ is called the Lion and at some point He shows Himself to the writer of that book as a Lamb, but this does not mean that He also took on the body of a lion or of a lamb, the same way He took on the body of a man; these are just symbols."

"I see, so you mean that the icons of the Holy Trinity only represent some symbols?"

"There are two categories of icons that are called icons of the Holy Trinity. The first category includes the icon painted by Saint Andrew Rublev in the 15th century, most likely between the years 1408 and 1427, and other icons that reproduce or imitate it. In that icon, the meeting of the patriarch Abraham with God by the oak of Mamre is represented, and the icon does not claim that it truly represents the Holy Trinity, but just a historical event, related in the Bible.[135] This icon is accepted by the entire Orthodox Christian world, although some claim that its correct name is not 'Holy Trinity,' but 'The Hospitality of Abraham.' Here's what Saint John of Damascus, a great defender of the icons, says about that vision of Abraham:"

> Abraham did not see the Nature of God, for no one has seen God at any time, but an icon of God, and falling down he venerated it.[136]

"I see," Daniel said, "so it's just the representation of a historical event that really took place. But I remember that I also saw icons of the Holy Trinity in which God the Father is represented as a bearded old man. I take it that these belong to the second category?"

"Yes, these icons are somewhat more controversial and are not fully accepted in the entire Orthodox Christian world. In the years 1666 and 1667, a Church Synod held in Moscow decided that such representations should be forbidden, because no mortal man has ever seen God the Father. It was also decided that the Holy Spirit could be represented as a dove only in the icon of the Baptism of the Lord, because it was only then that He showed Himself as a dove.[137] But other theologians say that those icons are just a symbol, and that no one claims the absurdity that God the Father is an old man with a white beard. They mention a fragment from the book of Daniel:"

---

[135] Genesis 18:1-16. This is the beginning of the account:
«Then God appeared to him at the oak of Mamre, as he was sitting in the tent door during the noon hour. So he lifted his eyes and looked, and behold, three men stood before him; and when he saw them, he ran from the tent door to meet them, and bowed himself to the ground, [...] [.]»
[136] St. John of Damascus, *On Holy Images*.
[137] Leonid Ouspensky, Vladimir Lossky, *The Meaning of Icons*, revised SVS Press edition, St. Vladimir's Seminary Press, Crestwood, New York, 1999, pp. 201-202.

«I continued to watch until thrones were put in place, and the Ancient of Days enthroned Himself. His clothing was white as snow, and the hair of His head was like pure wool. His throne was a fiery flame, and its wheels a burning fire. A river of fire flowed from before Him. Thousands and thousands ministered to Him, and countless thousands stood before Him. The court was in session, and the books were opened.»

[...]

«I continued to observe the vision in the night, and behold, One like the Son of Man was coming with the clouds of heaven, until He came to the Ancient of Days and approached Him.»[138]

"I think it is now obvious from this quote," Michael said, "that those theologians claim that the *«Ancient of Days»* seen by the prophet Daniel is a symbol of God the Father, and that those icons are only representing a symbol and nothing more."

"What about statues?"

"This is a different issue. Here's what we found written in a footnote from a treatise on Orthodox Theology, a footnote that belongs, most likely, to Father Seraphim Rose, the translator and the editor of the first English edition of that treatise:"

> This distinction between the "worship" of God and the "reverence" or "veneration" shown for icons was set forth first by St. John Damascene in his treatises on the icons. See his *On the Divine Images*, translated by David Anderson (Crestwood, N.Y.: St. Vladimir's Seminary Press, 1980), pp. 82-88, and the introduction, pp. 10-11.

> Nothing is said in the Orthodox canons regarding the veneration of statues, such as came to be used in the religious art of the West in the Middle Ages and later centuries. However, the virtually universal tradition of the Orthodox Church of both East and West in the early centuries, and of the Eastern Church in later centuries, has been to allow as religious art two-dimensional depictions and bas-reliefs, but not statues in the round. The reason for this seems to lie in the realism that is inevitable in three-dimensional depictions, making

---

[138] Daniel 7:9-13.

them suitable for representing the things of this world of earth (for example, the statues of emperors), but not those of the heavenly world into which our earthly thinking and realism cannot penetrate. Two-dimensional icons, on the other hand, are like "windows to heaven" which are much more capable of raising the mind and heart to heavenly realities.[139]

8.6.3. Worship and Veneration

"I see," Daniel said. "One more question on this topic: Why do you, the Orthodox, like the Roman Catholics, worship the saints and the icons? The Protestants say that this is idolatry."

"This is a linguistic problem," Michael said. "It is regrettable, I think, that Romanian-speaking people often use the same verb, *to worship*, both for expressing the worship of God, and for expressing the honoring of the saints. But even from the first centuries of Christianity, the Greek and Latin speaking Church has used different verbs. The Greek word *latreia (λατρεία)* and the derived Latin word *latria* were being used to designate the worship of God and God alone. From this word is derived the word idolatry, which means worshipping idols. And for 'worshipping' the saints, the Church used the Greek word *douleia (δουλεία)*, and in Latin the words *veneratio* and *dulia*. In my opinion, a more correct translation of the term *dulia* would be *veneration* or *honoring*, but not *worship*. As for the Mother of God, a special word was being used, *hyperdulia*, that is, super-veneration, all-honoring. The same can be said about the icons, too; we do not *worship* the icons, but we venerate them, we honor them, the same way we honor the saints. We worship God alone, but we venerate His icons, His saints and their icons, and we super-venerate His Mother, whom we call the All-Holy Birthgiver of God, because she gave birth to God in the flesh."

---

[139] Protopresbyter Michael Pomazansky, *Orthodox Dogmatic Theology, A Concise Exposition*, 3rd edition, St. Herman of Alaska Brotherhood, Platina, California, 2005, p. 324.

"So actually this is only a linguistic issue," Daniel repeated.

"Yes, that's correct. Nowadays, efforts are made for the fixing of this problem, I mean sometimes it is attempted to use the verbs *to venerate* or *to honor* for saints or icons, but at the moment the verb *to worship* is still widely used."

"Wait a second, there's something I didn't understand. What does it mean that the Virgin Mary gave birth to God?"

"God the Son has always existed; He is born of the Father 'before all ages,'[140] before the creation of the world. And about two thousand years ago He was incarnate, that is, He took the body of a man, and was born, as a man, by the Virgin Mary. As God, He was born of the Father, without a mother. This is not a birth in the flesh, as living beings are being born in our world, this is about something entirely different, a birth that is far beyond our ability to comprehend. And as a man, He was born of the Virgin Mary, without having a human being as father."

"What about God the Father, who 'gave birth' to Him, or who created Him?" Daniel asked.

"No one; God the Father has always existed without being born of or created by someone else."

"So the Mother of God is more special than all the other saints because she gave birth to God?"

"I think you're asking the wrong question. She was chosen to give birth to God because she was, with the exception of Christ, the most pure and virtuous human being, that is, more special than the other people, to use your words. God, who can see into the future, knew this even before she was born, and for this reason He chose her to be His mother."

"Who are the 'brothers of the Lord,' about whom I heard that are mentioned in the Bible?"

"The word 'brother' is used in the Holy Scripture to designate other relatives, too, especially cousins. Next, there are ancient writings that tell us that Joseph, Virgin Mary's betrothed, was an old widower, and those 'brothers' were actually his children from the legitimate marriage that had ended with the death

---

[140] The Creed (The Symbol of Faith).

of his wife. The Virgin Mary, who had lived till the age of 15 close to the Temple in Jerusalem, had only been entrusted to him to take care of her, because she intended to never get married, and he was a very virtuous and trustworthy man. The Bible never mentions that there ever took place a marriage, but only a betrothal. Think about the words told to the Archangel Gabriel when he told her that she will give birth to a child:"

«Then Mary said to the angel, "How can this be, since I do not know a man?"»[141]

Michael went on:

"Could these be the words of a woman who expects to get married very soon? No, they couldn't. Then we also have in the Old Testament a prophecy that the Fathers of the Church have interpreted as referring to the fact that the Virgin Mary was a virgin for the rest of her life:"

«Then He brought me back to the outer gate of the sanctuary that faces toward the east, but it was shut. So the Lord said to me, "This gate shall be shut. It shall not be opened, and no man shall pass through it, because the Lord God of Israel will enter by it; therefore, it shall be shut. [...]"»[142]

"OK, I see," Daniel said.

"There are some people who interpret in a wrong way this verse: [Joseph] *«did not know her till she had brought forth her firstborn Son. And he called His name Jesus.»*[143] It is just an expression; the Lord has also said that *«I am with you always, even to the end of the age.»*[144] Should we understand that after the *«end of the age»* the Lord will not be with the faithful anymore? No, but exactly the opposite.[145]

---

[141] Luke 1:34.

[142] Ezekiel 44:1-2.

[143] Matthew 1:25.

[144] Matthew 28:20.

[145] More details can be found here:
http://orthodoxinfo.com/inquirers/evervirgin.aspx

"Let's get back, so you're not 'worshipping' the saints, but you pray to them. Do you pray to the saints in the same way as you pray to God?"

"No, of course not. From the saints we're only asking for intercession, that is, for them to join us in prayer to God. We even have an example in the Bible: At the wedding in Cana of Galilee, Christ's mother interceded for the miracle that the Lord worked at that time, namely for the turning of the water into wine.[146] When we ask for the prayers of the saints, we usually use sentences such as 'Lord Jesus Christ, for the prayers of Your all-holy Mother, have mercy on us,' or 'Saint Nicholas, pray to Christ God for us.'"

"Do you use to ask for forgiveness, too, from the saints?" Daniel asked.

"The saints cannot forgive sins, obviously, only God can do this. However, during the evening prayers we ask forgiveness from our guardian angel because we have saddened him during the day. And we do this exactly as if we were asking forgiveness from a brother whom we upset with something."

"However, doesn't it seem weird to kneel in front of an icon, or to kiss an icon that depicts Christ or a saint?"

"Not at all. The honor paid to the icon is actually paid to its prototype, that is, to Christ or to the saint or angel painted on it. Imagine that one kisses a photograph of his mother. Whom does that one love? The paper on which the image is printed, or his mother? Is that idolatry? In past times, people used to bow down, or even to kneel in front of the emperor or in front of a local ruler, from whom they were asking for a certain favor. Was that idolatry? In the Old Testament we read that a messenger of King Ahaziah knelt before the prophet Elijah, asking him to have mercy on him and on the 50 people who were accompanying him.[147] Was that idolatry? Only pride makes it seem to us that it is weird to kneel."

---

[146] John 2:1-11.
[147] 4 Kingdoms 1:13 (NKJV: 2 Kings 1:13).

"But I remember that somewhere in the Bible some people are praised for refusing to worship a carved image."[148]

"That would have been, indeed, a clear case of idolatry. The king had asked them to worship his false god and the image he had made. Orthodox Christians venerate only the icons of Christ and those of the saints and angels of God, and not the 'icons' or the statues of pagan gods and pagan emperors who were considering themselves to be gods."

8.6.4. Confession

"Why do you confess your sins to the priest? The Protestants say that this is an innovation and that there are no biblical references for this practice."

"The Bible is not a textbook with detailed instructions for all religious practices, as the Protestants started to believe about 500 years ago. Confession of sins has been done in the Church since ancient times, and there is no wonder that the Bible only contains a few indirect witnesses about this:"

«If you forgive the sins of any, they are forgiven them; if you retain the sins of any, they are retained.»[149]

«And I will give you the keys of the Kingdom of heaven, and whatever you bind on earth will be bound in heaven, and whatever you loose on earth will be loosed in heaven.»[150]

«Assuredly, I say to you, whatever you bind on earth will be bound in heaven, and whatever you loose on earth will be loosed in heaven.»[151]

"These quotes," Michael said, "do not contain a detailed description of the practice of confession of sins, because this is not the purpose of the Bible. The Bible only mentions the words by

---

[148] Daniel 3:1-30.
[149] John 20:23.
[150] Matthew 16:19.
[151] Matthew 18:18.

which the Lord gave authority to the bishops, the priests and their successors to bind and to loosen."

"But some priests are very sinful, do they still have this authority?"

"We are all sinners, more or less. But the sins of the priest are not an obstacle for the grace of God, which keeps working through him. Here's what we find in the Bible:"

> «*And one of them, Caiaphas, being high priest that year, said to them, "You know nothing at all, nor do you consider that it is expedient for us that one man should die for the people, and not that the whole nation should perish." Now this he did not say on his own authority; but being high priest that year he prophesied that Jesus would die for the nation, and not for that nation only, but also that He would gather together in one the children of God who were scattered abroad.*»[152]

Michael went on:

"Do you know who Caiaphas was? He was one of the enemies of Christ, one of those who plotted against Him. But behold, this Caiaphas uttered a true prophecy by virtue of the position he was occupying in the church hierarchy of that time. In the same way, a sinful priest can perform religious services, as long as he is not defrocked and he has the blessing of his bishop to serve."

8.6.5. Communion

"What about the practice of Communion?" Daniel asked. "Why do you say that Communion is the body and blood of the Lord?"

"Here we have even more biblical references:"

> «["] *I am the living bread which came down from heaven. If anyone eats of this bread, he will live forever; and the bread that I shall give is My flesh, which I shall give for the life of the world." The Jews therefore quarreled among themselves, saying, "How can this Man give us His flesh to eat?" Then Jesus said to them, "Most assuredly, I say to you,*

---

[152] John 11:49-52.

unless you eat the flesh of the Son of Man and drink His blood, you have no life in you. Whoever eats My flesh and drinks My blood has eternal life, and I will raise him up at the last day. For My flesh is food indeed, and My blood is drink indeed. He who eats My flesh and drinks My blood abides in Me, and I in him.»[153]

«And as they were eating, Jesus took bread, blessed and broke it, and gave it to the disciples and said, "Take, eat; this is My body." Then He took the cup, and gave thanks, and gave it to them, saying, "Drink from it, all of you. For this is My blood of the new covenant, which is shed for many for the remission of sins. ["] »[154]

"And here's a witness of this practice in the Church in the first decades after Christ:"

«The cup of blessing which we bless, is it not the communion of the blood of Christ? The bread which we break, is it not the communion of the body of Christ?»[155]

Michael went on:

"These are not just mere symbols. Let's read carefully: the Lord said *«For My flesh is food indeed, and My blood is drink indeed.»* For this reason, we believe that the bread and the wine become, through the prayer of the priest, truly the body and blood of Christ, although we see them further as bread and wine."

"Is this true for any piece of bread and any glass of wine?"

"No, obviously not. Only the bread and wine for which certain prayers are said are transformed this way. And this transformation can only be performed by a bishop or by a priest who acts as the representative of a bishop. And the bishop must have valid apostolic succession, that is, he should have been made a bishop by other valid bishops, and so on, all the way to the Holy Apostles, who were made bishops by Christ Himself. And there's something else I'd like to add here. The same way heaven is a pleasant experience only for those with an authentic Christian

---

[153] John 6:51-56.
[154] Matthew 26:26-28.
[155] 1 Corinthians 10:16.

life, so is Holy Communion beneficial only for those without serious sins, as the Bible also says:"

> *«Therefore whoever eats this bread or drinks this cup of the Lord in an unworthy manner will be guilty of the body and blood of the Lord. But let a man examine himself, and so let him eat of the bread and drink of the cup. For he who eats and drinks in an unworthy manner eats and drinks judgment to himself, not discerning the Lord's body. For this reason many are weak and sick among you, and many sleep.»*[156]

"I notice," Daniel say, "that this resembles a little the effect of the afterlife reality on the souls of the people. The same thing causes joy for the believers and suffering for the sinners."

"Yes, you noticed well," Michael approved. "And something else related to this: the canons of the Church forbid the commemoration during Holy Liturgy of those with serious sins, alive or deceased, and this is probably because it does no good for them. The well-known Russian hieromonk John Krestiankin says in a letter that commemoration at the Church prayer of one who killed himself is actually doing harm to him, and that we have to obey the rules that forbid this.[157] Those who have taken their own lives can only be commemorated in certain special prayers. Another example in which we see that the same thing can be beneficial for some people, but harmful for others, depending on their spiritual state."

"Should I take it then that all Church rules have a purpose of their own?"

"Of course."

8.6.6. Holy Objects

"Why do you keep objects that you consider to be 'holy' in churches? I'm talking about the earthly remains of the saints, or

---

[156] 1 Corinthians 11:27-30.

[157] Fr. John Krestiankin, *May God Give You Wisdom (The Letters of Fr. John Krestiankin)*, first English edition, St. Xenia Skete (and Sretensky Stavropegic Monastery), Wildwood, California, 2007, p. 202.

the pieces of wood that you say were once part of the cross on which Christ was crucified, or even certain objects that used to belong to the saints?"

"Even from ancient times, the believers noticed that various objects seem to 'borrow' something from the holiness of their owner:"

«Now Elisha died, and they buried him. Then in the following year, the raiding bands from Moab invaded the land. And it came to pass, as they were burying a man, they beheld a lightly armed band of raiders, and cast the man into the tomb of Elisha. When the man touched the bones of Elisha, he revived and stood up on his feet.»[158]

«Now a certain woman had a flow of blood for twelve years, and had suffered many things from many physicians. She had spent all that she had and was no better, but rather grew worse. When she heard about Jesus, she came behind Him in the crowd and touched His garment. For she said, "If only I may touch His clothes, I shall be made well." Immediately the fountain of her blood was dried up, and she felt in her body that she was healed of the affliction.»[159]

«And believers were increasingly added to the Lord, multitudes of both men and women, so that they brought the sick out into the streets and laid them on beds and couches, that at least the shadow of Peter passing by might fall on some of them. Also a multitude gathered from the surrounding cities to Jerusalem, bringing sick people and those who were tormented by unclean spirits, and they were all healed.»[160]

«Now God worked unusual miracles by the hands of Paul, so that even handkerchiefs or aprons were brought from his body to the sick, and the diseases left them and the evil spirits went out of them.»[161]

Michael went on:

"Then, in the tradition of the Church, we read that when the Cross of Christ was unearthed, there were actually three crosses found, and nobody knew which one had been the Lord's. But

---

[158] 4 Kingdoms 13:20-21 (NKJV: 2 Kings 13:20-21).
[159] Mark 5:25-29.
[160] Acts 5:14-16.
[161] Acts 19:11-12.

there was a funeral procession passing by, and they touched the dead man with each of the three crosses, and when they touched him with the Lord's cross, he came back to life, and thus they knew which cross was the right one. Obviously, the garment of Christ was just an object, it had no power of its own, but God healed the woman by means of it. The same for the bones of Elisha. Nor did the shadow of Peter have any power of its own; actually the shadow is not even an object, but only the absence of light in a certain area. Not even the apostles had any power of their own—the healing power was coming only from God. Both the saints and their objects are just mere intermediaries. For this reason, the objects that are considered to be holy do not always work miracles, on demand, but only when God so ordains, for the faith of the one who needs healing and, of course, if the healing is for his spiritual benefit."

"What about the remains of the Christian saints?"

"The same thing. The Christian Church noticed even from its beginnings that the earthly remains of the saints, called relics, often work wonders. Also, it was noticed that the bodies of many saints do not decompose, but this criterion is not enough to prove a person's holiness, because there are both natural and supernatural causes for why a body does not decompose. And of the supernatural causes, one is holiness, and another can be the burden of some very serious sins. For this reason, the Church carefully analyzes each case before recognizing one's sainthood."

"Do you worship... do you venerate the relics of the saints?"

"We honor them, we venerate them, but in no case do we worship them as we worship God."

8.6.7. About Sinful Believers

"The Protestants in our country are accusing you, the Orthodox, of not being true Christians. Very many of you drink too much and too often, are engaged in cohabiting relationships without being married, many Orthodox priests are greedy for money, and so on."

"Please remember what I have just told you: Not all those who declare themselves to be Christians are indeed so. If we go to America or other country where most of the population is Protestant, won't we notice the same thing, namely that most people declare themselves to be Christians, although among them we'll also find many of the sins enumerated before?"

"Yes, that's correct," Daniel admitted.

"And one more thing: Think about the situation in Israel at the time of Jesus, a situation that is very well described in the four Gospels. Weren't those Jews sinful? Doesn't the Savior say that in the Day of Judgment, it will be more tolerable for some pagans than for the population of some cities in Israel? Doesn't the Savior say to the Jews that «yet none of you keeps the law»?[162] Weren't most priests of the Jews among the greatest enemies of Christ? Yet still, despite all these sins, which was at that time the true religion? Were any of the religions of the pagans true? No, but Judaism, the religion of those sinners was the true religion at that moment of history."

"Is this why it is said to do what the priest is saying, but not what the priest is doing?"

"This was said by Christ Himself:"

«Then Jesus spoke to the multitudes and to His disciples, saying: 'The scribes and the Pharisees sit in Moses' seat. Therefore whatever they tell you to observe, that observe and do, but do not do according to their works; for they say, and do not do.»[163]

"And here's one more example," Michael went on. "If you were to find out that your mathematics teacher is a criminal, a serial murderer let's say, would that make the math he taught you false? Would the Pythagorean theorem cease to be valid for this reason?"

"Obviously not, this is a matter of logic; the veracity of a statement has nothing to do with the ethic or moral state of the

---

[162] John 7:19.
[163] Matthew 23:1-3.

person making that statement. OK, I understand now the difference between Orthodox and Protestants, but I still don't understand the difference between Orthodox and Roman Catholics."

8.6.8. About Roman Catholics

"First, we have to be careful about how we use the word 'catholic.' It is a word of Greek origin and it means 'universal,' 'whole,' lacking nothing. This word is also attributed to the Orthodox Church in some languages, like Greek and English. I mean, in Greek it is said that the Orthodox Church is 'catholic,' that is, whole, complete, it lacks nothing, and the term was already being used for hundreds of years when the Great Schism took place, in the year 1054. The Romanian language, however, predominantly uses the originally Slavonic term 'sobornic,' which means approximately the same thing.[164] And in order to avoid confusion, the religious institution whose headquarters are in the Vatican and that is now led by pope Francis, is officially named the Roman Catholic Church, and its members are called Roman Catholic believers."

"I see," Daniel said. "And what are the differences between the Orthodox and the Roman Catholics?"

"Up to the year 1054, when the split happened, also called the Great Schism, in Europe there was a single Christian Church. There were not two united churches, but there was a single Church in all of Europe. For this reason, the Roman Catholic saints canonized before 1054 are also recognized as saints by the Orthodox Church. The same is true for the Orthodox saints canonized before 1054; they are also recognized as saints by the Roman Catholics. I'll only give you two examples: Saint Gregory the

---

[164] Quote from the Orthodox Creed (The Symbol of Faith):

In Romanian: "una, sfântă, *sobornicească* şi apostolească Biserică."

In Greek: "mían, Hagían, *Katholikḗn* kaì Apostolikḗn Ekklēsían" ("μίαν, Ἁγίαν, *Καθολικὴν* καὶ Ἀποστολικὴν Ἐκκλησίαν").

In English: "one, holy, *catholic*, and apostolic Church."

Great, Pope of Rome, and Saint John Chrysostom, archbishop of Constantinople, are both recognized as saints by both the Orthodox and the Roman Catholics."

"And why was there a split in 1054?"

"In 1054 there were two main reasons. The first reason was related to the way the two sides saw the origin of the Holy Spirit, the third Person of the Holy Trinity. The Eastern Christians believed that the Holy Spirit originates, 'proceeds' only from the Father, as Christ also said:"

> *«But when the Helper comes, whom I shall send to you from the Father, the Spirit of truth Who proceeds from the Father, He will testify of Me.»*[165]

Michael went on:

"But Western Christians had added to the Symbol of faith, to the Creed, the Latin word *filioque*, and thus, though the Bible kept saying *«who proceeds from the Father,»* in the Western Creed the phrase had become 'who proceeds from the Father and the Son.' And the Orthodox East considered this change a wrong teaching, a heresy."

"And the second reason?" Daniel asked.

"The second reason was related to the authority of the bishop of Rome, namely the pope. The West considered the pope to be the supreme authority in the Church, some kind of a super-bishop, who had full rights in the entire Christian Church, being allowed to appoint and replace bishops anywhere and anytime, as he considered appropriate. But the East saw things differently: the pope of Rome was considered to be just the 'first among equals,' as today is considered to be the Patriarch of Constantinople, who had taken the pope's place after the Great Schism."

"Are these all of the differences?" Daniel asked.

"Besides these two major differences, after 1054 new ones have been added, and thus the distance between the East and the West grew larger and larger: the doctrine of Purgatory, Immacu-

---

[165] John 15:26.

late Conception, papal infallibility, and a few more. For one looking from the outside, Orthodoxy and Roman Catholicism may
seem very similar, but in reality it is not really like that. If you
look, for example, at the way in which the Orthodox and the Roman Catholics see the sacrifice of Jesus Christ on the cross, you'll
think they are two completely different religions."

"Really?" Daniel wondered. "How do the two ways of seeing
the crucifixion differ so much?"

"In short, the Roman Catholics and some Protestants understand the sacrifice of Christ this way: The sins of men are an
insult, an offense against God. This offense is infinitely greater
than the offense against a simple man, because God is also infinitely greater than a simple man. This offense must be punished,
that is, God is somehow obliged, forced to punish the sinners.
But it is impossible for men to ever be able to redeem by themselves the guilt of sins; man is a finite being, and the offense
against God is infinite, because God is infinite, too.[166] Therefore,
Christ came to earth, He was incarnate and was crucified for us,
that is, He was punished in our place, the sinners. God the Father
accepted the sacrifice of His Son and He forgives all sinners who
repent, because the sins were paid for by Jesus Christ.[167]"

"I think I've heard this explanation before," Daniel said.
"Probably from a Protestant. And how do the Orthodox see
things?"

"I'm not a theologian, but I'll briefly explain to you what I
understand from what the Orthodox theologians say: Sin is not
an offense against God, but a disease of the human soul. God
hates sin, indeed, but not because it affects Him in any way, but
because of the effects sin has on His creation, the man. Christ,

---

[166] This idea was probably influenced by the judicial systems that
considered a crime to be more serious if the victim was a more important person.

[167] According to the *Catechism of the Catholic Church*:
    http://www.vatican.va/archive/ccc_css/archive/cate-
chism/ccc_toc.htm
    This theory was developed especially by Anselm of Canterbury
(1033-1109).

God the Son, did not come into the world in order to restore the wounded honor of God the Father, He did not suffer in order to satisfy God's obligation to punish sinners, but in order to heal man's sick nature. His death on the cross was indeed a necessary sacrifice for the salvation of the people, for the restoration of the human nature corrupted by the sin of Adam and Eve, but not because God the Father was obliged, forced by some strict rules to punish someone for our sins. Indeed, Christ had to suffer for the sins of mankind, as it is written in so many places in the Bible, but not because God felt the need to take revenge on someone. God does not suffer from spiritual diseases, as we do, God is not like those people who cannot find peace till they take revenge on their enemies. Such an idea is absurd. Here's what Father Professor Basil (Vasile) Mihoc tells us about the mystery of the salvation of men:"

> Saint Gregory [the Theologian] tries to explain this mystery by that which in theology is called the ontological aspect of redemption, I mean the fact that Christ's Sacrifice has a direction toward His own human nature. It was necessary that the human nature assumed by Him through Incarnation was healed of its fall by the obedience till death of the One Who has assumed it and by His victory over the tyrannical devil. But the mystery can only be partially comprehended. 'Let the rest of the mystery be venerated silently,' concludes Saint Gregory.[168]

Michael went on:

"You notice that we again encounter the idea that we cannot understand everything with our mind, and that we simply have to accept some things by faith, without being able to explain them in detail."

"Yes, indeed…"

"It is still possible that in this fleeting life we are punished by God for our sins, with diseases, accidents, or in other ways,

---

[168] Translated from this Romanian article:

http://ziarullumina.ro/slujirea-rezuma-implinirea-legii-100247.html

but I don't think these punishments are caused by God's 'anger' or by His desire for 'revenge.' These punishments have the purpose of correcting us, of doing *us* good; they have the purpose of preventing us from going to hell. Do you remember what I was telling you about people on the first spiritual level, who do good and abstain from evil for fear of being punished? Well, I think that, more or less, most of us are still a little bit lagging behind on this level."

"I notice," Daniel said, "that the Roman Catholic vision about Christ's sacrifice does not match very well the vision of hell that you presented to me earlier. As I understand it, if Christ had to suffer and die because God the Father was angry and He had to punish someone for men's sins, if He had to avenge His wounded honor, then maybe the suffering of those who end up in hell is not caused by their spiritual diseases, but they are being eternally and on purpose tormented by a vengeful God, Who takes revenge this way for having been offended."

"Indeed, this is so. For this reason, this Roman Catholic and Protestant doctrine seems unacceptable to me. And, obviously, we can't really argue scientifically for or against the two visions. But *something* inside us will be attracted either toward one, or toward the other. And this is, I think, what God is looking for in a man."[169]

---

[169] Although the mystery of man's salvation through the Crucifixion and Resurrection of Christ cannot be fully understood by the human mind, for a better clarification one can read:

St. Athanasius the Great (of Alexandria), *On the Incarnation.*

St. Gregory the Theologian (of Nazianzus), *Oration on Easter* (possibly also titled *Word on Easter*), XLV, 22; *Patrologia Graeca* (P.G.), 36, 653.

Fr. Dumitru Staniloae, *Jesus Christ or Man's Restoration* (in Romanian), Basilica Press, 2013.

Fr. Prof. Dumitru Staniloae, *The Experience of God / Orthodox Dogmatic Theology*, Holy Cross Orthodox Press.

Clark Carlton, the books mentioned in section 8.6.10. (*Books*), especially *The Truth* and *The Life.*

8.6.9. Religious Exclusivism

"Tell me please," Daniel said, "why is your Church so exclusivist? Although I don't go to church or read religious books or articles, I know that many Orthodox Christians have a somewhat hostile attitude toward other Christians, including toward Roman Catholics, and they are against common prayers, I mean they refuse to pray together with a Roman Catholic. From the point of view of some of them, all Protestant denominations are just some sects, and the pope of Rome is either the Antichrist,[170] or a forerunner of him. Even more, some Orthodox say that all Roman Catholics and all Protestants are going to hell, that only the Orthodox can be saved, and that all non-Orthodox are anathematized. What is actually the anathema?"

"Almost every religion, monotheistic or not, and almost every Christian confession is exclusivist in its own way. Look, for example, at June 29, 2007, when Pope Benedict XVI approved a document that claims that the Roman Catholic Church is the only true church, with the Orthodox Churches being 'defective,' and the other denominations not being true churches."

"And what is the Orthodox position?"

"The Eastern Orthodox Church is the only true Church of Christ. All other Christian denominations are affected more or less by various wrong teachings, known as heresies. Therefore, common prayers together with those belonging to other Christian denominations are forbidden by the Apostolic canons, which are about two thousand years old. I used the complete official name, 'The Eastern Orthodox Church,' in order to distinguish it from the institution that calls itself 'The Oriental Orthodox Church,' and which broke away from our Church after the year 451[171], that is about 600 years before the Great Schism."

---

[170] Antichrist: the one who is against Christ, who will come before the end of times and will attempt to deceive the entire world.

[171] Following the Council of Chalcedon:
https://orthodoxwiki.org/Fourth_Ecumenical_Council

"Aha, so is it officially forbidden to pray together with a Roman Catholic?" Daniel asked.

"Yes, it is forbidden both for a layman, and even more for a priest to perform any religious service together with a priest belonging to any other Christian denomination. This rule is usually observed, but not quite all the time."

"What about anathema? Is there such a thing?"

"Yes, anathema means separation, exclusion from the Church, and it is usually used to remove wrong teachings, or heresies, from within the Church. Anathema has two main purposes: first, to warn the one being anathematized that he is outside the Church of Christ and that he has to repent and return to the true faith. And the second purpose is to warn the members of the Church that a certain person, or group of persons, are no longer members of the Church, and that his or their opinions and teachings must be disregarded. Anathema does not mean a lack of Christian love, as some people say, but on the contrary. Think about it, if you tell a sick man that he is healthy and he needs no treatment, is that a proof of love? Wouldn't that instead lead to his death? Wouldn't it be better if he were told that he is sick and he needs treatment? This is the purpose of anathema."

"And what about the salvation of the non-Orthodox? Is it true that they are losing their souls?"

"I think that those who claim that all non-Orthodox will end up in hell are speaking with too much certainty about things that are not in their power to know. Other persons much more equipped to speak about this issue are not that sure. Here's for example what Saint Silouan the Athonite says:"

> Father Cassian used to say that all heretics would perish. I do not know about this — my trust is only in the Orthodox Church [...] .[172]

"Saint Silouan only trusts in the Orthodox Church, but he cannot say that all the rest will end up in hell. Now here's what

---

[172] Archim. Sophrony Sakharov, *St. Silouan the Athonite*, p. 483.

Saint Theophan the Recluse says, answering a question about the salvation of the non-Orthodox:"

> You ask, will the heterodox be saved.... Why do you worry about them? They have a Savior Who desires the salvation of every human being. He will take care of them. You and I should not be burdened with such a concern. Study yourself and your own sins.... I will tell you one thing, however: should you, being Orthodox and possessing the Truth in its fullness, betray Orthodoxy, and enter a different faith, you will lose your soul forever.[173]

"And here's what says Father Justin Pârvu, who is considered to be a model worth following by many Orthodox Christians of today. Although he was firmly against conducting prayers and religious services with Roman Catholics, Father Justin does not say that they are certainly going to lose their souls, but he says:"

> They remain with their ideas, maybe they'll be saved that way [...].[174]

"Somehow the three quotes seem unclear to me," Daniel said. "What should I understand from them?"

"Here's what I understand from what the saints and the other voices of authority are saying: All non-Orthodox are indeed outside the true Church. However, where each one of them will end up after death is something that God alone knows, and it is not our business to judge these things. But we have to keep in mind Saint Theophan's warning: The Orthodox who betray their faith are losing their souls."

"I understand," Daniel said. "From each one it is asked according to how much it was given him. Most non-Orthodox were

---

[173] Quoted in Metropolitan Philaret Voznesenskii, *Will the Heterodox Be Saved?* (leaflet #L213, St. John of Kronstadt Press); quoted in Patrick Barnes, *The Non-Orthodox (The Orthodox Teaching on Christians Outside of the Church)*, Regina Orthodox Press, Salisbury, MA, 1999, p. 107.

[174] Graţia Lungu Constantineanu, *Fr. Justin Pârvu*, p. 192.

born this way and they are in no way guilty of the schisms that took place hundreds of years ago."

"Exactly. We have so many examples in which we see that God is extremely tolerant to those who unknowingly make mistakes. However, nowadays, almost everyone can use books or the Internet for gathering information, so sometimes this is not just about not knowing, but also about the lack of will to find out the truth. But in the end, only God can judge these things."

8.6.10. Books

"In conclusion," Daniel said, "are these the main differences between the Orthodox, on the one hand, and the Roman Catholics and Protestants, on the other?"

"I presented the differences to you briefly and superficially, because I'm not an expert in theology. But if you're interested and you want to read more, there are very many good books that explain all these things in a detailed manner. Finding the true religion is impossible if we try to find it only by our own means. But we are not alone; God helps us at every step, and if we really are looking for the Truth, God will place in our way the right arguments at the right time. All that is needed is for our inner *something* to accept them. Each man is unique in his own way; there are no two identical men. Some people begin to believe when they understand that the theory of evolution is a lie. Other people begin to believe when they see or hear about a miracle. And still other people will not believe regardless of how many arguments they see. God knows what arguments to present to each one, as long as he is predisposed to accept them. I will enumerate briefly the books in which I found the arguments that seemed to me to be the best. It is possible that you'll also consider them to be as good as I did, or not. If not, don't worry, God will place in your way other arguments, suited for you. All you have to do is to accept them. And meanwhile, be careful, the devil might also offer you some arguments of his own."

"I'm tempted to ask you again, why does it have to be that difficult? Why does God allow the devil to offer me his false arguments, too? What if I can't tell them apart?"

"I'll give you the same answer. In my opinion, the smarter and the more superior we think we are compared to other people, the harder it is for us to tell the arguments apart. But I believe that if we start to think that we're not at all superior to those who lived hundreds of years ago, if we look for help from God and not from our intellect, then God will help us and it will be much easier for us to make the right choices."

Daniel pulled a phone from his pocket.

"I'm taking notes," he said.

"First, a book I found very interesting is *Becoming Orthodox*[175], written by Peter Gillquist, a former American Protestant. The author recounts how he studied the history of the Church and came to the conclusion that the Orthodox Church is the only unchanged church in history. At the end of his spiritual journey, in the year 1987, Peter Gillquist together with about two thousand other people converted to Orthodoxy."

"Together with two thousand people?" Daniel wondered.

"Yes, there was a group of about two thousand people who were looking for the true Church. It is a very interesting book. Then I found very useful the books written by Clark Carlton[176], an American author and a former Baptist who has converted to Orthodoxy."

---

[175] Peter Gillquist, *Becoming Orthodox (A Journey to the Ancient Christian Faith)*, revised edition, Conciliar Press, Ben Lomond, California, 1992.

[176] *The Faith: Understanding Orthodox Christianity*, Regina Orthodox Press, 1997.

The Way: What Every Protestant Should Know About the Orthodox Church, Regina Orthodox Press, 1997.

The Truth: What Every Roman Catholic Should Know About the Orthodox Church, Regina Orthodox Press, 1999.

The Life: The Orthodox Doctrine of Salvation, Regina Orthodox Press, 2000.

"I got it," Daniel said. "I really want to read the first one, you've made me curious. About the others, I'll see later."

"Other people might recommend other books, which seemed to them more useful. As I was saying, each man is sensitive to certain arguments. Some people would object and would say that the value of the writings of these modern authors cannot be compared to the value of the writings of the ancient saints. I perfectly agree, but these modern authors were very useful to me in those moments of my life when I was myself looking for the true religion, and this because they were speaking a language that I could understand. And I don't mean Romanian, English or any other modern language."

"I think I understand what you mean," Daniel said, "modern man, who has a modern way of thinking and of seeing things, understands more easily something written by another modern man, than something written a thousand years ago."

"Something like that," Michael admitted. "If you become a believer, then certainly you'll appreciate more the Holy Scripture and the writings of the saints, like Saint Paisios of Mount Athos, Saint John Chrysostom, and many others. Then you'll probably also appreciate the writings of other Christians, usually monks, who at this moment are not considered to be saints, like Father Seraphim Rose from America, Father Cleopa from Romania, and many, many others. God will take care that you encounter the right book at the right time."

8.7. Other Questions

8.7.1. The Movie Zeitgeist

"Tell me please," Daniel said, "what do you think about the movie Zeitgeist? In the first part it makes some statements about religion."

"The statements made at the beginning of that movie are simply lies. No, they are not mistaken interpretations of some ancient writings, they are lies, in the true sense of the word. For example, the movie claims that there are certain similarities between Jesus Christ and some gods of the ancient peoples. Here's what it says about the Egyptian god Horus:"

> Broadly speaking, the story of Horus is as follows: Horus was born on December 25th of the virgin Isis-Meri. His birth was accompanied by a star in the East, which in turn, three kings followed to locate and adorn the new-born savior. At the age of 12, he was a prodigal child teacher, and at the age of 30 he was baptized by a figure known as Anup and thus began his ministry. Horus had 12 disciples he traveled about with, performing miracles such as healing the sick and walking on water. Horus was known by many gestural names such as The Truth, The Light, God's Anointed Son, The Good Shepherd, The Lamb of God, and many others. After being betrayed by Typhon, Horus was crucified, buried for 3 days, and thus, resurrected.[177]

"Indeed," Daniel noticed, "it resembles very much the biblical account about Jesus Christ."

"It resembles it that much because it is a lie. According to the Egyptian mythology, Horus was not born on December 25th, but during the summer. His father, Osiris, had been killed, but his mother, Isis, used a magic ritual to bring Osiris back to life for a short period of time, and in that short period the two of them conceived Horus. The mythology describes very well this episode, from which it can be seen very clearly that Isis was not a virgin when she gave birth to Horus. In the mythology there are neither references to a star in the East, nor to the three kings, nor to the 'new-born savior,' nor to the fact that he ever walked on water, nor to the fact that he had become a teacher by the age of 12, nor to the fact that he was baptized at the age of 30. All these

---

[177] https://en.wikiversity.org/wiki/Zeitgeist_the_movie/Transcript

are nothing but blatant lies. Also, the mythology does not mention anywhere that he was betrayed and crucified; actually the mythology doesn't mention anywhere that Horus ever died, let alone that he was raised after three days."

"I never thought that a documentary movie could present such obvious lies…"

"The documentary lies about the other deities, too. Attis dies every winter and is 'resurrected' every spring. He is not crucified, and winter does not last for three days. Krishna is the eighth son of princess Devaki and her husband, Vasudeva, so he was not born of a virgin. Indian mythology mentions no star in the East, no crucifixion and no resurrection of Krishna. Greek mythology makes no claim that Dionysus would have been born of a virgin, but it does claim that his father, Zeus, had other sons, too, so obviously this semi-god could not be the only son of his father, as the movie Zeitgeist alleges. Neither was Mithra born of a virgin, nor did he have 12 disciples. And so on, lies so obvious, that they can easily be spotted by anybody who knows a few things about the ancient mythologies. You can search the Internet for "Zeitgeist debunked" or "Zeitgeist lies" and you'll find countless articles that analyze in detail each lie in this movie."

8.7.2. Old Testament Law

"Tell me please," Daniel said, "why is the Old Testament so different from the New one? In the Old Testament the law was very harsh, one could be sentenced to death even for offenses that today can be considered to be minor, for example adultery. Some people say that the God of the Old Testament doesn't really look like the God of the New Testament."

"God is one and the same, only the people are different. The Old Testament Law was an inferior law, given to people who simply could not handle something better. The coming of Christ abolished the Old Law, as He Himself tells us very clearly. Here's a quote from the Old Testament:"

«If a man takes a wife and marries her, and it should be she finds no favor before him, because he found something shameful in her, and he writes her a certificate of divorce, puts it in her hands, and sends her out of his house, and she departs from his house and marries a different man, [...] »[178]

"And here's what Christ tells us in the New Testament:"

«The Pharisees also came to Him, testing Him, and saying to Him, "Is it lawful for a man to divorce his wife for just any reason?" And He answered and said to them, "Have you not read that He who made them at the beginning 'made them male and female,' and said, 'For this reason a man shall leave his father and mother and be joined to his wife, and the two shall become one flesh'? So then, they are no longer two but one flesh. Therefore what God has joined together, let not man separate." They said to Him, "Why then did Moses command to give a certificate of divorce, and to put her away?" He said to them, "Moses, because of the hardness of your hearts, permitted you to divorce your wives, but from the beginning it was not so. And I say to you, whoever divorces his wife, except for sexual immorality, and marries another, commits adultery; and whoever marries her who is divorced commits adultery. "»[179]

Michael went on:

"So we are told pretty clearly that in the Old Testament certain things were permitted because those people were not capable of receiving a higher teaching. Here's other examples:"

«You have heard that it was said to those of old, 'You shall not murder, and whoever murders will be in danger of the judgment.' But I say to you that whoever is angry with his brother without a cause shall be in danger of the judgment. And whoever says to his brother, 'Raca!'[180] *shall be in danger of the council. But whoever says, 'You fool!' shall be in danger of hell fire.»*

[...]

---

[178] Deuteronomy 24:1-2.
[179] Matthew 19:3-9.
[180] Raca: sometimes translated as "stupid" or "worthless."

«You have heard that it was said to those of old, 'You shall not commit adultery.' But I say to you that whoever looks at a woman to lust for her has already committed adultery with her in his heart.»

[...]

«Again you have heard that it was said to those of old, 'You shall not swear falsely, but shall perform your oaths to the Lord.' But I say to you, do not swear at all: neither by heaven, for it is God's throne; nor by the earth, for it is His footstool; nor by Jerusalem, for it is the city of the great King. Nor shall you swear by your head, because you cannot make one hair white or black. But let your 'Yes' be 'Yes,' and your 'No,' 'No.' For whatever is more than these is from the evil one.»

«You have heard that it was said, 'An eye for an eye and a tooth for a tooth.' But I tell you not to resist an evil person. But whoever slaps you on your right cheek, turn the other to him also. If anyone wants to sue you and take away your tunic, let him have your cloak also. And whoever compels you to go one mile, go with him two. Give to him who asks you, and from him who wants to borrow from you do not turn away.»

«You have heard that it was said, 'You shall love your neighbor and hate your enemy.' But I say to you, love your enemies, bless those who curse you, do good to those who hate you, and pray for those who spitefully use you and persecute you, that you may be sons of your Father in heaven; for He makes His sun rise on the evil and on the good, and sends rain on the just and on the unjust. For if you love those who love you, what reward have you? Do not even the tax collectors do the same? And if you greet your brethren only, what do you do more than others? Do not even the tax collectors do so? Therefore you shall be perfect, just as your Father in heaven is perfect.»[181]

"What?" Daniel said. "The law that God gave to the Hebrews in the Old Testament was not good, or was incomplete?"

"It was good for them, for their level. Now, for us, certain aspects of it are not good anymore. But others are still good, for example the Ten Commandments."

"How is it possible that some aspects were good at some point, and now they are not good anymore?"

---

[181] Matthew 5:21-48.

"Saint John Chrysostom answers exactly this question of yours:"

"But how," one may say, "should the same thing become at one time good, at another time not good?" Nay, I say the very contrary: how could it help becoming good and not good, while all things are crying aloud, that they are so: the arts, the fruits of the earth, and all things else?

See it, for example, taking place first in our own kind. Thus, to be carried, in the earliest age of life, is good, but afterwards pernicious; to eat food that hath been softened in the mouth[182], in the first scene of our life, is good, but afterwards it is full of disgust; to be fed upon milk and to fly to the breast, is at first profitable and healthful, but tends afterwards to decay and harm. Seest thou how the same actions, by reason of the times, appear good, and again not so? Yea, and to wear the robe of a child is well as long as you are a boy, but contrariwise, when you are become a man, it is disgraceful. Wouldest thou learn of the contrary case too, how to the child again the things of the man are unsuited? Give the boy a man's robe, and great will be the laughter; and greater the danger, he being often upset in walking after that fashion. Allow him to handle public affairs, and to traffic, and sow, and reap, and great again will be the laughter.[183]

"And the same Saint John says in some other place:"

So that from all considerations it is clear, that not from any badness in itself doth it [the Old Testament] fail to bring us in [into the Kingdom of heaven], but because it is now the season of higher precepts.

---

[182] St. John Chrysostom is probably referring to some mother's custom of them first chewing the food for the babies who they're teaching how to eat. This is still being practiced, pretty rarely, usually at the age of several months, when, without necessarily ceasing breastfeeding, the babies also begin to eat other food besides milk.

[183] St. John Chrysostom, *Homilies on the Gospel of Matthew*, Homily XVII.

And if it be more imperfect than the new [Testament], neither doth this imply it to be evil: since upon this principle the new law itself will be in the very same case. Because in truth our knowledge of this, [knowledge given by the New Testament,] when compared with that which is to come, is a sort of partial and imperfect thing, and is done away on the coming of that other. *«For when,»* saith he [Paul], *«that which is perfect is come, then that which is in part shall be done away:»*[184] even as it befell the old law through the new [Testament]. Yet we are not to blame the new law for this, though that also gives place on our attaining unto the Kingdom: for *«then,»* saith he [Paul], *«that which is in part shall be done away:»* but for all this we call it [the New Testament] great.[185]

"And here's another observation of the same Saint John Chrysostom about the sacrifices that were being offered during the Old Testament period:"

The precepts then uttered had reference to the weakness of them who were receiving the laws; since also to be worshipped with the vapor of sacrifice is very unworthy of God, just as to lisp is unworthy of a philosopher.[186]

8.7.3. Old Testament Worship

"And what was the use of all those religious rules about the sacrificing of sheep, goats and other animals? Some of them were eaten, others were killed and then burned in a fire."

"What does your inner *something* tell you? Does God need sacrificed animals?"

"It tells me that there has to be another explanation…"

---

[184] 1 Corinthians 13:10.

[185] St. John Chrysostom, *Homilies on the Gospel of Matthew*, Homily XVI.

The notes in [brackets] are taken from the Romanian translation, which seems to be a little bit more explicit.

[186] Ibid., Homily XVI.

"Yes," Michael confirmed. "Here's what God says:"

«I will not accept a young bull from your house,
Nor he-goats from your flocks.
For all the wild animals of the forest are Mine,
The cattle and the oxen in the hills.
I know all the birds of heaven,
And the ripe fruit of the field is with Me.
If I were hungry, I would not tell you;
For the world is Mine, and all its fullness.
Will I eat the flesh of bulls,
Or drink the blood of goats?»[187]

"Then why was God asking for such things in the Old Testament?" Daniel asked. "What was the purpose of those rituals?"

"God did not and does not need anything. Therefore, I believe it was the souls of the people that needed to offer those sacrifices. When they were offering to God from all their hearts whatever they had that was of the greatest value in their herds, then their souls were making great spiritual progress. For this reason, I think, God was asking for sacrifices in the Old Testament, for the good they were doing to those souls. Here's what Saint John Chrysostom tells us:"

> For it is too monstrous, enjoying as we do His bounty in deed every day, not so much as in word to acknowledge the favor; and this, though the acknowledgment again yield all its profit to us. Since He needs not, be sure, anything of ours: but we stand in need of all things from Him. Thus thanksgiving itself adds nothing to Him, but causes us to be nearer to Him.[188]

"And here's what Saint Paisios of Mount Athos says:"

> During another visit by us, in 1988, we asked [Saint Paisios of Mount Athos]: "Father, how should we thank God for some problem, that has been troubling us for

---

[187] Psalms 49:9-13.
[188] St. John Chrysostom, *Homilies on the Gospel of Matthew*, Homily XXV.

this many years and now it has been resolved, in a way?" And the Starets replied: "Even recognition alone, my son, is enough. And, if recognition wasn't beneficial for us, not even that would have been required; it is required from us because it is beneficial for us."[189]

Michael went on:

"So here's why we use to glorify God and to praise Him, not because He needs our praises, but because our souls need to do this. Our souls make spiritual progress this way."

"Is it also true about prayer? I always wondered why believers are always praying; doesn't their God, if He exists, know what they need?"

"Of course God knows. Here's what Christ said:"

«[Y]our Father knows the things you have need of before you ask Him.»[190]

"Then why do you guys always pray, if God already knows?"

"God doesn't need our prayer, it is our souls that need the prayer. Our souls make spiritual progress when we truly pray. This is why we were told *«pray without ceasing.»*[191] Once I encountered these words:"

There is no need of other sins: the lack of prayer kills the soul slowly and surely. Regardless of the quantity or quality of the efforts of the body or the mind.[192]

"They were written by a person totally unknown to me," Michael went on, "and I don't know whether they were her words

---

[189] Nikolaos A. Zournatzoglou, *Pilgrims' Accounts, Elder Paisios the Athonite*, Vol. 2 (in Romanian).

[190] Matthew 6:8.

[191] 1 Thessalonians 5:17.

[192] Rassophore* Neonila, *Against Modern Cosmology (The Separation of Science from Scripture)* (in Romanian), "Atitudini" periodical, no. 21/2012, pp. 94-95.

* Rassophore (or rassaphore): monastic rank, just before becoming a monk.

https://orthodoxwiki.org/Monastic_Ranks#Rassaphore

or whether she was quoting them from somewhere. But *something* inside me felt they were true and I did not forget them."

"I understand," Daniel said. "Is the opposite also true? I mean those who blaspheme, swear or insult God in other ways, are they actually doing harm to their own souls?"

"Yes, obviously. Here's what Saint John Chrysostom says:"

> For no harm at all ensues unto God by their blasphemy, that thou shouldest be angered, but he who blasphemed hath himself also received the wound. Wherefore groan, bewail, for the calamity indeed deserves tears.[193]

Michael paused for a few seconds, then said:

"God does not suffer at all from spiritual diseases, from passions, as we suffer. God does not get angry as we get angry. God does not want to take revenge on the one who blasphemes Him, as we feel the need to take revenge on those who upset us."

"Then why is it said that certain sins draw the punishment of God even from this life?"

"Because God desires the good for the soul of each man, and for this reason some are punished in this life with diseases, accidents and other things like this in order to be corrected, to stop sinning."

"Is this why so many bad things are happening in the world, I mean accidents, diseases, natural cataclysms? For correcting the sinners?"

"For turning the sinners to the right way and for the healing of their souls. God's main goal is to help us save our souls, so we'll have a happy eternal life. But we are more preoccupied with this fleeting life. We don't want to understand that the troubles sent or allowed by God in this life help us to save our souls, if we approach them in a spiritual manner. When he was on his death-bed, with many clergy and faithful gathered around him, Saint Nephon was asked:"

---

[193] St. John Chrysostom, *Homilies on the Gospel of Matthew*, Homily XXIX.

"Father, I wonder, does an illness benefit man in anyway?" the patriarch asked the saint at one point.

"And Saint Nephon replied:"

"Yes, my lord. Just as gold heated in the fire expels rust, so it is with man also, if he thanks God for his sickness, he sheds his sins."[194]

"And Saint Andrew of Caesarea says about the 'mental powers', that is, the angels, that they:"

give thanks to God for the punishment of those who have transgressed the Divine commandments, so that at least in part they may receive the forgiveness of sins [.][195]

Michael went on:

"So the angels rejoice that the sinners are punished in this life, exactly because this punishment is beneficial for their souls, and it diminishes a little the eternal suffering to which they are headed. This is not about a desire for revenge. The troubles we encounter in this world help the healing of our souls, the same way as bitter medicines and painful surgeries help the healing of our bodies. Think about this for a moment: If the Roman Catholic and Protestant explanation of Christ's sacrifice were correct, if indeed Christ was punished in our place, then all human sins would be paid for already, and there would be no reason for people, or at least for the 'already saved' Christians, to keep on suffering in this life. Thus, if suffering were indeed useless and it didn't have any effect on salvation, then the almighty God could simply eliminate it, without this having any effect on their 'already secured' place in heaven. But their explanation is wrong, and people keep on suffering in this ephemeral life because sin is a disease of the soul, and suffering helps the healing of their souls."

"Why is it a sin to work on Sundays and other holy days?"

---

[194] *Stories, Sermons, and Prayers of St. Nephon: An Ascetic Bishop*, p. 130.

[195] St. Andrew of Caesarea, *Commentary on the Apocalypse*, chapter 48; quoted in Archim. Averky Taushev, *The Apocalypse in the Teachings of Ancient Christianity*, St. Herman of Alaska Brotherhood, 1998, p. 217.

"God is not affected in any way if we work on a Sunday, but our souls are much harmed. Sunday must be dedicated to going to church and to other religious activities, not to shopping."

"Is it a sin to go shopping or to the restaurant on a Sunday?"

"Think about it, one does not work on Sunday, because it is a sin, but he goes shopping, or to a movie, or to the restaurant, namely he takes advantage of the fact that someone else, the cashier or the waiter, is working on Sunday. Doesn't it seem to you that something is wrong here?"

"Indeed, it doesn't seem quite right. But what if I get sick?"

"This is a different issue; the Savior, too, healed sick people during the Sabbath day."

8.7.4. Old Testament Wars

"And what about the conquest of Canaan, when the Israelite army, with the help of God, literally exterminated almost the entire population of the Promised Land?"

"God is the One Who gives life, and He is also the One Who takes it away when He knows that it has to be taken. God can use various methods for this: He can send an earthquake, an accident, a disease, or the Israelite army led by Joshua. The Old Testament says very clearly that God decided to wipe those peoples off the face of the earth because of their sins:"

«Do not say in your heart, after the Lord your God consumes these nations before you, saying, "Because of my righteousness the Lord brought me in to inherit this good land"; but because of the ungodliness of these nations, the Lord will destroy them before your face. It is not because of your righteousness or the uprightness of your heart that you are going in to inherit their land, but because of the ungodliness of these nations, the Lord will destroy them before your face, that He may establish His covenant He swore to your fathers, to Abraham, Isaac, and Jacob. Thus you will know today, the Lord your God is not giving you

this good land to inherit because of your righteousness, for you are a stiff-necked people.»[196]

"So it was also about the fulfilling of a divine promise," Daniel noticed.

"Yes, but God knew what sins those people were going to commit, long before promising their land to the descendants of Israel."

"And what were those sins?"

"The Bible tells us that among their most serious sins were the human sacrifices, especially the sacrificing of children. If you want, we can make an analogy to the extermination of the South and Central American peoples by the Europeans. Although it is not written in any holy book, we can imagine that God allowed the European conquistadors to do this not because they were virtuous, but because of the sins of those peoples, who were practicing human sacrifices and cannibalism."

"Yes, I understand the idea," Daniel said. "But together with the sinful adults, the Hebrews also exterminated many children who were not guilty at all."

"God takes care of the souls of all people. The souls of those children will probably spend eternity in a much better state than the souls of their parents. If God decided those children should not live any longer, it means that this was better for their souls."

"If it is so, can I ask you why didn't the sinful adults die when they were children, too?"

"Let's not imagine that we know better than God how long each one has to live. Nobody dies by chance, and nobody is born by chance in the midst of a sinful or faithful people. Everything happens with the knowledge and permission of God."

"Didn't the same thing happen later to the Hebrews, too?" Daniel asked.

"Yes, the same thing happened to them, too. Later on, when their sins exceeded certain limits, they were occupied by the Assyrians, the Babylonians, and by other empires. Everything that is allowed by God to happen happens for very good reasons.

---

[196] Deuteronomy 9:4-6.

Sometimes those reasons are revealed to us, too, other times they aren't. But even when we don't know the reasons, *something* inside us should, however, tell us that God never makes mistakes:"

> *«And they overtook Adoni-Bezek in Bezek, and stood in formation against him; and they slaughtered the Canaanites and the Perizzites. Then Adoni-Bezek fled, and they pursued him and caught him and cut off his thumbs and big toes. And Adoni-Bezek said, "Seventy kings with their thumbs and big toes cut off used to gather the things under my table; God has repaid me for what I have done." They then brought him to Jerusalem, where he died.»*[197]

8.7.5. Unknown Mistakes

"You told me once that God is very understanding toward those who make mistakes unknowingly."

"Yes, of course," Michael confirmed. "But, as far as I understand, not toward the proud ones who think they are smart:"

> *«Jesus said to them, "If you were blind, you would have no sin; but now you say, 'We see.' Therefore your sin remains. ["]»*[198]

> *«And that servant who knew his master's will, and did not prepare himself or do according to his will, shall be beaten with many stripes. But he who did not know, yet committed things deserving of stripes, shall be beaten with few. For everyone to whom much is given, from him much will be required; and to whom much has been committed, of him they will ask the more.»*[199]

"Is this also true for those who make mistakes out of stupidity? I mean for those who could know the truth, but they lack the intellectual capacity required to comprehend it?"

"Of course," Michael replied. "Heaven is for everybody, for the experts in quantum mechanics, for the mentally retarded, and for all the other people, regardless of their intellectual level. Here's a story recounted by Saint Paisios of Mount Athos:"

---

[197] Judges 1:5-7.
[198] John 9:41.
[199] Luke 12:47-48.

I remember an elderly monk at Esphigmenou Monastery[200] on Mount Athos, who was so simple, that he thought 'Ascension'[201] was the name of a woman Saint. He prayed to her on his komboschoini, "Saint of God, intercede for us!"

"You mean he thought that there was a woman saint named 'Ascension'?" Daniel asked, finding it hard to believe.

"Yes, something like that. But let us go on:"

Once, he had to feed a sick Brother in the infirmary and had nothing to offer him. He immediately went down the stairs, opened a window overlooking the sea, stretched his arms out and said, 'Ascension, my Saint, give me a little fish for the Brother.' And right away, as if by miracle, a big fish jumped out of the sea and into his hands. The others who saw him were astonished, but he simply looked at them smiling, as if he were saying 'What's so strange about what you've just seen?' And then look at us. We may know everything about the life and martyrdom of the Saints, or about when and how the Ascension took place and yet, we cannot even catch a tiny little fish! These are the strange and paradoxical things of the spiritual life, which the reasoning of those intellectuals that are centred on themselves and not on God, cannot explain, because their knowledge is of this world and sterile; their spirit is ill with secularism and their mind void of the Holy Spirit.[202]

"A truly remarkable happening," Michael went on. "From the point of view of science, that old man might have been categorized as an idiot or mentally retarded. But from God's point of view, maybe he was a saint."

"Yes, indeed…"

---

[200] Saint Paisios used to live in the Esphigmenou Monastery between the years 1953 and 1956.

[201] The Feast of the Ascension of the Lord, celebrated every year 40 days after Pascha (Easter).

[202] Elder Paisios of Mount Athos, *Spiritual Counsels*, vol. 1 (*With Pain and Love for Contemporary Man*), Holy Monastery "Evangelist John the Theologian," Souroti, Thessaloniki, Greece, 2006, p. 230.

"And here's another similar occurrence, which took place a long time ago:"

In Egypt, in whose ancient Christian past there had once been many grand monasteries, there once lived a monk who befriended an uneducated and simple peasant farmer. One day this peasant said to the monk:

"I too respect God Who created this world! Every evening I pour out a bowl of goat's milk and leave it out under a palm tree. In the evening God comes and drinks up my milk! He is very fond of it! There's never once been a time when even a drop of milk is left in the bowl."

Hearing these words, the monk could not help smiling. He kindly and logically explained to his friend that God doesn't need a bowl of goat's milk. But the peasant so stubbornly insisted that he was right that the monk then suggested that the next night they secretly watch to see what happened after the bowl of milk was left under the palm tree.

No sooner said than done. When night fell, the monk and the peasant hid themselves some distance from the tree, and soon in the moonlight they saw how a little fox crept up to the bowl and lapped up all the milk till the bowl was empty.

[The peasant was struck by this discovery as by thunder.²⁰³]

"Indeed!" the peasant sighed disappointedly. "Now I can see that it wasn't God!"

The monk tried to comfort the peasant and explained that God is a spirit, that God is something completely beyond our poor ability to comprehend in our world, and that people comprehend His presence each in their own unique way. But the peasant merely stood hanging his head sadly. Then he wept and went back home to his hovel.

---

²⁰³ The statement in [brackets] is taken from the Romanian edition.

The monk also went back to his cell, but when he got there he was amazed to see an angel blocking his path. Utterly terrified, the monk fell to his knees, but the angel said to him:

"That simple fellow had neither education nor wisdom nor book-learning enough to be able to comprehend God otherwise. Then you with your wisdom and book learning took away what little he had! You will say that doubtless you reasoned correctly. But there's one thing that you don't know, oh learned man: God, seeing the sincerity and true heart of this good peasant, every night sent the little fox to that palm tree to comfort him and accept his sacrifice.[204]

"Impressive, indeed," Daniel said.

"Each man is unique in his own way; there are no two identical people. Some have more physical strength, others have less. Some have a greater intellectual strength, others a less great one. Some are closer to God, others further away. Categorizing people by their physical or intellectual strength is possible from a scientific standpoint, but is totally irrelevant from a spiritual standpoint, as you have just seen. And categorizing people by how close or far away they are from God is something only God can do."

"There's something else I want to know," Daniel said, "if God is so good, why do people talk so often about the 'fear of God'?"

"According to the Holy Fathers, there are, broadly speaking, three spiritual levels on which believers can be situated. The first level, the lowest one, is the level of the slaves of God, and those on that level do good deeds and abstain from bad deeds for fear of being punished, in this life or in the next one. The second level is that of the servants of God, and those on that level do good deeds and abstain from bad deeds in the hope that they will be rewarded, in this life or in the next one. In other words, they are like servants who work in order to get paid. The third level is that of the sons of God, and those on that level do good deeds and

---

[204] From the *Prologues*; quoted in Archimandrite Tikhon (Shevkunov), *Everyday Saints and Other Stories*, Pokrov Publications, 2012.

abstain from bad deeds out of love for God and for other people, without thinking about punishments or rewards. God would like for all people to be on the third level, but He also accepts those on the levels two and one."

"Aha, so fear is present only on the lowest level."

"The three levels are not clearly delimited, and there is a possibility for someone to be on two or even on all three at the same time. A certain fear also exists on levels two and three, but not necessarily the fear of being punished, but instead the fear of falling into sin and losing God."

"And based on these criteria, can a Christian tell where he is situated?"

"To protect ourselves against pride, it is better that we always consider ourselves to be on the lowest level, and in no case to consider ourselves on a higher level than other people. The Holy Fathers teach us to always see ourselves as more sinful than the others. Pride is extremely dangerous, and as it brought the devil down from heaven, so can it bring us down, too."

8.7.6. About Birth Control

Daniel asked:

"Why is the Orthodox Church, like the Roman Catholic one, against methods of contraception? How can a family afford nowadays to have four, five or more children? I don't have children, but I know from those who do that it is very hard to raise a child, especially from a financial point of view."

"First, the Church is against abortions. The human embryo has a soul even from the moment of conception, and aborting him is a crime, because it is the killing of an unborn human being."

"I understand this. But what about contraceptive methods?"

"There are two categories of methods, the abortifacient (or abortive) ones, and the non-abortifacient (or non-abortive) ones. The first category includes the coil and the other intrauterine devices that prevent the embryo from attaching to the mother's uterus. This way, a few days after conception, the embryo dies and he is ejected. This is a crime, too, the same as abortion. Also in this category are the contraceptive pills, and here I mean not only the morning after pill, whose clear purpose is the abortion of the embryo, but also other contraceptive pills, which are taken on a daily basis in order to prevent conception."

"What is the problem with those pills?"

"Their leaflet usually does not explain the way they work, but you can find it in the specialty literature. For example, here are some details about the ethinyl estradiol and desogestrel combination, present in many contraceptives:"

> Ethinyl estradiol and desogestrel is a combination drug that contains female hormones that prevent ovulation (the release of an egg from an ovary). This medicine also causes changes in your cervical mucus and uterine lining, making it harder for sperm to reach the uterus and harder for a fertilized egg to attach to the uterus.[205]

"The fertilized egg is an embryo, a human being who has a soul," Michael said. "If he cannot attach to the uterus because of the contraceptive pill, he dies and the organism of the mother expels him."

"I didn't know that these pills have such side effects. However, their main effect is that of preventing ovulation, and in that case there is no abortion, because there is no conception."

"We all know that these pills are not 100% efficient and sometimes the women who use them do get pregnant. In those cases, all three protection systems enumerated before failed: The ovulation did take place, the sperm got where it was supposed to, and the embryo managed to attach. But besides these cases, it is possible that there are millions of other cases in which only the first two systems failed: The ovulation did take place, the sperm got where it was supposed to, the conception took place, but the embryo died because he could not attach to the uterus."

---

[205] http://www.drugs.com/mtm/ethinyl-estradiol-and-desogestrel.html

"But aren't there also cases in which the embryo cannot attach because of natural causes?"

"This is also possible, but it is like comparing a death caused by a disease to a death caused consciously with a firearm. God is the One Who gives and takes life, not us."

"OK, I understand this, but what is wrong with the non-abortive methods, with the condom, for example?"

"The Church has always been against any contraceptive method. Even in Old Testament times we see that Onan died because he did not want to get his wife pregnant, but *«he emitted his semen on the ground.»*[206] And this practice, including the use of a condom, is condemned even today."

"But why? The two of them are not causing harm to anybody. Where would we get if all families had ten children each?"

"My opinion is that the purpose of these rules is not necessarily to produce families with ten or more children, but to contribute to the gradual killing of the sexual desire, desire which can cause us serious troubles if we take it with us in the afterlife. Here's what Saint John Chrysostom says:"

> So marriage was granted for the sake of procreation, but an even greater reason was to quench the fiery passion of our nature. Paul attests to this when he says: *«But to avoid immorality, every man should have his own wife.»*[207] He does not say: for the sake of procreation. Again, he asks us to engage in marriage not to father many children,[208] but why?

> So *«that Satan may not tempt you,»*[209] he [Paul] says.

> [...]

> At the beginning, as I said, marriage had these two purposes [procreation and quenching the fiery passions] but now, after the earth and sea and all the

---

[206] Genesis 38:7-10.

[207] 1 Corinthians 7:2.

[208] In other translations: "not with the main purpose of fathering many children."

[209] 1 Corinthians 7:5.

world has been inhabited, only one reason remains for it: the suppression of licentiousness and debauchery.[210]

Michael went on:

"I think that it is a very serious sin for one to consider himself smarter and above the canons of the Church. One who breaks certain rules forced by circumstances, but with humility, aware of the sin he is committing, and who tries hard to correct himself, commits, I think, a way lesser sin than one who breaks the same rules thinking that they are useless and that he knows better. The first one, the humble one, could be helped by God to correct himself, but the second one, the 'smart' one, I think is at risk of being partially abandoned by God till he changes his opinion about himself."

"It is hard for me to understand how marriage helps put out the sexual desire."

"The husband is only allowed to look at his wife. Christ Himself has told us that to merely look lustfully at another woman is a sin.[211] The same for the wife—she can only look at her husband. However, with the passing of time, the two of them get bored of each other, they get old, the beauty of youth withers away, and thus both become unattractive from a sexual point of view. This is one of the factors that contributes to putting out the desire. Then, with age, there come various diseases, some of which can force them to abstain from sexual contact. Diseases do not come by chance, but from God. Then, both of them have to dress decently, especially the woman, to not wear provocative clothes that ignite sexual desire. Then there come the children who, as you also said, bring along a lot of hardships. These hardships are, in my opinion, another factor that contributes to putting out the sexual desire. And children don't come by chance, either, but when God sends them. And thus, in time, and with

---

[210] St. John Chrysostom, *On virginity; Against remarriage*, (Studies in Women and Religion, vol. 9), Edwin Mellen Press, 1983, p. 27.

The notes in [brackets] are taken from the Romanian translation, which seems to be a little bit more explicit.

[211] Matthew 5:27-28.

the help of God, the spouses cleanse themselves of this desire. It is a slower, more humane, if I can phrase it that way, cleansing than the way of the monks, who have absolutely no kind of sexual contact."

"I see that this explanation matches well the vision about heaven and hell that you presented to me earlier. In a way, now it makes sense: If one has a strong sexual attraction toward his wife and he dies with that desire, what is he going to do in the afterlife? Even if the two of them will be together, they won't be able to have sexual relations anymore... And that makes me wonder: What happens to those who are married and die young, before putting out this desire?"

"As I have already told you, nobody dies by chance. If it were profitable for the soul to live ten more years, he will live ten more years. With the exception of suicides, of course. Besides this, sexual desire is not the same for everybody. For some it is stronger, for others it is weaker, some need a longer time to put it out, and others less. Some families try for many years to have children and they don't succeed, while others succeed in just a few days. These are not random events, all of them are so ordained by God."

"The way you describe the Christian family does not really resemble modern families," Daniel said.

"This is true, modern people, though most of them say they believe in God, ignore the teachings of the Church and, instead of letting the desire die slowly, by itself, they do their best to keep it alive and even ignite it more than it already is. Thus, modern man has produced erotic movies, provocative and scanty clothing, lipstick and makeup, perfumes, modern hairstyles, plastic surgery, modern music, dances, potency pills, birth control pills, and so on. From this point of view, the madness of modern man seems to have no limits. Think about this one: In 1957 Elvis Presley was only filmed from the waist up, his moves being considered to be way too indecent to be broadcast on television. What do we see today on TV? Here are other examples: In 1907, Australian swimmer Annette Kellermann was arrested in the United States for wearing on the beach a one-piece bathing suit, a suit that today is considered to be exaggeratedly decent.[212] The flapper dress was considered indecent at the beginning of the 20th century. Tight clothing, including sweaters, was considered indecent even during the 40s and the 50s. And today? What do we see today on the streets and on the beaches? Not only is modern man's madness shocking, but it's also shocking the speed at which this madness is increasing."

"Indeed," Daniel said, "modern society seems to pay no attention to the afterlife. But if there really is an afterlife and if it is eternal, as believers say, then I don't think there can be any greater preoccupation in this life than the preparation for the eternity that will follow."

"That's correct. A logical conclusion for anyone. But modern society is pursuing *totally* different goals. Here's another example: from a young age we are told that we have to fight to overcome others, to be better than they are. It starts with kindergarten, then with school, and so on. Also when entering college, when looking for a job, everywhere there's a limited number of available positions. And in order to succeed in life, from a worldly perspective, we have to always be better than others, so we can occupy the tax-free position at college, or the job opening. But this seems to me to be a terrible thing, from a Christian perspective. What are we going to do in the afterlife if, instead of seeing other people as our brethren, we see them as competitors we have to overcome? What are we going to do after death, if we take this spiritual disease with us? From the words of Christ, I understand that in heaven there are no such 'competitions' between saints:"

«At that time the disciples came to Jesus, saying, "Who then is greatest in the Kingdom of heaven?" Then Jesus called a little child to Him, set him in the midst of them, and said, "Assuredly, I say to you, unless you are converted and become as little children, you will by no means enter the Kingdom of heaven. Therefore whoever humbles himself as this little child is the greatest in the Kingdom of heaven. ["] »[213]

---

[212] https://en.wikipedia.org/wiki/Annette_Kellermann
[213] Matthew 18:1-4

«Jesus called them to Himself and said, "You know that the rulers of the Gentiles lord it over them, and those who are great exercise authority over them. Yet it shall not be so among you; but whoever desires to become great among you, let him be your servant. And whoever desires to be first among you, let him be your slave—just as the Son of Man did not come to be served, but to serve, and to give His life a ransom for many."»[214]

«For he who is least among you all will be great.»[215]

Michael went on:

"Indeed, modern man seems to be living *only* for himself, for satisfying his material desires. 50 or 100 years ago people were not like this. Who were the most negative characters of the 20th century? Only God knows for sure, but I would say that the Nazis and the Communists were among them, I mean among the worst. But look, even those Nazis and Communists were capable of fighting, suffering and dying for their absurd ideals. But modern man many times pursues only personal and material ideals."

"Are you thinking about what Jesus said about some people from that time, that in the afterlife they will end up in a worse state than those in Sodom?[216] Do you think that many modern men may end up in the afterlife in a worse state than the Nazis and the Communists?"

"Let's not think about something like that, it would mean to judge people and only God can do that."

8.7.7. About Repentance

"One last question," Daniel said, "can anyone be saved, no matter how many sins he has committed?"

"Yes, there is no limit for how much God can forgive, all that is needed is for the man to repent. No matter how many sins one has committed, God accepts him. The Bible and the tradition

---

[214] Matthew 20:25-28.
[215] Luke 9:48.
[216] Matthew 11:20-24.

of the Church offer us several examples of sinners who have repented. In the Old Testament, the Prophet David[217] and King Manasseh.[218] David had caused the death of a man in order to take his wife, and Manasseh, as a king, had done a lot of unlawful things, which I'm not going to enumerate now. In the New Testament, the apostles Peter[219] and Paul[220], and the robber crucified next to Christ.[221] Peter had denied Christ, and Paul had fought against the Christians in the beginning. We also find many other examples in the *Lives of Saints*. Saint Mary of Egypt[222] used to be a prostitute, and Saint Barbarus[223] used to be a robber and had killed many people."

"Can one still hope for the mercy of God after such sins?"

"Certainly. Judas, the one who betrayed Christ, could have repented, too, if he hadn't hung himself. Even Hitler could have repented. These examples are given to us so that nobody grows despondent over his salvation, no matter how many and how serious the sins he has committed. However, let's not imagine that we can sin at will and then repent. First, we don't know how long we're going to live and whether we'll have time for repentance. Second, many times repentance takes a very long time and it is very painful, according to the sins that were committed. This is why it is better not to sin."

"Can you give me some examples of long and painful repentance?" Daniel asked.

"Don't necessarily think about physical suffering; there can also be spiritual suffering, as God ordains for the healing of the

---

[217] 2 Kingdoms 12:1-25 (NKJV: 2 Samuel 12:1-25).

[218] 2 Chronicles 33:1-25.

[219] Matthew 26:69-75.

[220] Acts 8:1 - 9:43.

[221] Luke 23:39-43.

[222] *Lives of Saints*, April 1st. She lived during the 4th and 5th centuries.

[223] *Lives of Saints*, May 6th. It is possible that he was called Barbarus because he was of barbarian origin, but this is just a personal opinion. He lived during the 9th century, and his relics are located in Greece, in the Kellios Monastery in Thessaly, near the city of Larissa.

sick soul. The prophet David had to suffer for almost all of the remainder of his life because of his sin. King Manasseh was captured, cuffed and thus taken to Babylon. The tradition of the Church tells us that Peter cried every time he heard a rooster crowing. Saint Mary of Egypt, after repenting, spent the rest of her life in the desert, as a hermit. And Saint Barbarus walked about only on his elbows and knees for the remainder of his life, three years in a village inhabited by people, and another 12 in the wilderness:"

> After Barbarus went out of the village with the beasts, walking about after their likeness, and feeding on raw greens like them, he came to a grove and lived there for 12 years, naked and without clothing; and his skin became like palm bark, scorched by the heat of the sun, and cracked by the frost, blackened all over like coal. Thus blessed Barbarus willingly made himself a martyr. After fulfilling the 12 years of suffering in the wilderness, he was informed by divine revelation that his sins were forgiven and that he was going to end his struggle of repentance by blood–like a martyr.[224]

"And how did he die?" Daniel asked.

"He was killed with arrows by some people who mistook him for a wild animal. Then he was buried, and at his grave miraculous healings started to happen, then his incorrupt body was discovered, gushing forth myrrh. Thus, people knew that God accepted his repentance and that his soul was healed of passions. However, most murderers don't become saints, and some of them don't even save their souls, but instead they end up in hell. It all depends on each one's repentance."

"Why did he walk about on his elbows and knees? Was he sick, did he have an accident, or was this a penance imposed on him for his outrageous sins?"

---

[224] Ibid. Translated from the Romanian edition.

"There are no such *epitimies*.[225] He himself chose this canon, and the priest approved his choice. This is an important detail, usually Christians can only choose *epitimies* with the blessing of the priest."

"I notice, however, that the repentance of the robber crucified next to Christ was not that long and painful," Daniel said.

"We cannot judge this. We don't even know the sins of the robber and how long he had already been in jail for them. Maybe he had not committed any murders; how can we know? Then, the Bible only says that the robber was saved, not that he also became a saint."

"So a repented robber can end up in heaven. But I wonder, what is going to happen if he encounters in heaven victims of his, people from whom he has stolen, or whom he has killed, or close relatives of those killed by him."

"You see, this is why God tells us we have to forgive everybody. What if we die harboring hatred toward someone, and then we encounter that person in the afterlife? How are we going to get rid of hatred then, because there is no repentance? Are there in heaven conflicts and hatred amongst those in there? Certainly not. Only those without spiritual diseases are admitted to heaven. God tells us very clearly that we won't enter into heaven if we don't forgive from all our hearts."[226]

"What does it mean to forgive from all your heart?"

"We don't have an exact definition, but I think we can imagine that it means to come to see that person like a brother of ours, who has never done anything wrong to us. To be glad of his presence."

"This seems impossible to me," Daniel said.

---

[225] Epitimia: the canon, the penance that the spiritual father prescribes to the one who confesses his sins. It can mean: prayers, fasts, giving alms to the poor, etc.

Epitimia is not a punishment, but a medicine. It is not prescribed in order to punish the sinner, but in order to help the healing of his soul.

[226] Matthew 6:14-15; 18:35.

"For our human powers, it is impossible, indeed. If we are put in such a situation, we can try to forgive, to forget the evil. But no matter how hard we try, we will soon realize that our forgiveness is not perfect, that we will never truly love the one forgiven that way, and that we wouldn't feel good in his presence if we were to meet him, in this world or in heaven. Then we are at a crossroads. We can choose to not obey God and to refuse to forgive; we know the consequences. Or we can limit ourselves to a partial forgiveness and say 'I forgive him, but I don't want to ever see him again.' It is a dangerous approach, I think; what if we'll hear the same from the Lord, namely 'I forgive you, but I don't want to ever see you again'? The Lord said *with what judgment you judge, you will be judged; and with the measure you use, it will be measured back to you,*[227] so what if we are forgiven the same way we forgive others? Forgiveness is very important; some Holy Fathers were saying that the one who does not forgive his neighbor is cursing himself when he says the Our Father prayer, I mean when he pronounces the words *And forgive us our debts, as we forgive our debtors.*[228] He is asking from God the same kind of forgiveness that he is offering to others."

"And what is the solution? We cannot forgive from all our hearts, and without this forgiveness we cannot enter into heaven. So what do we do?"

"We need humility and repentance. We need to admit that no matter how hard we try, we succeed at almost nothing, and that we need God. Then God will help us, over time, and will Himself do in our souls the change that we cannot do. Then we'll truly feel that we have forgiven that person and that we would feel good in his presence if we were to meet, on earth or in heaven."

"I understand why humility is needed," Daniel said. "But why is there also need of repentance?"

---

[227] Matthew 7:1-2.
[228] Matthew 6:12.

"Considering that nothing happens by chance, I think we should ask ourselves why exactly did we end up in such a seemingly impossible situation, in which we have to forgive someone who has done so much harm to us? Did we have a good opinion about ourselves? Did we think that we were true and virtuous Christians? Well then, now we are put to the test, to prove how virtuous we are and to truly forgive the one who has done wrong. For this reason, I think that we also need repentance. But the best thing for us is to repent in advance, that is, to not ever think that we are good and virtuous Christians."

"Do we also have to forgive one who has harmed us and has never asked forgiveness? If I understand correctly, not even God forgives the sinners who don't repent. Why do we have to forgive one who does not repent?"

"For three reasons. First: Maybe he does repent, but his repentance is only seen by God. Second: Maybe he did not upset us on purpose, and he does not realize that he did something wrong and that he has to apologize. And third: Maybe he did nothing wrong, and it is just *something* inside us that thinks he is guilty. You remember, our inner *something* can be wrong many times, especially when our soul has not been cleansed of passions."

"I understand," Daniel said, "but sometimes it's hard for me to accept that those who upset me do it unintentionally."

"Why? It can happen to anyone to upset someone else without actually having this intention. Here's an example: A friend of mine was visited in his office by a coworker, and they talked for a few minutes. In that office there was a chair, and my friend invited his coworker a few times to have a seat, but she refused every time. Only when she left did he realize why she hadn't sat in the chair: The chair was equipped with armrests, and she was overweight and simply couldn't fit between them. He was very sorry for making her feel bad, but it was not an intentional mistake. He was too occupied with the work-related discussion and he simply didn't notice that the width of his coworker was greater than the width of the chair. And here's another example: I know someone who has a certain memory problem. Although he re-members very well, for years, what he reads, or what he talks about with other people, it is very hard for him to remember peo-ple's faces, and usually he needs to see someone many times till he is able to recognize him if he sees him accidentally. Thus, it happens rather often that he encounters people who recognize him, but whom he does not recognize. Therefore, maybe some people form a bad opinion of him; maybe they think he ignores them on purpose, that he pretends that he does not recognize them. In reality, the man just has a visual memory problem, a minor health problem, we could say. So here's one more reason for which we should judge no one and forgive our neighbor, as God has also told us."

"The Orthodox Church and the Roman Catholic one con-sider those killed because of their faith to be saints, especially those martyred in the first centuries of Christianity. How does this square with the idea that sin is a disease of the soul and that salvation consists in spiritual healing, in the cleansing of passions? What if one of those martyrs had not been healed enough? How could he become a saint?"

"Nobody has ever gotten by chance in the situation to choose between his life and death for the faith. I believe that death for the faith is only offered by God to one who is prepared. The Church teaches those in such a situation to not betray the faith, to confess that they are Christians and to accept the tortures and death. But at the same time, the Holy Fathers warn them to not get themselves on purpose in such a situation, to not offer themselves on purpose to be martyred. Besides this, in the tradi-tion of the Church we are told that for one who is full of passions, death for the faith brings no benefit:"

> And the one who has remembrance of evil in his soul, whether he eats, or he sleeps, or he walks, he is consumed as by rust; and sin is always inseparable with him, and his prayer

becomes curse[229]; and all his labor becomes unacceptable, even if he were to spill his blood for Christ.[230]

He that lovest not his neighbor so offends God, as to find no help even in his own martyrdom [.][231]

---

[229] Psalm 108:6-7.

[230] *Egyptian Paterikon* (in Romanian), second part (unnamed elders), the chapter on longsuffering and not remembering evil.

[231] St. John Chrysostom, *Homilies on the Gospel of Matthew*, Homily XLI.

9. Epilogue

Daniel looked at his watch. It was late and it was beginning to get dark.

"Thank you for your time, I found out a lot of new things today."

"Have you begun to become a believer, or do you still remain a nonbeliever?"

"It is too early to pronounce a decision; certainly now I have many things I have to think about and many arguments I have to take into consideration. Obviously, things are not as simple as they seem to a nonbeliever at first glance."

"I hope you'll make the right decision," Michael said. "Now it's the time for me to go, too. If you still have any questions, now you know where to find me. And if you have any questions for which I did not give you satisfactory answers, don't worry, God will offer you the right answers at the right time, either by means of a book, or by means of an article, or by means of another man, or by other means. All that is needed is for your inner *something* to accept those answers. And when you become a believer, we won't be using the term *something* anymore, we'll call it the *soul*."

"I also hope that the decision I make will be the correct one. Good bye."

"Good bye and good night."

Was this book helpful? If so, please consider:

Recommending or **lending** it to a friend who might find it helpful, too.

Writing a short review on amazon.com:
   https://www.amazon.com/dp/154108635X/

Following the author's Facebook page, where you can find out about updates, new editions, new releases, or other information related to the topics addressed in this book:
   https://www.facebook.com/Bogdan.John.Vasiliu

Sending constructive feedback directly to the author:
   Bogdan.John.Vasiliu@outlook.com

Thank you!

42717764R00191

Made in the USA
Middletown, DE
19 April 2017